Ethical Practice in Forensic Psychology

SECOND EDITION

Ethical Practice in Forensic Psychology

A Guide for Mental Health Professionals

Shane S. Bush, Mary Connell, and Robert L. Denney

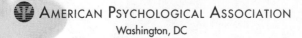

AMERICAN PSYCHOLOGICAL ASSOCIATION
Washington, DC

Published by
American Psychological Association
750 First Street, NE
Washington, DC 20002
https://www.apa.org

Order Department
https://www.apa.org/pubs/books
order@apa.org

In the U.K., Europe, Africa, and the Middle East, copies may be ordered from Eurospan
https://www.eurospanbookstore.com/apa
info@eurospangroup.com

Typeset in Meridien and Ortodoxa by Circle Graphics, Inc., Reisterstown, MD

Printer: Sheridan Books, Chelsea, MI
Cover Designer: Gwen J. Grafft, Minneapolis, MN

Library of Congress Cataloging-in-Publication Data
Names: Bush, Shane S., 1965- author. | Connell, Mary, author. | Denney, Robert L., author.
Title: Ethical practice in forensic psychology : a guide for mental health professionals / Shane S. Bush, Mary Connell, and Robert L. Denney.
Description: Second edition. | Washington, DC : American Psychological Association, [2020] | Includes bibliographical references and index.
Identifiers: LCCN 2019022623 (print) | LCCN 2019022624 (ebook) | ISBN 9781433831171 (paperback) | ISBN 9781433831188 (ebook)
Subjects: LCSH: Forensic psychology—Moral and ethical aspects. | Forensic psychologists—Professional ethics. | Forensic psychology—Practice.
Classification: LCC RA1148 .B86 2020 (print) | LCC RA1148 (ebook) | DDC 614/.15—dc23
LC record available at https://lccn.loc.gov/2019022623
LC ebook record available at https://lccn.loc.gov/2019022624

http://dx.doi.org/10.1037/0000164-000

Printed in the United States of America

10 9 8 7 6 5 4 3 2 1

*To psychologists working in forensic settings who,
faced with complex ethical situations and
potential incentives for ethical misconduct,
nevertheless aspire to the highest standards
of ethical practice.*

IMPORTANT NOTICE

The statements and opinions published in this book are the responsibility of the authors. Such opinions and statements do not represent official policies, standards, guidelines, or mandates of the American Psychological Association (APA), the APA Ethics Committee or Ethics Office, or any other APA governance group or staff. Statements made in this book neither add to nor reduce requirements of the APA's (2017) *Ethical Principles of Psychologists and Code of Conduct* (APA Ethics Code), nor can they be viewed as a definitive source of the meaning of the APA Ethics Code Standards or their application to particular situations. Each ethics committee or other relevant body must interpret and apply the APA Ethics Code as it believes proper, given all the circumstances of each particular situation. Any information in this book involving legal and ethical issues should not be used as a substitute for obtaining personal legal and/or ethical advice and consultation prior to making decisions regarding individual circumstances.

CONTENTS

ACKNOWLEDGMENTS

We are indebted to the many authors who have previously written about psychological ethics, and we are particularly grateful to those who have explored ethical issues in forensic psychology and related psychological specialties. Without their work, this book would not have been possible. We are also appreciative of the many colleagues with whom we have discussed cases and debated controversial ethical issues; the development and application of professional ethics is an evolving process, and such discussions keep the evolution alive. Additionally, we are grateful to the legal system for allowing us to contribute to what we hope are just determinations and quality consultative and clinical services. Finally, we appreciate the support that APA Books, particularly acquisitions editor Susan Reynolds, has provided us over the years.

Ethical Practice in Forensic Psychology

Introduction

Thoughts of forensic involvement evoke mixed reactions from psychologists. Some psychologists find forensic practice very appealing, others are extremely frightened by the prospect of being involved in the legal system, and still others fall somewhere in between. Psychologists involved in forensic practice perform wide-ranging professional services in varied settings, with a broad spectrum of referral sources and examinees. Yet, providing forensic services tends to be quite different from providing the clinical services for which most practitioners were trained. In forensic practice, psychologists are likely to confront competing expectations from the consumers of our services, the profession of psychology, and the guardians of public welfare. Successfully negotiating competing expectations in an adversarial context is required for both professional survival and the protection and benefit of those receiving services. Although psychologists who are drawn to forensic activities will undoubtedly face the unique ethical challenges associated with forensic practice, many psychologists with little or no interest in professional legal involvement will also find themselves thrust into the adversarial process and confronting ethical challenges for which they are not adequately prepared.

The practice of psychology in forensic contexts can be both rewarding and challenging. Successful negotiation of the challenges can itself be rewarding. To establish ethical practices and successfully negotiate the challenges, psychologists involved in forensic practice activities must have both a personal commitment to maintaining high standards of ethical practice and the information and tools needed to achieve and maintain ethical practice. This book

http://dx.doi.org/10.1037/0000164-001
Ethical Practice in Forensic Psychology, Second Edition: A Guide for Mental Health Professionals, by S. S. Bush, M. Connell, and R. L. Denney

is intended to help fulfill both of those requirements by emphasizing the importance of and modeling high standards of ethical practice, as well as by serving as a source of information and some of the tools needed to achieve and maintain ethical practice.

It has been said that ethics papers and books raise more questions than they answer (Goodman, 1998). The extent to which that is true of this text, like most ethical matters, depends upon what questions are asked. If one asks, "What are the ethical issues of greatest concern in forensic psychology?" or "What model can one follow to negotiate ethical challenges in forensic psychology?" then this text will likely provide the answers sought. In contrast, if one asks for guidance to an ethical dilemma, such as, "What should I do when I'm asked to have my evaluation of an examinee recorded?" then the information provided may be less specific than desired. The specific ethics questions with which psychologists struggle do not lend themselves to cookbook answers that apply to everyone. Nevertheless, through use of a structured decision-making process, the ethical issues can be clarified and good solutions can be established. Our vision for the book is to provide essential information and tools that promote the ethical practice of forensic psychology.

GOALS OF PUBLICATION

This second edition provides an update on common ethical issues confronting psychologists practicing in forensic contexts, including updated illustrations of ways to negotiate ethical challenges in civil, criminal, and family law cases. With this book, we strive to present and integrate the principles and standards provided in the American Psychological Association's (APA's; 2017a) *Ethical Principles of Psychologists and Code of Conduct* (APA Ethics Code) with many of the other guidelines that have relevance for forensic practice in order to form a more proactive, long-term, and positive approach to ethical practice. A number of important resources have emerged since the first edition of this book was published more than a decade ago, including the revised *Specialty Guidelines for Forensic Psychology* (SGFP; APA, 2013), the *Standards for Educational and Psychological Testing* (SEPT; American Educational Research Association, APA, & National Council on Measurement in Education, 2014), and new position statements/practice guidelines promulgated by the APA (e.g., *Assessment of Older Adults With Diminished Capacity* [American Bar Association (ABA)/APA, Assessment of Capacity in Older Adults Project Working Group 2008]) and other professional organizations that are directly relevant to forensic practice. Additionally, journal articles and book chapters in subspecialty areas (e.g., forensic practice with older adult and pediatric populations) have advanced the understanding of ethical issues in forensic psychology and have been integrated into this edition of the book. Furthermore, as the forensic psychologist's under-standing of relevant ethical issues evolves, so does the field of psychological ethics in general. Scholarly publications that contribute knowledge to gen-eral ethical psychological practice (e.g., the work by Knapp, VandeCreek, &

Fingerhut, 2017, on positive ethics) are relevant for, and should apply to, forensic practice.

The overarching purpose of this book is to provide information and a decision-making process that assists psychologists engaged in forensic practice activities to (a) understand relevant ethical issues; (b) aspire to practice in a manner that is consistent with high standards of ethical practice; and (c) anticipate, avoid, and address ethical challenges. To achieve the overarching purpose, this book (a) describes ethical issues involved in forensic psychology; (b) reviews ethical requirements, professional guidelines, and other published literature relevant to forensic psychology; (c) provides an ethical decision-making model; (d) describes ethical decision making in forensic psychology from the perspective of positive ethics; and (e) illustrates the application of the decision-making model through clinical vignettes that represent a sample of ethical challenges experienced in different subspecialties of forensic psychology. The present edition incorporates the ethical and professional resources and thinking that have emerged since the first edition was published. It integrates evolving psychological ethical principles with the evolution of forensic psychology, relying on contemporary theory and research, where it exists. Although the wide variety of potential forensic activities for psychologists prohibits exhaustive coverage of issues and practices, it is hoped that readers will benefit from an enhanced understanding of relevant ethical issues and the structured approach to ethical decision making.

In addition to updating the text based on new and revised ethical and legal materials that have become available since publication of the first edition, notable changes in this edition include (a) a description of ethics as a foundational competency; (b) increased focus on evidence-based practice; (c) increased emphasis on cultural considerations, technology, and teaching and supervision; (d) modification of the decision-making model and implementation of a mnemonic to facilitate recall of the decision-making steps; and (e) revision and updating of case analyses based on the new resources and decision-making mnemonic.

Coverage of ethical issues and challenges involves consideration of areas of controversy that, by definition, lack universal agreement. As a result, readers may disagree with some points made or positions taken in this book. In ethical decision making, there can be more than one sound decision or course of action for a given situation. Well-reasoned, evidence-based divergence of opinions enhances ethical thinking and promotes the evolution of forensic psychology.

ETHICS AS A FOUNDATIONAL COMPETENCY

Professional competence is the foundation of ethical practice in psychology in general and in specialties such as forensic psychology specifically. Professional competence establishes the foundation upon which practitioners of forensic psychology can provide services that are informative and beneficial to referral sources and triers of fact. However, professional competence is not a unitary concept, and it is not as easily defined as some practitioners and consumers might wish. Multiple competencies underlie the forensic practitioner's various activities and responsibilities. Rodolfa et al. (2005) provided a conceptual framework for competency development in psychology in general. Known as the cube model, this conceptual framework covers both foundational competencies (knowledge, skills, attitudes, and values) and functional competences (professional activities, e.g., forensic psychological evaluations). Fouad et al. (2009) explained how competency benchmarks are attained at different stages of training and professional development. Packer and Grisso (2011) and the American Board of Forensic Psychology (ABFP; 2015) described functional and foundational competencies for forensic practitioners.

Consistent with the cube model, ABFP (2015) described core competencies in forensic psychology. Foundational competencies include (a) relationships, (b) individual and cultural diversity, (c) ethics legal standards policy, (d) professionalism, (e) reflective practice/self-assessment/self-care, (f) scientific knowledge and methods, (g) interdisciplinary systems, and (h) evidence-based practice. Functional competencies include (a) assessment, (b) intervention, (c) consultation, (d) research and/or evaluation, (e) supervision, (f) teaching, (g) management/administration, and (h) advocacy. For each of the foundational and functional competencies, behavioral anchors are provided that further describe and clarify the forensic specialist's required knowledge or skills. As the cube model and ABFP illustrate, the ability to practice in an ethical manner is a core foundational competency.

The functional competencies include assessment strategies, forensic consultation, and supervision, training, and management. The foundational competencies consist of ethics, interpersonal dimensions of the forensic relationship, and laws relevant to the practice of forensic psychology.

Other documents, such as the *Education and Training Guidelines for Forensic Psychology* (Forensic Specialty Council, 2007), outline training goals and the sequential organization of training, including doctoral and internship level training, and the accreditation requirements for forensic psychology residency programs. The authors explained that

> A basic principle of Forensic Psychology is that the quality of the forensic work is limited by the underlying foundational competency (i.e., the science and professional practice of psychology) of the forensic psychologist. It is therefore essential for practitioners to first obtain a broad and general education in both scientific psychology and in the foundations of practice. This generalist training should then be augmented by exposure to the forensic area, at the graduate and internship levels, followed by specialized training at the postdoctoral level. (Forensic Specialty Council, 2007, p. 3)

When career paths within forensic psychology change or consultation is requested in an aspect of forensic practice in which one's experience is limited, competence must be attained in the new areas of practice. The APA Task Force on the Assessment of Competence in Professional Psychology stated that the assessment of professional competence, including ethical competence, should be a multitrait, multimethod, and multi-informant process that occurs throughout one's career (Kaslow et al., 2007). Board certification by way of a reasonably rigorous formal peer review process (e.g., as conducted by the American Board of Professional Psychology [ABPP]) provides evidence of professional competence in a psychological specialty, which can be readily understood by other professionals and the public. Additionally, the recent implementation of maintenance of certification requirements by ABPP helps demonstrate a commitment to a career-long pursuit of professional competence.

Achieving and maintaining an awareness of common ethical challenges and an understanding of ethics-related resources reflects an essential aspect of foundational competence and helps forensic practitioners pursue high standards of practice, reduce the likelihood of ethical conflicts, and resolve ethical dilemmas when they occur. The ability to develop and maintain ethical competence is a dynamic and ongoing process. Because ethics codes and professional guidelines are periodically drafted and updated, changes in clinical practice occur, and new laws are implemented, forensic practitioners must integrate the evolving requirements into their professional activities.

Ethical decision making would be much simpler if all ethics questions could be resolved with bottom-line answers. Bottom-line answers provide direction for resolving specific ethics questions and can be applied consistently across settings and contexts. For some ethics questions, such as, "Is it appropriate to have sex with a therapy client?" the bottom-line answer is obvious and can be applied consistently. However, more ambiguous variations may emerge, such as, "Is it appropriate to have sex with the attorney who retained me and is technically my client but is not a recipient of clinical services? And does the 2-year abstention rule apply even though the case has been settled?" Although bottom-line ethics may be refreshing and appreciated, the considerable variability of case details renders such an approach insufficient in most situations. For this reason, a structured approach to ethical decision making, such as through use of a decision-making model, helps facilitate the decision-making process and the generation of sound solutions to challenging situations.

ETHICAL ISSUES AND CHALLENGES

Bush (2015) described 10 ethical and professional issues that are of primary importance in forensic practice contexts. The list is based on the assumption that the psychologist is competent to perform the service being provided. If competence is lacking, it is unlikely that the service provided or conclusions offered will be of value to the trier of fact, and considerable harm could result. The order of importance of the issues covered in this list will vary depending on the forensic practice context, and issues not on this list may be of considerable importance to some forensic practitioners.

- Third-party requests for services
- Multiple relationships/conflicts of interest
- Informed consent/notification of purpose (including privacy and confidentiality)

- Test security/release of test data
- Explaining assessment results
- Contingency fees
- Impartiality/bias
- Third-party observers
- Accuracy and truthfulness in public statements (reports and testimony)
- Addressing ethical misconduct

Forensic practitioners should understand the potential relevance of these issues in their professional activities, anticipate challenges, and establish procedures for addressing dilemmas when they arise.

UNDERSTANDING, ADOPTING, AND APPLYING PROFESSIONAL RESOURCES

Psychologists have at their disposal a variety of ethics resources for determining appropriate professional behavior. The views psychologists take of professional ethics have a considerable influence on their professional behavior. Those who view ethics solely as a means of establishing and enforcing minimal standards of practice fail to appreciate that professional ethics, including the APA Ethics Code, represent an attempt to translate core ethical principles and their underlying human values into operationally defined guidelines for psychologists. Professional codes of ethics, despite their essential contribution to guiding behavior, need not always be the final word on how best to resolve an issue.

Practitioners of forensic psychology have an obligation to the profession and those who are served not to simply be guided by that which is ethically permissible but to seek that which is ethically preferable. The extra steps required to determine and pursue ethically preferable courses of action may require additional effort in the short term, but from that effort comes greater benefit to the forensic practitioner, forensic psychology, consumers of forensic psychology services, and the general public in the long run. While professional ethics codes are a primary resource for psychological practice, they typically provide only the ethical floor and do not address the more specific needs of psychological specialties. Therefore, psychologists providing forensic services benefit from an understanding and use of ethics resources that extend beyond ethics codes.

POSITIVE ETHICS AND THE 4 As OF ETHICAL PRACTICE

Ethics codes used for disciplinary purposes represent the minimum standards of professional conduct. This remedial perspective on psychological ethics focuses more on ways to avoid harming others than on ways to promote well-being. In contrast to remedial ethics, positive ethics represents a voluntary commitment to pursuing ethical ideals, motivated by deeply held moral principles (Knapp et al., 2017). Positive ethics is proactive; practitioners strive to promote exemplary professional behavior rather than only reacting when faced with ethical challenges. From the perspective of positive ethics, ethics codes represent a starting point, from which higher standards of practice are pursued (Knapp et al., 2017). When considering ethical issues, the question to ask is not, "What must I do according to the Ethics Code?" but, "What can I do that reflects the highest standard of ethical practice?" As Beauchamp and Childress (2013) noted, "If we expect only the moral minimum of obligation, we may lose an ennobling sense of excellence" (p. 49).

Positive ethics involves a deeper level of integration, the integration of practitioners' personal ideals with their professional lives (Knapp et al., 2017). Although most members of a society, including professional societies, share common values (e.g., competent adults should have the right to make decisions about matters that affect their lives, as reflected in the bioethical principle *respect for autonomy*), individuals vary in the extent to which they embrace different values. Differences in life experiences, cultural backgrounds, religious beliefs, and other unique variations in one's life influence the personal values that guide one's personal and professional decisions. Practitioners who perceive a connection between their personal values and the values underlying their ethical obligations may be more likely than practitioners who lack such a connection to experience a strong commitment to their professional ethics. The pursuit of ethical ideals can require more time and expense than is required to comply with enforceable ethical standards, causing some practitioners to choose not to pursue such ideals. However, time and expense requirements are poor reasons for electing not to pursue ethical ideals.

Bush (2009) described the *Four As of Ethical Practice* as a framework for conceptualizing ethical practice. The four As are *Anticipate, Avoid, Address*, and *Aspire*. Practitioners strive to (a) A*nticipate* and prepare for ethical issues and challenges commonly encountered in their specific practice contexts, (b) A*void* ethical misconduct, (c) A*ddress* ethical challenges when they are anticipated or encountered, and (d) A*spire* to the highest standards of ethical practice. In this way, the four As are consistent with positive ethics. Remaining mindful of the four As of ethical practice can facilitate appropriate professional activity, as well as the modeling of ethical behavior for students and trainees, other forensic specialists, and interdisciplinary professionals.

AUDIENCES

The book is intended both as (a) a resource for the forensic psychology practitioner, which is defined broadly to include all psychologists working in the various legal contexts, including civil, criminal, and family/child custody law; and (b) a text for forensic psychology students and trainees. In addition to psychologists who deliberately pursue professional involvement in the legal system, some clinicians inadvertently find themselves involved in the legal matters of their patients. Involvement of a clinician may be either requested or required.

For example, a neuropsychologist may be subpoenaed to testify about the evaluation findings of a patient who sustained a traumatic brain injury in a motor vehicle collision. Such engagement in the legal system, although not forensic practice by most definitions, nonetheless requires an understanding of the relevant professional, ethical, and legal issues. Those with little forensic experience but who are anticipating involvement in, or have been unexpectedly thrust into, a legal matter will acquire the ability to apply appropriate professional resources to ethical challenges associated with specific practice activities.

The critical reader may find legitimate points of disagreement with positions taken in the text, given the broad range of contexts and services in which forensic practice takes place. Nevertheless, an increased understanding of the ethical issues that pertain to forensic psychology in general will assist psychologists in all forensic contexts to better serve those with whom they interact professionally. For the purposes of this text, the term *forensic psychologist* is used broadly to refer to those psychologists who perform forensic activities; it is not used solely to denote those with specialized training or board certification in forensic psychology.

CONTENTS AND FORMAT

There are many possible ways to organize a forensic psychology ethics book, including organizing the material around (a) the steps in the forensic evaluation process (e.g., the referral, data collection); (b) forensic topics areas, such as civil litigation and criminal litigation; (c) the relevant ethical issues and principles; or (d) threats to the validity of the data or the opinions provided, such as inadequate competence and compromised objectivity. We chose to organize the material around the steps in the evaluation process, because it provides clear reference points for practicing psychologists who are considering ethical issues or facing ethical challenges. Although practitioners may not always immediately be aware of the relevant ethical issues and principles or the underlying threats to the validity of data and opinions, they do know the practice activity in which they or their colleagues are engaging. Thus, organization along these lines facilitates reference to the material that is most relevant at a given time. The material was not organized according to forensic topic areas because the considerable overlap of relevant ethical issues across topic areas would require excessive redundancy in the coverage of material. The emphasis on the evaluation process is not meant to minimize the importance of ethics for the many nonevaluation forensic activities (e.g., treatment, trial consultation) in which psychologists engage; it simply reflects an element of practice that we have found to be a focus for many forensic psychologists. It is hoped that the ethical issues examined and the decision-making process described in the context of the forensic evaluation can be readily applied to a broad range of forensic practice activities.

Following this introduction, Chapter 1 provides an overview of the inter-face of law and psychology. The chapter includes a description of a structured, systematic ethical decision-making model with the corresponding mnemonic *CORE OPT*. The seven steps of the model are (1) *C*larify the ethical issue; (2) identify *O*bligations owed to stakeholders; (3) utilize ethical and legal *R*esources; (4) *E*xamine personal beliefs and values; (5) consider *O*ptions, solutions, and consequences; (6) *P*ut plan into practice; and (7) *T*ake stock, evaluate the outcome, and revise as needed. All of the case examples pre-sented in the book are analyzed according to this model. Although applying the model can help psychologists develop ethical practices and arrive at sound solutions to ethical challenges, ethical behavior also requires personal integ-rity and a commitment to high standards of ethical practice.

Chapters 2 through 7 examine the various components of the forensic evaluation process, including the referral, collection and review of informa-tion, the evaluation, documentation of findings and opinions, and testimony and termination. Although much of the information applies to psychologists working in forensic treatment settings and as trial consultants, the book is structured primarily around the forensic evaluation. Issues related to neuro-psychological evaluations in forensic contexts are covered. Case illustrations are provided to demonstrate application of the issues examined and the ethi-cal decision-making process. Case illustrations cover three broad topic areas: personal injury litigation, criminal litigation, and child and family law. Chap-ter 7 covers the ethical challenges inherent in addressing ethical misconduct by colleagues performing forensic work. Forensic psychologists are likely exposed to more of the work of colleagues than psychologists practicing in any other specialty areas. That exposure, combined with the natural emotional reactions and the potential for bias that may emerge in adversarial situations, contribute to a context in which allegations of ethical misconduct may abound. This issue raises a need for attention to be given to the sensitive topic of responding to apparent ethical misconduct by forensic psychology colleagues. The chapter includes a checklist for reporting ethical violations that shares some similari-ties with the *CORE OPT* model. The Afterword offers concluding remarks, with an emphasis on the personal commitment needed by forensic psychologists in order to establish and maintain ethical conduct.

The book includes "excerpts" from fictional psychological and neuropsycho-logical reports. These "excerpts" were created by the authors and represent an amalgam of reports by numerous psychologists that the authors reviewed over the years. Similarly, case illustrations provided in the book were created by the authors and represent an integration of scenarios encountered in practice and/or imagined by the authors. Despite any unintended similarities, excerpts and case illustrations do not represent the reports or practice of any given psychologist.

1

The Interface of Law and Psychology

An Overview

The profession of psychology has much to offer the legal system and those with possible or clearly identified psychological difficulties who find themselves negotiating the legal system. As a result of the contributions made by psychologists to legal matters, forensic psychology emerged as a distinct specialty area within the broader field of psychology. Forensic psychology, although defined in multiple ways by different authors, includes both scholarly and applied activities and represents the intersection of psychology and the law (Bartol & Bartol, 2019; Cutler & Zapf, 2015; Melton et al., 2018; Otto & Ogloff, 2013; Packer & Grisso, 2011; Roesch, Zapf, & Hart, 2010).

The *Specialty Guidelines for Forensic Psychology* (hereinafter referred to as the *Guidelines*; APA, 2013) emphasize the applied aspects of the specialty in the following fairly broad definition:

> *forensic psychology* refers to professional practice by any psychologist working within any subdiscipline of psychology (e.g., clinical, developmental, social, cognitive) when applying the scientific, technical, or specialized knowledge of psychology to the law to assist in addressing legal, contractual, and administrative matters . . . Psychological practice is not considered forensic solely because the conduct takes place in, or the product is presented in, a tribunal or other judicial, legislative, or administrative forum. (p. 7)

In this chapter, we describe (a) primary subspecialties within forensic psychology, (b) forensic roles for psychologists, (c) the adversarial environment, (d) the need for information on ethics in forensic psychology, (e) the application of general bioethical principles in forensic arenas, (f) the application of

http://dx.doi.org/10.1037/0000164-002
Ethical Practice in Forensic Psychology, Second Edition: A Guide for Mental Health Professionals,
by S. S. Bush, M. Connell, and R. L. Denney

psychological ethics in forensic arenas, (g) the *Specialty Guidelines for Forensic Psychology* and other relevant professional guidelines, and (h) the importance of understanding jurisdictional laws. The chapter also presents an ethical decision-making model for forensic psychology, and it describes appropriate risk management strategies for forensic practice.

PRIMARY SUBSPECIALTIES WITHIN FORENSIC PSYCHOLOGY

The clinical and experimental forensic arenas are themselves composed of psychologists from diverse psychological specialties, such as counseling, developmental, and social psychology. Thus, forensic psychologists may have multiple professional identities representing both their primary areas of training and experience and their subsequent application of their knowledge and skills to forensic matters.

Subspecialties within forensic psychology can be conceptualized in multiple ways, such as by a related psychological specialty (e.g., forensic neuropsychology, forensic geropsychology), the administrative context in which psychological evaluations are performed (e.g., claims for Social Security disability, workers' compensation, or Veterans Affairs), or, as described by Bartol and Bartol (2019), the nature of the forensic involvement. Bartol and Bartol presented the following five forensic psychology subspecialties: (a) police and public safety psychology, (b) legal psychology (e.g., child custody, competency to stand trial, not guilty by reason of insanity defenses, civil capacities, court mandated psychotherapy), (c) psychology of crime and delinquency, (d) victimology and victim services (e.g., personal injury), and (e) correctional psychology. There are many settings in which such subspecialties are practiced.

FORENSIC ROLES FOR PSYCHOLOGISTS

Psychologists practice and conduct research in both civil and criminal legal arenas. Civil law includes matters of family law; administrative proceedings (e.g., workers' compensation, commitment for mental health treatment, and decisional capacity/competency issues); and tort law, such as personal injury litigation. Common purposes of civil law are to assign responsibility for harm, resolve disputes, and provide compensation to someone injured by another's behavior (see https://legaldictionary.net/civil-law/).

Family law, a type of civil law, differs from other civil matters in several important ways. In family law matters, the court is generally called upon to resolve disputes having to do with the following: (a) marital dissolution, where there may or may not be a finding of fault; (b) determinations regarding parenting relationships, such as parenting agreements following divorce, adoption proceedings, or proceedings to terminate parental rights; and (c) matters of juvenile justice that do not fall within the purview of criminal law, owing to the status of the actor as a minor.

In contrast to civil law, criminal law is based on the concept of moral blameworthiness (Behnke, Perlin, & Bernstein, 2003). When an individual has been found guilty of a crime, a moral sanction applies, including removal from society if that is deemed necessary by the court. Criminal law determines the guilt or innocence of a defendant and provides a consequence if the accused is found guilty. Psychological expertise and services can be found across the continuum of criminal law procedures. According to the American Bar Association's (ABA's; 2016) *Criminal Justice Standards on Mental Health*, mental health professionals serve the administration of criminal justice through the following roles: evaluative expert, scientific expert, consultative, treatment, and policy (ABA Standard 7-1.3, p. 3). Because these roles involve differing and sometimes conflicting obligations and functions, these professionals as well as courts, attorneys, and criminal justice agencies need to be clear about the nature and limitations of the roles assumed by mental health professionals. Because much of the role confusion for psychologists involves distinctions between forensic (e.g., evaluative expert) and clinical (e.g., treatment) practices, these issues are the focus of the following sections.

Forensic Evaluation Services

For criminal forensic purposes, the ABA (2016) defines the evaluative expert role as

> Evaluating and offering legally relevant expert opinions and testimony about a particular person's past, present or future mental or emotional condition, capacities, functioning or behavior, and about the effects of interventions, treatments, services or supports on the person's condition, capacities, functioning or behavior. (p. 3)

Although it may at first appear that a treating clinician could offer such information to the court, theoretically with greater accuracy because treating clinicians often have known and worked with the patients longer than an evaluative expert could, the nature of the information obtained, the manner in which it is obtained, and the relationship with the person being evaluated differ in significant ways between forensic and clinical evaluations.

Differences begin with the language used to describe the evaluation. Psychological evaluations performed by practitioners who are hired as independent contractors by third parties, such as disability insurers, attorneys, or the courts, are often referred to as *forensic evaluations, independent psychological examinations,* or *independent medical examinations* (IMEs). Attorneys and courts tend to refer to such evaluations as *forensic,* whereas disability insurance carriers tend to describe such evaluations as *IMEs.* Differences between forensic and clinical evaluations also include the nature of the requested evaluation, which has theoretical and practical implications for the manner in which the task is approached. With forensic evaluation services, context affects (a) the goals of the evaluation, (b) the psychologist's role, (c) the assumptions the psychologist makes about the accuracy of information received from the examinee, (d) alliances formed and obligations owed, and (e) methodology employed by the psychologist.

As Melton et al. (2018) stated, "the purposes and uses of forensic evaluations differ qualitatively from the purposes and uses of evaluations developed for treatment purposes" (p. 10). The purpose of a forensic evaluation is to assist the legal decision-maker, who may be a judge, jury, mediator, or other hearing officer. This forensic purpose stands in contrast to the clinician's goal of assisting the patient. Accepting that the psychologist's primary obligation is to the legal decision maker rather than to the examinee may be a difficult transition to make for psychologists who have been clinically trained. However, it is necessary for examining psychologists to understanding that the retaining party is the client and that the examinee is neither a patient nor the client of the examining psychologist. Exceptions may exist in forensic treatment settings in which evaluations may be performed to facilitate clinical services rather than to inform legal decisions.

The goal of the psychologist retained to serve as an expert witness is to provide information useful to the trier of fact in its effort to answer a specific legal question, such as the presence or absence of psychological injury or the examinee's competency to stand trial. Thus, the psychologist's task "is an exercise in consultation and dissemination of information" (Melton et al., 2018, p. ix). To be able to disseminate useful information to the trier of fact, the psychologist assumes the role of "seeker of truth" and judicial educator (Denney, 2012a; Denney & Sullivan, 2008). The opinions provided are not designed to "help" the examinee; in fact, in many instances, the opinions offered conflict with the examinee's wishes.

The psychologist retained to serve as an expert witness cannot assume that the information received from the examinee is complete or accurate. Examinees may not even be voluntary participants in the evaluation. The possible outcomes of litigation can create tremendous motivation for the examinee to attempt to manipulate the evaluator and to affect the outcome of the evaluation. It would be naïve and forensically misguided to trust the presentation of such highly invested examinees without corroboration; a degree of skepticism can promote accurate diagnoses and conclusions.

The alliances that a psychologist maintains and the obligations owed to those involved differ depending on the context in which the services are provided. Although a psychologist providing treatment typically forms a therapeutic alliance with the patient and is invested in promoting the well-being of the patient, such an alliance with, and investment in, a forensic examinee would not be appropriate. The psychologist retained as an expert witness forms an alliance with the truth, and the primary obligation is to the trier of fact. The investment in determining and reporting the truth may make problematic the establishment of rapport between examiner and examinee. Rapport may be misconstrued as an offer of advocacy and may lure the examinee into a level of disclosure that is not in the examinee's best legal interest. A posture of respectful receptivity with an arms-length, or dispassionate, mien may be the most appropriate posture to assume during the forensic evaluation.

The context in which the evaluation is performed also affects the methodology employed by the psychologist. Forensic psychological evaluations require a broader base of information sources than is typical of clinical practice, a base that extends well beyond the self-report of the examinee (Denney, 2012a; Denney & Sullivan, 2008; McLearen, Pietz, & Denney, 2004; Melton et al., 2018). A multimethod, multisource examination is required for forensic examinations (Heilbrun, 2003). In contrast to the urgency that is often required in the provision of clinical evaluation services, psychologists practicing in many forensic contexts must take the time necessary to ensure that the broad base of information that is needed (e.g., interviews, observations, records, test data) can be obtained and thoroughly reviewed before conclusions are offered. Of course, evaluations in some forensic contexts can be time sensitive as well; however, in situations in which the broad information base is not available, conclusions should be tempered accordingly, with limitations described in the report.

The Distinction Between Expert Witness and Treating Clinician

The distinction between the roles of "treating clinician" and forensic psychological "expert" has long been a focus of discussion in forensic psychology ethics (e.g., S. A. Greenberg & Shuman, 1997, 2007; Neal, 2017; Otto, Goldstein, & Heilbrun, 2017; Saks, 1990; Strasburger, Gutheil, & Brodsky, 1997). In the treatment role, psychologists can be called to testify as either fact witnesses or expert witnesses. Fact witnesses limit their testimony to what they know firsthand, do not rely on hearsay information, and have little freedom to draw conclusions or provide opinions. Treating psychologists who testify as expert witnesses are called *percipient experts* (Caudill & Pope, 1995). They are considered experts because of their specialized training and/or experience but were not retained for the purpose of litigation. Treating psychologists generally avoid providing ultimate issue opinions, aware that offering expert testimony about such forensic issues is risky. This topic, which has been a source of divergent opinions in forensic psychology, is covered in more detail in Chapter 6.

Opinions about the clinical interpretation of data are relevant contributions, but the treating therapist rarely has accomplished an arms-length, comprehensive assessment that would lead to defensible opinion on the psycholegal issue. Although there is controversy about whether the treating clinician should offer opinion on the ultimate issue before the court, the treating clinician must limit opinion to that for which adequate data has been gathered. For example, a therapist may believe that visitation with a parent the therapist has never met would be damaging, based on the child's and possibly the other parent's presentation, but the therapist must recognize that as an advocate for the patient and without hearing the "other side of the story," such an opinion would be insufficiently developed. The interpretation of data collected in therapy is more subjective and potentially less reliable than data gathered from a range of sources, such as objective measures, records, and collateral consultation. Even with careful statement of limitations, the therapist testifying about matters before the court must be aware of the potential for the court to misconstrue or misuse the opinion data. The therapist who has risked this misuse of data may find little support in the professional community for offering opinion derived through provision of psychotherapy as an expert evaluation of the forensic issue (Heilbrun, 1995, 2001; Melton et al., 2018).

The distinction, then, is between being an expert clinician and being a forensic examiner for the purpose of developing an expert opinion, to be offered to the court, on a psycholegal matter. Both may function as experts in the court, and the clinician may be able to provide expert opinion on the clinical data, but generally the clinician has insufficient data to offer an opinion on the matter before the court.

To facilitate clinical treatment, the treatment provider may develop diagnostic impressions prior to or without performing a complete review of relevant records, interviewing collateral sources of information, conducting thorough psychodiagnostic testing, or otherwise performing an evaluation adequate to answer questions before the court "with a reasonable degree of certainty." In contrast to the clinical role, the forensic psychological expert role requires (a) review of all materials and completion of all procedures upon which to base an opinion sufficient to withstand judicial scrutiny, and (b) an objective and judgmental position that may be impossible for the typically accepting and nonjudgmental clinician to achieve (Guideline 4.02.01: Therapeutic–Forensic Role Conflicts).

The term "treating clinician" has at times been used inappropriately to describe all clinical activities, such as clinical diagnostic evaluations that do not involve remedial intervention or advocacy (Bush, 2005c). Although clinical evaluations are typically performed to facilitate therapy, they are not intended to be therapeutic in and of themselves. Thus, the goals, assumptions, and alliances of the clinical examiner may more closely parallel those of the forensic examiner than those of the treating therapist.

The distinction between "treating clinician" and "expert witness" is limited and is insufficient to understand the forensic roles of psychologists. Heilbrun (2001) described five possible roles for mental health professionals in forensic assessment contexts: clinical or court-appointed evaluator, defense/prosecution/plaintiff's expert, scientific advisor to the court, consultant, and fact witness. This broad description of roles better reflects the breadth of psychologists' potential professional forensic involvement.

Blurring of Professional, Clinical, and Forensic Roles

The role held by the psychologist has implications for objectivity and accuracy in the presentation of information to the court and, by extension, the accuracy of judicial determinations. The *Ethical Principles of Psychologists and Code of Conduct* (APA Ethics Code, 2017) states that

> (a) A multiple relationship occurs when a psychologist is in a professional role with a person and (1) at the same time is in another role with the same person, (2) at the same time is in a relationship with a person closely associated with or related to the person with whom the psychologist has the professional relationship, or (3) promises to enter into another relationship in the future with the person or a person closely associated with or related to the person. (APA Ethics Code, Standard 3.05, Multiple Relationships)

APA Ethics Code, Standard 3.05 also states that psychologists should strive to avoid entering into such relationships, if the relationship "could reasonably be expected to impair the psychologist's objectivity, competence, or effectiveness in performing his or her functions as a psychologist, or otherwise risks exploitation or harm to the person with whom the professional relationship exists."

Blurring of professional, clinical, and forensic roles has the strong potential to invoke conflicts of interest that negatively affect one or more of the roles. Psychologists have a responsibility to recognize the potential for conflicts of interest in dual or multiple relationships with parties to a legal proceeding and to seek to minimize their effects (APA Ethics Code, Standard 3.05, Multiple Relationships, & Standard 3.06, Conflict of Interest; Guideline 4.02, Multiple Relationships). In general, to maximize objectivity, these roles should not be combined in a single case (Denney, 2005a; Heilbrun, 2001); however, some exceptions exist.

One potential exception to the principle of avoiding dual or multiple relationships may be seen in the psychologist who transitions from the role of examiner to that of trial consultant after all evaluation-related responsibilities have been completed. For example, a psychologist retained by a criminal defense attorney to conduct an evaluation and provide verbal feedback, who is asked to not write a report, and who will not later testify, might appropriately transition to the role of consultant. The psychologist in this scenario will have completed the role of examiner and will no longer be required to maintain impartiality.

Other situations in which a psychologist may find the unavoidable need to provide multiple services to a party in a legal proceeding include small forensic hospital settings, small communities, and psychiatric emergencies in which patient welfare is given priority over the forensic service. Additionally, military court-martial participation by psychologists designated as expert forensic consultants/testifying experts may call for blending of roles (Connell, 2019; Gottlieb & Younggren, 2019). When circumstances call for blending of roles or provision of multiple services, the onus is on the forensic psychologist to actively monitor for the insidious effects of bias or allegiance and to limit roles in order to retain objectivity.

Some forensic mental health professionals want to have it both ways, to be healers and to serve or influence the adversary system (Stone, 1984). L. R. Greenberg and Gould (2001) took the position that, in some situations, psychologists may ethically have it both ways. They described a "hybrid role" in which the treating psychologist whose patients have impending or ongoing litigation should (a) be sensitive to the unique experiences and needs of such patients, (b) be aware that the litigation will likely impact the therapy, and (c) possess many of the practice-related traits of the forensic examiner, while maintaining firm limits regarding the nature of the opinion testimony provided. Although the treating psychologist may provide to the court their opinions regarding diagnosis, treatment, and prognosis, "the treating expert generally declines to express opinions on psycholegal issues (e.g., custody recommendations and parental capacity)" (L. R. Greenberg & Gould, 2001, p. 477). When overlapping or multiple roles are adopted, the manner in which the overlap or different roles are managed distinguishes ethical conduct from misconduct. An awareness of competing obligations and a demonstrated commitment to maximizing objectivity serves the psychologist well.

Although psychologists may define the factors that comprise a forensic psychological evaluation and the factors that characterize a competent expert witness, it is ultimately the court that determines what evidence will be allowed and who will be considered an expert in a particular case. The adversarial system is designed to provide the checks and balances for determining the adequacy (relevance and reliability) of the psychologist's work product. It is the psychological sophistication of the attorneys, trial consultants, and trier of fact involved in the case that determine the effectiveness of the adversarial system for cases in which psychological functioning is at issue. It is the responsibility of the psychologist to provide education to those who do not appreciate the threats to impartiality and to attempt to maintain clear distinctions in professional roles. For example, a family court judge may suggest that the custody evaluator who conducted a court-ordered evaluation of all parties to a parenting dispute take on the role of treatment provider to assist one parent and child to reunify; it falls upon the forensic psychologist to explain to the judge why adoption of this second role could be problematic for the parent (who may harbor antipathy toward the forensic evaluator for the findings of the initial evaluation) and for the examiner who may have some investment in a treatment outcome that supports the opinions offered to the court.

The Guidelines address the issue in the following manner:

> When requested or ordered to provide either concurrent or sequential forensic and therapeutic services, forensic practitioners are encouraged to disclose the potential risk and make reasonable efforts to refer the request to another qualified provider. If referral is not possible, the forensic practitioner is encouraged to consider the risks and benefits to all parties and to the legal system or entity likely to be impacted, the possibility of separating each service widely in time, seeking judicial review and direction, and consulting with knowledgeable colleagues. When providing both forensic and therapeutic services, forensic practitioners seek to minimize the potential negative effects of this circumstance. (Guideline 4.02.01, Therapeutic-Forensic Role Conflicts)

In addition to potentially biasing relationships between psychologists and examinees, it is advisable for psychologists to maintain independence from the retaining party (Packer & Grisso, 2011). Despite what can be appropriately close working relationships between practitioners and attorneys, psychologists should remain mindful that the attorney's primary obligation is to prevail in the case, whereas the psychologist's primary obligation is to educate the trier of fact in as complete and objective manner as possible (Packer & Grisso, 2011). Psychologists who are aware that pressure, whether subtle or overt, and financial incentive may be used to influence their opinions can prepare to negotiate such influences when they are encountered.

THE ADVERSARIAL ENVIRONMENT

Expert witnesses play a prominent role in the American litigation process (Crown, Fingerhut, & Lowenthal, 2003); however, the adversarial nature of the U.S. legal system presents unique challenges for psychologists. A primary issue that is unique to many forensic situations is that the practitioner's opinions may be challenged or questioned. The "opponent" mounting this challenge is an individual or team of individuals who question the practitioner's methods, opinions, and/or qualifications. A psychologist retained by the defense attorney in a civil case or by the prosecution in a criminal case to provide an "independent" opinion is viewed by some examinees as an opponent, a perception that may alter the examinee's behavior during the exam. The perception of the psychologist as an opponent leads to many of the ethical dilemmas that are faced by forensic psychologists.

The adversarial environment may also pit psychologists against those who have retained their services. The attorney who has retained a psychologist to perform an evaluation has an allegiance to the client and must diligently advocate for the client. In contrast, the examining psychologist has a responsibility to remain objective. Although retained by the attorney, the psychologist has an allegiance to the trier of fact. This inherent clash between the attorney as advocate and the expert witness, whose single most important obligation is to approach each question with independence and objectivity, can become a source of ethical conflict for psychologists (Crown et al., 2003; Packer & Grisso, 2011). Such conflict sometimes arises from the real and perceived incentive or other subtle or obvious pressures from the attorney advocate to influence the opinions of the objective expert.

Psychologists are not always adequately prepared by their education and training for these challenges. Thus, for many psychologists, the transition from the classroom or clinical setting to a forensic environment may involve a substantial paradigm shift and a corresponding struggle with the ethical, moral, and legal issues involved (Martelli, Bush, & Zasler, 2003). A logical approach to both advancing ethical practice and availing the legal system of one's expertise is to develop an increased sensitivity to, and understanding of, the disparities between conflicting interests and ethics and to maintain a personal commitment to ethical practice.

THE NEED FOR INFORMATION ON ETHICS IN FORENSIC PSYCHOLOGY

The pulls to sacrifice objectivity, the differences between clinical and forensic activities, and the enticement to step beyond the boundaries of one's competence all provide fertile soil for ethical misconduct. Particularly in today's health care environment, where shrinking or unpredictable reimbursement for clinical services is often coupled with increased time-consuming clerical requirements, the lure of higher fees for one's professional services may draw inadequately prepared clinicians into professionally dangerous waters. Similarly, financial incentives may lead even the most qualified forensic psychologist into unethical behaviors that are harmful to the involved parties, the legal system, and the profession of psychology. Awareness of the common ethical challenges in forensic psychology helps psychologists examine their own practices and the practices of colleagues; familiarity with ethical, legal, and professional resources provides a foundation for addressing the challenges.

APPLYING GENERAL BIOETHICAL PRINCIPLES IN FORENSIC ARENAS

All ethical principles are based on fundamental human values. Values that a society deems important, such as the right to self-determination and the right to quality health care, are applied to specific industries and professions. Beauchamp and Childress (2013) offered a model of biomedical ethics that has been widely adopted by scholars and practitioners in a variety of health care specialties, including psychology. The model comprises moral principles, including respect for autonomy, nonmaleficence, beneficence, and justice. Psychologists may recognize nonmaleficence, beneficence, and justice from the APA Ethics Code's General Principles. Respect for autonomy, also present in the APA Ethics Code's General Principles, is embedded in Principle E (Respect for People's Rights and Dignity).

Respect for autonomy refers to an appreciation of the individual's right to self-determination—the ability to make decisions regarding one's life. Nonmaleficence is closely related to the Hippocratic Oath's mandate to "first, do no harm." Beneficence takes clinician responsibility a step further by encouraging the practitioner to promote that which is beneficial to the patient. In health care settings, justice typically refers to the equitable distribution of the burdens and benefits of care (Hanson, Kerkhoff, & Bush, 2005). Biomedical ethical principles can be readily applied to most ethical challenges in clinical psychology, where the clinician's goal is to help patients, avoid harm, respect the wishes of patients regarding their treatment, and practice in a just and fair manner. However, in an adversarial judicial system, the application of these principles may initially appear to be far more challenging.

In forensic practice, psychologists have a responsibility to respect the rights of examinees and other clients to determine their involvement in psychological services. Examinees participate in forensic evaluations more or less of their own accord, albeit at times under the threat of negative consequences should they choose not to participate. In legal contexts, the concepts of nonmaleficence and justice are closely tied. Forensic practitioners are mindful of the ethical principle of doing no harm, and yet the results of forensic examinations and testimony can thwart the interests of the examinee in ways that are maximally harmful. These include possible life or death determinations in capital cases, termination of parental rights, loss of insurance coverage for a claimed disability, and many other potential consequences. The practitioner's obligation is to address the psycholegal question in an objective way with candor. The outcome of the legal matter may depend somewhat or to a great extent on that input, but practitioners have fulfilled their professional obligation when they adhere to those ethics. The issue of self-determination can and should be addressed in the way we gain consent or assent for services, which is addressed more fully in other chapters of this book.

Forensic psychologists have a responsibility to treat examinees with courtesy, dignity, and fairness. Beyond the possibility of evoking emotional reactions to evaluation questions or tasks, practitioners must not bring direct harm to examinees during evaluations. Nevertheless, the results of forensic psychological evaluations and subsequent testimony have the potential to result in considerable negative effects on the lives of examinees. It is the psychologist's responsibility to perform a fair evaluation and present the findings objectively and dispassionately. The legal decision maker then has the task of achieving a just outcome. An examinee who believes he has been treated fairly and respectfully is less likely to perceive the examiner as being maleficent, even given an unfavorable determination.

For forensic examinations, helping the examinee is not a primary goal of the examiner. Helping the trier of fact to make an appropriate determination, taking into account the examinee's cognitive or psychological functioning, is a goal. The examinee may or may not benefit from the examination findings. Thus, the principle of beneficence as it relates to forensic psychological services may generally fall within the ambit of the justice system rather than the individual examinee.

The adversarial process is built upon the assumption that right will prevail if the responsibilities of all participants are fully discharged. It is not the forensic psychologist's responsibility to ensure retention by the party deserving to prevail. It is the forensic psychologist's responsibility to thoroughly and adequately perform his or her duties; if the resultant outcome favors the "unjust," the psychologist can forgo a sense of personal responsibility for the injustice.

The differences between clinical and forensic contexts notwithstanding, we believe that the Beauchamp and Childress model (2013) is useful in forensic psychology and have chosen to use their model in the more comprehensive decision-making model that is presented in this chapter.

Applying Psychological Ethics in Forensic Arenas

The 2002 edition of the APA Ethics Code was the 10th version of the code, reflecting the continuing evolution and maturation of the profession of psychology. The APA Ethics Code has been subsequently amended twice (APA, 2017a). The APA Ethics Code applies to all psychology specialty areas, including forensic psychology. However, different sections may hold more or less relevance for various aspects of forensic practice than they do for clinical psychology or other areas of practice. For example, it may be more common to have one's credentials called into question (Standard 2.01, Boundaries of Competence) in forensic practice than in routine clinical practice. The aspirational general principles and enforceable standards provide important guidance that can be supplemented by additional resources.

A Note About Nonmaleficence

Health care ethics typically emphasizes the long-held value that avoiding bringing harm to others is a primary goal. The obligation to do no harm represents half of the first APA General Principle (Beneficence and Nonmaleficence). However, in most forensic contexts, one party or the other is harmed by the outcome, and forensic psychologists often contribute directly to such an outcome. For example, the outcome of a psychological evaluation in the context of a criminal death penalty case could eventually lead to the person's execution or lifelong incarceration. However, if the defendant does not end up being executed or spending the rest of his life incarcerated, the family of a murdered victim may forever experience feelings of injustice. In personal injury litigation, multimillion-dollar awards may hang in the balance, to be swayed by the conclusions of a psychological evaluation, with either the plaintiff or an insurance carrier being harmed by the result. In child custody cases, family relationships and the well-being of children are at stake, typically with one parent and sometimes one or more children believing that they have been harmed by the outcome.

Thus, forensic practitioners should understand that their opinions can contribute to harmful outcomes for one party or the other (Bush, 2018b). Nevertheless, when competent services have been provided, it is not the psychological service that is harmful; it is the outcome of the legal matter. The psychologist's primary ethical obligation is to seek truth within the bounds of scientific understanding, which assists the court in the pursuit of justice; the psychologist's obligation is not to a particular party in the matter. Providing competent services in an unbiased manner that is beneficial, rather than harmful, to the judicial decision-making process is consistent with ethical practice and should be the goal of the psychologist.

SPECIALTY GUIDELINES FOR FORENSIC PSYCHOLOGY: A BRIEF OVERVIEW

The Guidelines were designed to be consistent with the APA Ethics Code while providing more specific guidance to forensic psychologists than is offered in the APA Ethics Code. The goals of the Guidelines were

> to improve the quality of forensic psychological services; enhance the practice and facilitate the systematic development of forensic psychology; encourage a high level of quality in professional practice; and encourage forensic practitioners to acknowledge and respect the rights of those they serve. (APA, 2013, p. 7)

The Guidelines consist of an introductory section followed by eleven guidelines, each with multiple subsections. The 11 guidelines are listed in Exhibit 1.1 and are referred to throughout the book. The Guidelines provide an essential resource as a supplement to the APA Ethics Code. Although the ethical standards of the APA Ethics Code are enforceable rules of conduct and the Guidelines are aspirational, forensic practitioners nevertheless benefit from considering the Guidelines a valuable resource for informing professional behavior and should be prepared for explaining why they deviated from these expectations.

RELATED PROFESSIONAL GUIDELINES

The Introduction and Applicability section of the APA Ethics Code states, "psychologists may consider other materials and guidelines that have been adopted or endorsed by scientific and professional psychological organizations . . ."

EXHIBIT 1.1

The 11 Specialty Guidelines for Forensic Psychology

 1. Responsibilities
 2. Competence
 3. Diligence
 4. Relationships
 5. Fees
 6. Informed Consent, Notification, and Assent
 7. Conflicts in Practice
 8. Privacy, Confidentiality, and Privilege
 9. Methods and Procedures
10. Assessment
11. Professional and Other Public Communications

Data from APA (2013).

during the process of making decisions about professional behavior. To go a step further, we suggest that forensic psychologists *must* consider guidelines promulgated within their areas of specialization and appropriately endorsed by recognized organizations leading the field to which they apply. The intentionally general nature of the APA Ethics Code offers a solid foundation for many aspects of forensic practice, but more specific application of ethical principles and acceptable practice parameters is required and can be found in a number of publications from APA and other professional organizations. Table 1.1 provides a summary of some of the available guidelines from psychological organizations. Some of these guidelines undergo periodic revision, so psychologists should periodically check the websites and publications of the sponsoring organizations to ensure that they are in possession of the most recent versions of the documents. Although the focus of Table 1.1 is on position statements generated by psychological organizations, many informative papers are also available from related professions, such as psychiatry, counseling, and medicine, as well as legal societies.

TABLE 1.1. Professional Guidelines and Position Statements Relevant to Forensic Psychology

Organization	Year	Title
AACN	2001	Policy Statement on the Presence of 3rd Party Observers in Neuropsychological Assessments
	2003	Official Position of the American Academy of Clinical Neuropsychology on Ethical Complaints Made Against Clinical Neuropsychologists During Adversarial Proceedings
	2009	American Academy of Clinical Neuropsychology Consensus Conference Statement on the Neuropsychological Assessment of Effort, Response Bias, and Malingering
	2010	Official Position of the American Academy of Clinical Neuropsychology on Serial Neuropsychological Assessments: The Utility and Challenges of Repeat Test Administrations in Clinical and Forensic Contexts
	2015	Official Position of the American Academy of Clinical Neuropsychology Social Security Administration Policy on Validity Testing: Guidance and Recommendations for Change
AACN, ABN, SCN (APA Division 40), & NAN	2018	Deciding to Adopt Revised and New Psychological and Neuropsychological Tests
AAPL	2005	Ethics Guidelines for the Practice of Forensic Psychiatry
	2015	Practice Guideline for Forensic Assessment
ABA & APA	2008	Assessment of Older Adults With Diminished Capacity: A Handbook for Psychologists
ABN	2014	Policy statement of the American Board of Professional Neuropsychology regarding third party observation and the recording of psychological test administration in neuropsychological evaluations
AERA, APA, NCME	2014	Standards for Educational and Psychological Testing

TABLE 1.1. Professional Guidelines and Position Statements Relevant to Forensic Psychology *(Continued)*

Organization	Year	Title
APA	1994	Guidelines for Child Custody Evaluations in Divorce Proceedings
	1999	Test Security: Protecting the Integrity of Tests
	1999	Guidelines for Psychological Evaluations in Child Protection Matters
	2007	Record Keeping Guidelines
	2007	Statement on Third Party Observers in Psychological Testing and Assessment: A Framework for Decision Making
	2010	Guidelines for Child Custody Assessment
	2013	Specialty Guidelines for Forensic Psychology
	2017a	Ethical Principles of Psychologists and Code of Conduct
	2017b	Professional Practice Guidelines for Occupationally Mandated Psychological Evaluations
ASAPIL	2014	Psychological Assessment of Symptom and Performance Validity, Response Bias, and Malingering
ASPPB	2005	ASPPB Code of Conduct (currently under revision)
CPA	2001	Practice Guidelines for Providers of Psychological Services
	2017	Canadian Code of Ethics for Psychologists—4th Edition
NAN	2000	Presence of 3rd Party Observers During Neuropsychological Testing: Official Statement of the National Academy of Neuropsychology
	2000	Test Security: Official Position Statement of the National Academy of Neuropsychology
	2003	Informed Consent: Official Statement of the National Academy of Neuropsychology
	2003	Test Security: An Update. Official Statement of the National Academy of Neuropsychology
	2005	Independent and Court-Ordered Forensic Neuropsychological Examinations: Official Statement of the National Academy of Neuropsychology
	2005	Symptom Validity Assessment: Practice Issues and Medical Necessity
	2009	Secretive Recording of Neuropsychological Testing and Interviewing
	2012	Conflict of Interest Inherent in Contingency Fee Arrangements
SCN (Division 40)	2007	Disclosure of Neuropsychological Test Data
SCN (Division 40), APPCN, & AACN	2007	Disclosure of Neuropsychological Test Data

Note. AACN = American Academy of Clinical Neuropsychology; AAPL = American Academy of Psychiatry and the Law; ABA = American Bar Association; ABN = American Board of Professional Neuropsychology; AERA = American Educational Research Association; APA = American Psychological Association; ASAPIL = Association for Scientific Advancement in Psychological Injury and Law; ASPPB = Association of State and Provincial Psychology Boards; NAN = National Academy of Neuropsychology; NCME = National Council on Measurement in Education; SCN = Society for Clinical Neuropsychology (APA Division 40). Complete references are available in the reference section. Note that some of the papers are referenced according to the contributing authors from the organizations rather than the organizations themselves. From *Ethical Decision Making in Clinical Neuropsychology* (2nd ed., pp. 26–31), by S. S. Bush, 2018, New York, NY: Oxford University Press. Copyright 2018 by Oxford University Press. Adapted with permission.

CONSIDERATION OF JURISDICTIONAL LAWS

The Introduction and Applicability section of the Ethics Code instructs psychologists to consider applicable laws and psychology board regulations during their ethical decision-making process. Packer and Grisso (2011) highlighted the issue this way:

> All psychologists must be familiar with the laws that govern their practice. However, the level of knowledge required for forensic practice is significantly higher because the very nature of forensic psychological practice involves interface with the law. Forensic psychologists must develop competencies related both to the application of psychological expertise to legal concepts, as well as the legal issues related to the practice of psychology. (p. 164)

Specific statutes and case law are covered in relevant sections throughout this book. We now turn to a brief overview of the sometimes confusing Health Insurance Portability and Accountability Act (HIPAA) requirements.

HIPAA

At the federal level, HIPAA took effect in April 2003 and has been a source of confusion for forensic psychologists. This legislation was intended to simplify and protect the confidentiality of electronic billing and transmission of health information, as well as to provide increased patient access to their medical records, including the right of patients to amend their medical records to correct errors. Although those goals may seem logical and straightforward, the legislation evolved into a complex series of administrative rules, with exceptions for certain settings.

Of particular relevance to forensic practice is the determination of whether HIPAA applies to forensic services and, if so, to what extent. HIPAA states that information compiled in anticipation of use in *civil, criminal, and administrative* proceedings is not subject to the same right of review and amendment as is health care information in general (HIPAA, 1996).

Connell and Koocher (2003) opined that forensic practice may not be subject to HIPAA because (a) forensic services are designed to serve a legal purpose, rather than a therapeutic purpose; (b) forensic services are provided at the request of a party or entity outside of the health care system; (c) forensic services fall outside of health insurance coverage, because they do not constitute health care; (d) forensic psychologists do not ordinarily transmit data electronically except in the specific ways for which consent has historically been obtained from the examinee; and (e) no new protections or rights accrue to examinees by way of HIPAA compliance (i.e., no new right of access and amendment of information gathered in anticipation of litigation).

Legitimate arguments, also noted by Connell and Koocher (2003), posit that forensic practitioners indeed need to become HIPAA compliant. Such arguments include (a) the observation that assessment and diagnosis with respect to an individual's mental condition or functional status may, in fact, constitute health care, according to HIPAA; and, as a result, psychologists who provide forensic assessment services may be considered by HIPAA to be covered entities; (b) to obtain health care information about an examinee from other service providers, forensic psychologists must provide assurance that the information will be handled in a secure way; and (c) the question of whether forensic psychologists are covered entities will likely fall to case law for resolution, and it may prove less expensive and burdensome to become compliant than to become the case that decides the issue. Borkosky, Pellett, and Thomas (2014) explained that HIPAA has no exclusion criteria based on type of service, only inclusion criteria for providers. They concluded, "the evidence strongly suggests that, for those forensic mental health practitioners who are *covered entities*, HIPAA does apply to forensic evaluations" (p. 1, emphasis in original).

Scholars continue to consider the HIPAA Privacy Rule to be complex, difficult to understand, and unclear, especially as applied to forensic practice (e.g., Knapp, VandeCreek, & Fingerhut, 2017). It has been reported that one's entire practice is subject to the requirements of HIPAA if, at the time that a given service is provided, the HIPAA rule is applicable for even one patient (Bennett et al., 2006; Knapp et al., 2017). Therefore, psychologists whose practices consist of both direct forensic activities (e.g., hired by attorneys or appointed by courts to accomplish assessment) and clinical activities that occur in medicolegal contexts are more likely to be subject to HIPAA requirements than those whose practice is solely forensic in nature. These authors have recommended that even psychologists who are not covered by HIPAA may be well served by complying with its standards.

Of course, many laws, not just HIPAA, govern the privacy of and patient access to records. State laws address these issues in various ways and may establish guidelines that are more protective of patient privacy. It has been reported that 47 states "have statutes or rules that are consistent with, or *more stringent* than HIPAA records release requirements" (Borkosky et al., 2014, p. 5, emphasis in original). When considering the applicability of overlapping state and federal laws, the more stringent of the two applies. Thus, when HIPAA and state laws conflict, it is prudent to adhere to the law that is most protective of health care information. Consultation with professional organizations and legal resources in the jurisdictions in which one practices will typically result in the most appropriate practices for a given psychologist.

Conflicts Between Ethics and Law

Jurisdictional laws, regulations, and other governing legal authority provide requirements for professional behavior that must be followed. However, sometimes laws or other sources of legal authority conflict with each other or with professional ethics. When laws and ethics conflict, psychologists should make known their commitment to professional ethics and take reasonable steps to resolve the conflict (Standard 1.02). Psychologists pursuing the highest standards of conduct may strive to compromise with legal authorities when the APA Ethics Code requires a higher standard of professional behavior than does the law. In many instances, efforts to compromise result both in the legal system receiving the information or action it requires and in the preservation of the integrity of psychological information or techniques. Although all such attempts may not meet with equal success, the attempts themselves help to educate others about the ethical concerns of psychologists and demonstrate the psychologist's commitment to high practice standards.

APPLYING RISK MANAGEMENT STRATEGIES IN FORENSIC PRACTICE

In 1984, Alan Stone wrote, "The philosophers say life is a moral adventure; I would add that to choose a career in forensic psychiatry is to choose to increase the risks of that moral adventure" (p. 73). Psychologists engaging in forensic professional activities enter an environment with moral, ethical, and professional challenges that are often quite different from those found in clinical practice. These challenges and their associated potential ethical pitfalls put the unprepared psychologist at considerable risk for at least allegations of professional misconduct if not actual professional misconduct. A significant contribution to decreasing one's vulnerability to professional misconduct can be made by striving to understand the laws that govern one's practice. As Sales and Miller (1993) indicated, however,

> most professionals do not know about, much less understand, most of the laws that affect their practice, the services they render, and the clients they serve . . . not knowing about the laws that affect the services they render can result in incompetent performance of, and liability for, the mental health professional. (p. 1)

Bennett et al. (2006) defined *risk* as "the calculation that a particular . . . service will lead to a good or bad outcome and that the outcome will have positive or negative consequences" (p. 11). They also noted that "ultimately risk management is a business decision in which you decide how much time and effort to put into implementing risk management principles into your professional practice" (p. 9). For forensic psychologists invested in minimizing risk, continuing education in the areas of one's psychological specialty, the laws that regulate one's practice, the interface of the specialty practice with the legal system, and risk management itself are all necessary to maximally reduce the likelihood of engaging in professional misconduct. However, knowledge is not enough. Forensic psychologists must be committed to applying that knowledge in a manner that is consistent with ethical practice.

Where professional competence has been established and is being maintained, the greatest risk to ethical misconduct in forensic psychology seems to be the potential influence of bias. Assessment of one's performance and attitudes, through both self-assessment and peer review, helps to identify and address biases that could otherwise lead to risk mismanagement. For example, a strong or inflexible belief in the value of a particular methodology or symptom etiology or course, while sufficient much of the time, could result in inaccurate or inappropriate determinations in a given case. Bias in this context, however, refers not only to a philosophical preference for one aspect of the professional literature or another, but also to bias in favor of the retaining party resulting in the intentional selection of instruments that may result in favorable outcomes or the modification of opinions or testimony designed solely to support the position of the retaining party. Bias can exert its influence even when the psychologist is well armed with information about the professionally correct course of action.

To justify one's positions and behaviors, clear and detailed documentation of the rationale should be maintained. As Behnke and colleagues (2003) stated, "*the process by which a clinician decides what to do* becomes as important as the decision itself" (emphasis in original; p. 13). Documentation that the psychologist understood the values at stake and followed a rational process of ethical decision making will, if necessary, inform any outside reviewer that the ethical challenge was addressed in a thoughtful and systematic manner. Such documentation of the decision-making process is the forensic psychologist's best protection against liability (Behnke et al., 2003). Bennett and colleagues (2006) highlighted the unique risk management usefulness of documentation with this warning: "From a legal perspective, the general rule is 'if it isn't written down, it didn't happen.' Records are given deference in disciplinary actions" (p. 45).

When issues of professional liability are in doubt, psychologists are well served by consulting their professional liability insurance carrier and perhaps their personal attorney as well. In considering the consultation, it is essential to keep in mind that the interests of the attorney or insurance carrier may overlap with one's own, but in some respects, may not, and at the end of the day, one must be comfortable that the action to be taken reflects the values and ethics held to be meaningful.

AN ETHICAL DECISION-MAKING MODEL FOR FORENSIC PSYCHOLOGY

Determining a course of professional behavior that not only avoids ethical misconduct according to an ethics code but also adheres to high aspirational principles requires a commitment to ethical ideals. Determining such a course of action requires access to the necessary tools, and it requires effort and time. Some practitioners may find adherence to the letter of enforceable ethical standards to be sufficient. In our view, however, it is difficult to justify choosing not to pursue the highest standard of ethical behavior available to psychologists. As Knapp and VandeCreek (2003) stated, "Ethics Codes of professions are, by their very nature, incomplete moral codes" (p. 7). Positive ethics requires a shift from an emphasis on misconduct and disciplinary action to an emphasis on the pursuit of one's highest ethical potential (Knapp et al., 2017). The forensic psychologist must understand not simply that certain practices are unethical but also why they are unethical.

The ability to develop ethical practices and arrive at sound ethical decisions is facilitated through use of systematic decision-making process. A variety of ethical decision-making models have been proposed by psychology scholars. The models vary in terms of the steps outlined by the drafters and the focus, depending on the specific context in which the model is being proposed. Having considered a number of models in preparation for the first edition of this work, we (Bush, Connell, & Denney, 2006) developed an eight-step model that incorporated steps common to existing models as well as components that were found to be lacking in those models. The model was designed to provide forensic psychologists with a structured, evidence-based means of establishing ethical practices and avoiding or resolving ethical challenges. Given the complexity of many ethical challenges and the range of information and consultation that may be needed to determine an appropriate course of action, it may be beneficial, consistent with the four As of ethical practice (described in the Introduction), for practitioners to anticipate potential ethical needs and challenges and determine in advance optimal courses of action. The original eight steps of the forensic psychology ethical decision-making model were as follows: (a) identify the problem, (b) consider the significance of the context and setting, (c) identify and utilize ethical and legal resources, (d) consider personal beliefs and values, (e) develop possible solutions to the problem, (f) consider the potential consequences of various solutions, (g) choose and implement a course of action, and (h) assess the outcome and implement changes as needed.

In the continuing evolution of ethical decision making, Bush, Allen, and Molinari (2017) reduced the model's eight steps to seven and provided a mnemonic to assist practitioners with remembering the steps. The updated model combines the previously separated steps of developing solutions and considering the consequences of the solutions, given that likely consequences often emerge as the possible solutions are generated. Additionally, focus of the second step was modified to more specifically address the obligations owed to the various parties within the context or setting. The mnemonic *CORE OPT* can help practitioners follow the ethical decision-making steps and arrive at a correct option. Table 1.2 lists the ethical decision-making steps according to the mnemonic and provides questions to be asked at each step in the decision-making process. Application of the model can help psychologists develop ethical practices and arrive at sound solutions to ethical challenges, but it is insufficient if the psychologist lacks personal integrity and a commitment to high standards of ethical practice.

Step 1: Clarify the Ethical Issues(s)

Some professional activities considered by or requested of forensic psychologists are clearly appropriate and ethical, and some are clearly not. However,

TABLE 1.2. Ethical Decision-Making Steps and Questions

CORE OPT mnemonic	Question
Clarify the ethical issue	What is the ethical issue?
Obligations owed to stakeholders	Who are the stakeholders, and what are my obligations to them?
Resources—ethical and legal	What references can inform me about the issue?
Examine personal beliefs and values	How might my values and beliefs affect my decisions?
Options, solutions, and consequences	What are my options?
Put plan into practice	Which option should I choose?
Take stock, evaluate outcome, and revise as needed	How did it work out, and is anything else needed?

Note. Adapted from *Ethical Practice in Geropsychology* (pp. 41–42), by S. S. Bush, R. S. Allen, and V. A. Molinari, 2017, Washington, DC: American Psychological Association. Copyright 2017 by the American Psychological Association.

many options available to practitioners are ambiguous or present complex layers to be considered. Forensic psychologists must keep in mind that a wide range of potential behaviors may be appropriate when considering courses of action and when reviewing the work of colleagues. A distinction may need to be made between ethical, legal, moral, and professional perspectives. These overlapping concepts may need to be parsed out in order to identify or clarify the ethical issue or dilemma.

Professional behaviors that are clearly ethical or unethical need little explanation or discussion. Blatantly unethical behavior harming others or obstructing just legal determinations may invoke a host of negative consequences. If one observes such behavior in a colleague, a course of action must be taken to remedy the situation. However, in the less clear circumstances often experienced in practice, a psychologist may encounter a request or a situation that arouses feelings of uneasiness, a sense that something may be wrong with the situation. In such situations, the psychologist must consider possible reasons for the unease and attempt to narrow down the possibilities, eventually focusing on those elements of the situation that are contributing to the initial feelings of discomfort.

To illustrate, a psychologist retained by an attorney to evaluate a plaintiff who has been experiencing posttraumatic stress from a motor vehicle collision may be asked by the attorney to describe the patient's severe symptoms, her total and permanent disability, and the causal link between the collision and the posttraumatic stress and disability. A request such as this, which may seem straightforward on the surface, may involve a host of issues that would need to be considered by the psychologist (e.g., regarding how clearly the causal link has been established or whether the psychologist believes it to be something that can be determined by virtue of the examination). The psychologist would benefit from determining, as specifically as possible, what it is about the situation that is troubling. The psychologist may feel uneasy about the appropriateness of writing such a report when the evaluation results may not support the facts as presented by the plaintiff's attorney. If such a situation had been considered in advance, the psychologist would likely have known exactly how to respond to the request. Consider next that the plaintiff's attorney, upon receiving the report, is very pleased with the conclusions and promises to send more cases to the psychologist but first asks that psychologist to make a couple minor edits, including deleting information about a prior traumatic event and postcollision substance abuse. The psychologist must determine whether complying with the request could simply reflect a professional choice or would have ethical or legal implications.

Step 2: Consider Obligations Owed to Stakeholders

Forensic psychologists work in a wide variety of settings and contexts, with differing roles and differing obligations to the parties and institutions involved. In any forensic role, there may be a number of individuals or institutions to whom or to which obligations are owed. Although differing by context, some possible parties to whom obligations may be owed include the following: referral source, client, examinee, surrogate decision makers, employing institution, profession of psychology, trier of fact, court, legal system, and society at large. In some contexts, these parties may overlap, whereas in others, they are distinct.

Just as there exists a range of individuals or institutions owed obligations, there is a range of obligations that may be owed. Professional activities that are appropriate in one forensic setting or one set of obligations may be inappropriate in others. In general terms, the forensic psychologist has an obligation to provide competent services that advance the interests of justice without bringing unjust harm to the individuals and institutions involved. The nature of the harm to be avoided has been specified as "unjust" harm. This clarification is provided because, due to the adversarial nature of the legal system, many of the opinions offered or determinations made by psychologists may be considered unfavorable and thus harmful to one of the parties involved in a case. Such opinions or determinations are only unethical if they were reached in an inappropriate manner.

Step 3: Utilize Ethical and Legal Resources

There exist many published resources, sometimes offering conflicting guidance, relevant to ethical issues encountered in forensic psychology. Nevertheless, by utilizing both the published and interpersonal resources described in this section, the forensic psychologist can likely establish a solid foundation for determining courses of action that are consistent with ethical practice. The various resources are presented here in an order consistent with a deductive or top-down method of ethical reasoning and decision making

(Beauchamp & Childress, 2013). This method involves applying a general rule to a specific case.

First, assess the foundational values. General bioethical principles, the ethics codes of professional organizations, and jurisdictional laws all reflect the values of a society. Examples of North American values include the right to self-determination and the right to adequate health care. These values underlie general bioethical principles, such as respect for a client's autonomy and the need to "do no harm" to the parties served by the health care professional. Determining the values underlying a given ethical standard or law helps to clarify the spirit behind the letter of the standard or law and, by extension, helps to clarify the appropriate course of action (Behnke et al., 2003). Behnke and colleagues (2003) advised that an ethical dilemma be approached by first asking the following questions, "What values are at issue? And how can I act consistent with those values?" (p. 225).

Second, determine the applicable bioethical principles. Beauchamp and Childress (2013) presented a model of bioethical principles reflecting society's fundamental values. Their model, which has been widely adopted across health care disciplines, posits four core principles: respect for autonomy, beneficence, nonmaleficence, and justice. As previously noted in this chapter, these principles are clearly evident in the APA Ethics Code.

Applying the Beauchamp and Childress (2013) model to ethical challenges in forensic psychology can be of considerable use in determining an appropriate course of action. However, dilemmas emerge or increase in complexity in situations in which one value is pitted against another. For example, from an ethical perspective, recommending that a particular parent be awarded custody based on the wishes of an older adolescent examinee may be consistent with respecting the adolescent's autonomy, but it may also result in psychological or other harm to the adolescent and others involved, if the decision is made solely on that factor. Weighing the relative importance of the principles involved and attempting to strike a balance that satisfies the greater good is the task of the forensic psychologist. Of course, such determinations need not, and often should not, be made in isolation.

Third, review relevant professional ethics codes. Ethics codes are developed to clarify and operationalize the concepts embodied in declarations of professional values (Beauchamp & Childress, 2013). The APA Ethics Code provides guidance for ethical psychological practice. Whereas the Code's General Principles are aspirational in nature, the ethical standards provide more concrete dicta for ethical practice and should be consulted to establish ethical practices and achieve ethical solutions. The standards are the enforceable minimum level of ethical conduct for psychologists who are APA members or whose state boards have adopted the APA Ethics Code as the professional regulations or rules of practice for licensed psychologists.

Fourth, psychologists must be familiar with the jurisdictional laws that regulate the profession of psychology where they practice. State and federal laws offer specific direction on how to manage fundamental aspects of psychological practice; however, specific practices pertaining to psychological specialty areas, such as forensic psychology, may not be adequately addressed by statutory or case law.

Fifth, refer to position statements ("white papers") of relevant professional psychological associations. Beauchamp and Childress (2013) noted, "Often no straightforward movement from general norms, principles, precedents, or theories to particular judgments is possible. General norms are usually only starting points for the development of norms of conduct suitable for specific contexts" (p. 2). Position statements offer clarification of details of practice areas that are beyond the scope of an ethics code. Many of these statements are listed in Table 1.1 and are readily available from the websites of the organizations authoring or endorsing them. The Guidelines provide ethical guidance specific to forensic activities, much of which overlaps substantially with the APA Ethics Code.

Sixth, review relevant scholarly publications, such as journal articles, books, and book chapters. General ethics texts provide coverage of ethical issues of concern to forensic psychologists and may offer vignettes specific to forensic practice. Forensic psychology books cover, to varying degrees, many of the practice issues that are of ethical concern, and some dedicate specific chapters to ethics. In addition, texts from related psychology specialty areas, such as child and family psychology and neuropsychology, include chapters that address forensically relevant ethical issues. Other forensic psychology ethics books are also available (e.g., Otto et al., 2017; Pirelli, Beattey, & Zapf, 2017). Thus, there exist many published resources that can assist the forensic psychologist striving to establish an ethical practice and anticipate or address ethical challenges.

Seventh, consult experienced and ethically knowledgeable colleagues. Such consultation may occur informally through discussions with colleagues, formally through contact with ethics committees, or both. Professional liability insurance carriers also typically have consultants available to advise their clients about risk management issues. The experiences of colleagues who have faced similar ethical challenges and the collective knowledge and experience of ethics committees may provide invaluable assistance to the psychologist facing an ethical dilemma. Consultation with others in one's own jurisdiction may offer the advantage of sensitivity to both the legal and ethical aspects of a case. However, one might also need, in certain circumstances, to seek consultation from outside the geographic area to preserve confidentiality of case involvement or of details of the matter. It is useful to establish several collegial consultative relationships and to seek expertise to address the relevant issues of the matter at hand. The consultation may be formalized, even on a case-by-case basis, by establishing a consultation agreement, retaining the consultant at an hourly fee, and requesting that the consultant maintain a record of the consultation. Such consultation can then be identified, if later needed, as one of the ways the psychologist strived to meet the ethical challenge in a professional and thoughtful way.

Step 4: Examine Personal Beliefs and Values

In addition to, or at times in contrast to, the collective values of a society, the psychologist may endorse a particular value to some degree along a continuum. Forensic psychologists have a responsibility to evaluate the degree to which their personal moral positions are consistent with those of the larger society and the organizations to which they belong. To the extent possible, they should attempt to understand their biases and the potential impact of their values and biases on their professional and ethical decision making. Psychologists may also draw on personal values other than those reflected in a model of professional ethics, such as those inspired by their religion or cultural background. It is critically important that forensic psychologists, whose work often involves matters laden with moral and values implications, attempt to understand the potential influences of their personal beliefs on their professional behavior.

Step 5: Consider Options, Solutions and Consequences

When confronted with an ethical dilemma, inaction is typically not an ethical option. The legal counsel that one may obtain would typically address the issue from a "risk management" perspective, arguing for temporary inaction or for avoidance of efforts at resolution that might incur liability, while the principles by which the psychologist practices may argue for action that remediates potential suffering or injustice on the part of a party in the situation. The complex dilemmas that pit one ethical principle against another, or ethical against legal obligations, may tax the most thoughtful practitioner.

Generating a list of possible solutions requires integration of the significance of the context and obligations owed, information obtained from available resources, and personal beliefs and values. In some situations, the best course of action may be clear upon such consideration. However, in other ethically challenging situations, practitioners may need to generate a number of potential solutions in as much detail as possible. Consider the example of the request to have a third party present during a forensic evaluation. Having considered the ethical and legal issues, there are a variety of options that the forensic psychologist might consider. Some of these options include (a) complying as requested, possibly with some conditions, such as the third-party observer remaining quiet and out of the examinee's line of sight; (b) refusing to perform the evaluation; (c) offering to allow the third-party observer to be present during the interview but not during testing; (d) offering to have the evaluation recorded; and (e) educating the involved parties about the ethical issues, including the impact of third-party presence on examinee performance, and suggesting that the request be rescinded.

Once possible solutions to the ethical problem have been developed, potential consequences must be considered. Both positive and negative consequences must be anticipated. In a manner similar to determining the relative importance of the underlying values, the potential positive and negative consequences of each action may need to be weighed to determine the best option. Attempting to negotiate a solution that is acceptable to all involved parties can foster good will and a spirit of cooperation with those with whom one wishes to work, whereas obstructive or oppositional attitudes are typically less beneficial. Thus, the potential consequences may extend beyond solely ethical considerations to those with business and other implications. Forensic psychologists must consider potential consequences, weigh their options, and pursue the option that is most consistent with high standards of ethical practice.

Step 6: Put the Plan Into Practice

Once potential solutions have been examined and consequences considered, the practitioner must select and implement the most appropriate course of action. The timing of the action may be critical to its success. Depending on the issues involved and the context, the course of action may need to occur quickly or may need to be delayed. Consultation with colleagues may be particularly valuable in weighing the best time to respond to situations in which timing must be taken into account. Advanced consideration of the types of ethical challenges that are likely to be encountered in a given practice context may help eliminate the panic that can be experienced and faulty decision making that can ensue when one must confront an urgent issue unprepared. The solution need not be perfect, because the reality of forensic practice seldom allows for such an option; however, the selected solution should be ethically sound and defensible.

Step 7: Take Stock, Evaluate the Outcome, and Revise as Needed

To ensure that the outcome was as anticipated and desired, the psychologist must evaluate the effectiveness of the decision or action. This process also affords the psychologist the opportunity to implement changes if needed. With many difficult ethical decisions in forensic psychology, the chosen action may be unsatisfactory to one or more of the parties involved. The psychologist should be prepared to receive and respond to feedback about the decisions made and actions taken. Being able to refer to the structured decision-making process and the evidence base (i.e., resources) that informed the decision helps the psychologist to explain how and why the decision was made. Documentation of the issues and process prepares the psychologist to address questions and defend one's choices and actions.

CONCLUSION

The interface of psychology and the law is unfamiliar territory for many, perhaps most, psychologists entering forensic practice. The ethical issues of most relevance and the manner in which ethical principles and standards are applied differ between clinical and forensic activities. Psychologists who successfully engage in forensic activities understand the importance establishing and maintaining ethical competence, including the value of a systematic approach to ethical decision making. As with clinical decision making, there are many resources that provide the evidence base needed for making sound ethical decisions. Psychologists who strive to anticipate ethical needs and challenges and to prepare practice activities to meet those needs and address the challenges are well positioned to apply their knowledge and skills in the interests of justice.

2

The Referral

The *Specialty Guidelines for Forensic Psychology* (SGFP; American Psychological Association [APA], 2013) state that "professional conduct is considered forensic from the time the practitioner reasonably expects to, agrees to, or is legally mandated to provide expertise on an explicitly psycholegal issue" (p. 7). When a practitioner is contacted and agrees to provide a forensic service or learns that a mandated service is required, a variety of ethical issues become relevant and need to be considered and addressed. Some ethical responsibilities begin immediately (e.g., confidentiality), whereas others begin after the agreement regarding compensation has been reached (SGFP Guideline 4.01: Responsibilities to Retaining Parties). Ethical issues most relevant to the referral involve (a) the relationship between the retaining party and the examiner, (b) objectivity, (c) advocacy, (d) professional competence, and (e) financial arrangements. This chapter describes ethical issues related to the forensic referral, including (a) the relationship between the retaining party and the forensic practitioner, (b) the importance of professional competence, and (c) the handling of financial arrangements. A case example is used to illustrate the relevant ethical issues using the ethical decision-making model.

THE RETAINING PARTY–EXAMINER RELATIONSHIP

The fundamental human value underlying the retaining party–examiner relationship is respect for autonomy, which may be operationalized in this regard by observing that all parties are entitled to a clear understanding of the

http://dx.doi.org/10.1037/0000164-003
Ethical Practice in Forensic Psychology, Second Edition: A Guide for Mental Health Professionals, by S. S. Bush, M. Connell, and R. L. Denney

expectations of the others involved in order to make a fully informed decision about whether to engage in the relationship. The court is entitled to expect from its experts the clarity of purpose upon which reliable testimony is based. In order to have clarity of purpose, all individuals in the process must have clearly defined roles. The ethical principle of respect for autonomy reflects this informed decision-making process.

When accepting a forensic case, psychologists should perform each step of their work in a manner that is defensible within the legal forum. The relationship between the retaining party and the examiner is the foundation upon which all forensic psychological services are based. A lack of clarity among involved parties regarding roles and responsibilities renders the working relationship vulnerable to subsequent misunderstanding and conflict and in itself represents possible ethical misconduct (see *Ethical Principles of Psychologists and Code of Conduct* [APA Ethics Code]; APA, 2017a; Standard 3.07, Third-Party Requests for Services; SGFP Guideline 4.01: Responsibilities to Retaining Parties).

Identifying one's role is not always as straightforward as might be anticipated. Clarifying the questions to answer or forensic issues in question in the context of a matter is essential to understanding one's role. The forensic issues may involve a plaintiff's or criminal defendant's cognitive or psychological functioning or the relationships among individuals. Improving the decision-maker's understanding of the plaintiff's or defendant's psychological functioning serves the larger legal question on which the case is based, such as the plaintiff's right to compensation, whether an accused is guilty, or the allocation of parental responsibilities in a way that serves the best interests of the child. Therefore, when identifying one's role, "an important first step is to identify the forensic issues contained in the legal questions that have triggered the need for the evaluation" (Heilbrun, 2001, p. 22).

An understanding of the nature of the information the psychologist gives the examinee and the extent to which information obtained during the evaluation process will be kept confidential, or conversely its discoverability, is established through discussions between the psychologist and the retaining party, and it derives at least partially from statutory or case law (Melton et al., 2018). Thus, the psychologist and the retaining party must achieve clarity regarding their mutual expectations from the outset. Clarifying these issues upon receipt of the referral, or as soon thereafter as possible, promotes a smoother working relationship between the retaining party and the practitioner as the case proceeds.

Objectivity in the Role of Forensic Expert

The ability of forensic practitioners to provide opinions that are objective and evidence based (rather than significantly influenced by partisanship, prejudice, or passion) is what gives value to the expert in legal matters. Efforts to identify and reduce or eliminate the impact of bias on forensic opinions promote objectivity. Nevertheless, threats to objectivity remain in forensic practice contexts, and both psychology as a profession and the legal system in which forensic psychologists work are becoming increasingly aware of the biases that influence forensic assessments and opinions (Neal & Grisso, 2014). When retained as forensic experts, psychologists should anticipate attempts by attorneys to elicit opinions for which adequate support may not exist (Barsky & Gould, 2002). This may even occur at trial when tensions are high and there is limited opportunity to re-examine and discuss expectations and resolve conflicting interpretations of the data. By anticipating this possibility at the outset, the psychologist may be better prepared to maintain previously agreed upon boundaries. The outcome of the litigation should not be the direct concern of the testifying expert. Rather, the expert's carefully developed opinion, and the sound data upon which it rests, should remain the focus. The practitioner's task is to assist the court by providing reliable information relevant to the matter at hand.

After summarizing field and experimental research findings on the issue of forensic identification and objectivity, Neal (2017) noted that forensic practitioners tend, unintentionally, to adopt the viewpoint of the retaining party. A tendency exists for otherwise neutral forensic practitioners to interpret case information in a manner supportive of the position of the retaining party. Psychologists working as forensic experts can maintain or improve objectivity by understanding the potential for such unintentional bias and taking steps to maximize their potential for arriving at impartial conclusions. Such steps include ensuring professional competence (discussed in this chapter) and engaging in self-examination.

Self-examination questions (e.g., Sweet & Moulthrop, 1999) and strategies (e.g., Neal & Brodsky, 2016) offer practitioners possible means of maximizing current and future objectivity. Sweet and Moulthrop (1999) offered nine self-examination questions to help forensic experts identify and reduce bias (see Exhibit 2.1).

Of particular relevance to our discussion here are these questions:

- "Do I almost always reach conclusions that are favorable to the side that has retained me?"

- "Have I taken a position, in very similar cases, when retained by an attorney from one side that I did not take when retained by the opposite side?"

- "Have I been reaching the same diagnostic conclusion at a much higher base rate than my colleagues or at a higher rate than described in the literature?"

It can be helpful for forensic practitioners to consider whether they are retained because their opinions tend to be predictable; that is, their opinions consistently reflect advocacy for a particular belief, or they consistently favor the retaining party, rather than being based on the facts of a given case and the established knowledge of the profession.

Alternatively, there are situations in which experts are known for their research findings and are brought into a legal situation because of their views

EXHIBIT 2.1

Self-Examination Questions Regarding Bias for the Expert Witness

1. Do I receive referrals from only plaintiff attorneys or only defense attorneys?
2. Do I almost always reach conclusions favorable to the side that has retained me?
3. Have I moved away from being an expert witness to being an advocate?
4. Do I form opinions of plaintiff or defense positions prematurely, without having enough facts for a solid opinion?
5. Have I taken a position, in very similar cases, when retained by an attorney from one side that I did not take when retained by the opposite side?
6. Do I routinely apply the same decision rules for establishing brain dysfunction no matter which side retains me?
7. Have I been reaching the same diagnostic conclusion at a much higher base rate than my colleagues or at a higher rate than described in the literature?
8. Has my initial written opinion been altered by the time of deposition or trial testimony?
9. Does my emotional response to a case cloud or distort my objectivity?

Note. From "Self-Examination Questions as a Means of Identifying Bias in Adversarial Assessments," by J. J. Sweet and M. A. Moulthrop, 1999, *Journal of Forensic Neuropsychology*, *1*, pp. 73–88. Copyright 1999 by Taylor & Francis. Adapted with permission.

of the science. In such instances, it is not inconsistent with ethical standards to provide an opinion relevant to the case at hand but which also reflects the psychologist's professional viewpoint regarding the scientific literature. For example, one can easily understand why Professor Elizabeth Loftus would be repeatedly hired by attorneys specifically because of her robust research regarding the problems inherent in claims of repressed memories of childhood abuse (e.g., Loftus & Ketcham, 1994). It would be much less likely for those advocating for the authenticity of such claims of remote memories to hire Professor Loftus as an expert witness for their cases. Likewise, it would be rather unlikely for prosecutors to hire Professor James Flynn to discuss why the Flynn Effect should not be used in a particular death penalty case given his research and published views (e.g., Flynn, 2007). In instances like these and others, having a record of testimony consistently for one side in forensic cases does not necessarily suggest an ethical concern. In both of the above examples, the ethical expert witness opines based on his or her genuine understanding of the scientific literature in a manner that is forthright, balanced, and dispassionate.

The third question posed by Sweet and Moulthrop (1999, as shown in Exhibit 2.1) warrants special consideration as well: "Have I moved away from being an expert witness to being an advocate?" Unlike the more obvious financial incentive to potentially bias an expert, there are instances in which a more cloaked, yet powerful, cause exists that can quickly move an unbiased expert witness into advocacy for a specific case outcome: sociopolitical advocacy. In the area of death penalty litigation and sex offender litigation, for example, we have observed individuals involved as expert witnesses who had strong sociopolitical opinions that were simply not consistent with having a balanced scientific opinion. There have been instances in which expert witnesses who had very clear moral objections to the death penalty take down their website blogs on the subject (corresponding to the time they were contracted as criminal defense witnesses in the case), then "bend" the truth, emphasize erroneous statistical principles, ignore established scientific consensus, and claim that their views on the death penalty did not bias their opinions.

It is not ethical for an expert to "drag the science through the mud" to achieve a sociopolitical outcome. Sociopolitical outcomes should be decided in the legislature, not in the courtroom. As noted in regard to a priori ethical considerations (Denney, 2005a, 2012b), "clinicians who are strongly opposed to the death penalty have too great a possibility of inadvertent bias to participate in capital cases as nonpartisan evaluators" (Denney, 2012b, p. 486). Likewise, it would be improper for a psychologist to take on a custody examination, if the psychologist held an a priori sociopolitical viewpoint that fathers should never have sole custody of very young children in the case of divorce. Such strong views have too great a likelihood of biasing the expert even before evaluating either parent.

Prior to accepting cases that involve emotionally charged outcomes (e.g., sex offenses, child abuse, death penalty), ethical examiners consider earnestly whether their strongly held sociopolitical viewpoints would inadvertently influence their ability to come to a proper opinion. If the psychologist cannot tolerate the possibility of having an opinion on either side of the issue, the psychologist should not take the case. The SGFP guidelines make this issue quite explicit: "Forensic practitioners refrain from taking on a professional role when personal, professional, legal, financial, or other interests or relationships could reasonably be expected to impair their impartiality, competence, or effectiveness" (SGFP Guideline 1.03: Avoiding Conflicts of Interest).

On the basis of interviews of board-certified forensic psychologists, Neal and Brodsky (2016) identified several bias-correction strategies, including seeking to disconfirm rather than confirm one's hypotheses, in part by considering the opposite of one's current thought patterns, and seeking to be appointed by the court rather than retained by one side of the adversarial process. Research (Murrie, Boccaccini, Guarnera, & Rufino, 2013) also revealed that use of standardized assessment measures, particularly those with less subjectivity in scoring, promotes objectivity; specifically, the more objective the test, the lower the risk for the influence of adversarial allegiance.

Advocacy in the Role of Trial Consultant

In assuming the role of trial consultant, the psychologist enters a relationship with an attorney that is different from that of a testifying expert, in that advocacy may more reasonably be expected in the former. Nevertheless, the psychologist should advocate for evidence-based decisions (which can include a critical review of the work of colleagues) rather than advocate for a specific outcome in the case. When retained as a trial consultant, the psychologist essentially joins the retaining attorney's team to bring psychological expertise to the partisan adversarial process. Impartiality is not required of the trial consultant, but the psychologist trial consultant who holds a place on the "trial team" is cautioned against agreeing to transition into or concurrently participate in the case as an examining or testifying expert (Brodsky & Gutheil, 2016). Some authors have maintained that a consultant can assume both a partisan role in assisting an attorney's case and an impartial evaluator role during trial preparation and then, at the time of trial, maintain only the role of impartial evaluator (e.g., Halleck, 1980). Separating the acceptable bias of the consultant from the necessary objectivity of the evaluator, however, may be difficult if not impossible. Heilbrun (2001) identified as an emerging principle the "single role" maxim that should be familiar to the practicing forensic psychologist, advising the forensic psychologist to decline a referral when impartiality would likely be jeopardized.

Psychologists may find this distinction between testifying expert and consultant difficult to maintain. For example, an attorney may ask a psychologist that she has retained as a testifying expert for feedback regarding the opposing expert's report, which invokes a discussion about a point of disagreement between the experts. The testifying expert, in explaining the source of the difference, essentially offers the attorney a roadmap for cross-examining the opposing expert. Although there is no clear line distinguishing the appropriate contribution of a testifying expert from that of a nontestifying, consulting expert, practitioners help clarify the appropriate course of action by examining their motivations. When motivated to clarify genuine professional disagreement and its genesis, as well as to assist an attorney in making appropriate use of one's opinion, the testifying expert is on solid ground. However, when the motivation is to contribute as a member of the trial team, sharing the attorney's goal of winning the case, the psychologist has become an advocate whose opinions should not be offered as objective expertise.

Attorneys may not observe this distinction between trial consultant and testifying expert in the same way forensic practitioners do. In fact, attorneys may consider consultation an essential part of the service they are seeking and may designate the expert as a consulting expert until an examination is completed and the report is received. Only when the attorney is clear about what the expert can and will say on the stand is the attorney inclined to designate the expert as a testifying expert. The recommended "one case–one role" rule of thumb does not preclude being designated as a consulting expert during the earlier stages of the case. It matters more how the psychologist carries out the role. The role of jury consultant or trial consultant that is specifically intended to be a behind-the-scenes assistant to help in such activities as deciding which experts to retain, deciding what materials to have the potential testifying expert(s) review, assisting with development of cross-examination ideas, identifying which jury members may be most likely to be sensitive to specific issues, and other such activities may be different in purpose and expected professional objectivity. However, to be maximally useful, the expert fulfilling this role may adhere closely to overarching psychological ethical principles and standards. For example, the expert trial consultant would not participate in distortion of psychological examination findings, construct questions or suggest arguments that would suggest psychological theories that are not validated, that are known to have been discredited, or that are not applicable in the case at hand. The consultant psychologist should not contribute to intentional misrepresentation or misconstruing of data.

In some institutional settings, it may be contemplated that forensic psychologists can fulfill several different roles on the same case. For example, in military courts-martial, the contractual obligation of the expert may be to serve as consultant assisting in trial preparation, a potential teaching expert who testifies on some specific issue, and/or an examining expert who may testify during the findings or the sentencing portion of the case. Navigating these multiple roles in a way that is consistent with professional ethics may be a challenge, but the expert who is aware of the reasons for caution and who exercises appropriate self-monitoring may be able to successfully navigate this terrain (Connell, 2019; Stein & Younggren, 2019).

Likewise, forensic psychologists working within the correctional environment, particularly with competency restoration cases, may find themselves in a potential dual role of treatment provider and subsequent examiner. In many settings, treatment provider roles and end of treatment assessment roles are kept separate; however, there are instances in which this practice simply may not be possible (e.g., where specialized expertise is required for both the treatment and assessment, such as with unique neuropathologies). Standard 3.06, Conflict of Interest, of the APA Ethics Code (2017a) and SGFP Guideline 1.03: Avoiding Conflicts of Interest, describe these general issues under the direction of avoiding conflicts of interest. Per SGFP Guideline 1.03, it is recommended that psychologists make known such potential conflicts as soon as they become aware of them. In both the courts-martial and correctional settings, examiners may not have the flexibility to completely avoid every potential dual role.

When such situations are unavoidable, peer consultation and/or review is a viable option to verify that potential affiliation bias has not unduly affected the examination process. For example, after providing months of cognitive remediation in the context of court-ordered competency restoration, a psychologist requested a formal peer review by a panel of forensic psychology colleagues in the facility. The issue related to the assessment of competence to proceed in a situation where there were no other options but to provide treatment and examination due to the lack of other neuropsychological experts in the facility. In this instance, the court appreciated the added protection against affiliation bias potentially tainting the examination findings.

Professional Competence

Psychological services, to be effective and useful to consumers, must be performed competently. Such professional competence is obtained through some combination of "education, training, supervised experience, consultation, study, or professional experience" (Standard 2.01a, Boundaries of Competence). Competence is not universal; that is, competence in one area of psychology does not imply competence in another area. This is true across and within specialty areas of practice. Within specialty areas, competence does not necessarily transfer across patient populations or clinical settings. This specificity of competence is particularly significant in forensic settings or contexts, where specialized knowledge of the rules or laws governing the activity is essential. Further, competence in a particular psychology specialty area does not necessarily translate into competence in performing that specialty in a forensic context or setting (Heilbrun, 2001; Sullivan & Denney, 2008). Psychologists who provide expert testimony without having had proper specialty training are practicing beyond the scope of their competence.

The concept of professional competence is based on the fundamental human value that people have the right to competently provided services. The bioethical principles of beneficence and nonmaleficence reflect this underlying value. Psychologists who lack the necessary competence to provide their services in forensic contexts may not be able to provide an acceptable level of accuracy and reliability, and they risk harming those with whom they interact professionally. For example, a forensic practitioner who uses outdated or unreliable instruments or techniques to arrive at opinions may provide erroneous testimony or, at the very least, may be easily discredited on the witness stand, causing harm to the retaining party who counted on the service to be competently provided.

Just as competence is not universal, it is not static. Competence must be maintained through continuing education and relevant professional activities (Standard 2.03, Maintaining Competence). Research continues to evolve and to illuminate matters of interest to forensic psychologists. New instruments may be incorporated in practice to assist psychologists in arriving at the most refined opinions possible. It is incumbent on testifying experts to stay abreast of current literature and assessment techniques in the areas in which they offer opinions. Massey (2017) noted, "perhaps the most important aspect of developing and maintaining competence is self-awareness and the willingness to continuously assess one's competence throughout one's career" (p. 51).

Difficulty may lie in determining what represents competence in forensic psychology. Psychologists who engage in forensic activities come from or represent a range of specializations. Such diversity is important for assisting the court with the range of questions that emerge; however, ambiguity regarding qualifications may emerge in individual cases. In fact, despite the existence of a division of the APA devoted to psychological and legal issues (Division 41/ American Psychology-Law Society) and the American Board of Forensic Psychology established by the American Board of Professional Psychology (ABPP), there remains debate within the field regarding the definition of "forensic psychology" (e.g., Bartol & Bartol, 2019). Although board certification in forensic psychology by the ABPP provides the clearest evidence of competence for forensic practitioners, such certification is not currently required and is held by only a very small percentage of psychologists providing services in forensic contexts. Board certification in a different psychological specialty provides evidence of competence in that specialty, which may assist the judge in determining whether to declare the holder of that certification an expert for purposes of the testimony being offered in a given case. However, holding board certification in a specialty other than forensic psychology does not necessarily imply forensic competence in that area. Further, it certainly does not convey competence to practice more broadly forensically.

SGFP Guideline 2.01: Scope of Competence states,

> When determining one's competence to provide services in a particular matter, forensic practitioners may consider a variety of factors including the relative complexity and specialized nature of the service, relevant training and experience, the preparation and study they are able to devote to the matter, and the opportunity for consultation with a professional of established competence in the subject matter in question. (p. 9)

In the individual case, it is the court that determines who qualifies as an expert for the matter at hand. Rule 702 of the Federal Rules of Evidence (FRE; House of Representatives, Committee on the Judiciary, 2018) and state laws define who is qualified to testify as an expert. The psychologist is responsible for accurate representation of the knowledge, skill, experience, training, and education that comprise the relevant credentials (Standard 5.01a, Avoidance of False or Deceptive Statements; FRE 702). Challenges to expertise can be raised by the other side in voir dire of the proffered expert. The court then makes a determination, based on the relevance of the expert's credentials to the matter for which testimony is to be offered, i.e., whether to qualify the witness as an expert whose opinion testimony will assist the trier of fact (FRE 702). A psychologist may be "qualified" or recognized by the judge as an expert in a specific field, such as child abuse or eyewitness identification, or may be qualified by the court more broadly as an expert in forensic psychology. Nevertheless, surviving voir dire on one's qualifications and being recognized as an expert in forensic psychology does not obviate professional requirements for establishing and maintaining competence.

Financial Arrangements

Forensic practitioners are compensated in different ways depending on the nature of the case and the referral source. For example, different billing and reimbursement practices occur for publicly funded court-ordered evaluations than for evaluations funded by a law firm, disability insurance carrier, or directly by the examinee (Otto et al., 2017). For publicly funded court-ordered evaluations, the psychologist may have little influence on the manner in which fees are determined or in which payment occurs. With other referrals, the psychologist often has the flexibility to choose to have a fixed fee or hourly rate, with or without advance payment. In considering billing options, the goal is not only to be adequately and fairly compensated for one's services but also to limit the potential to have one's opinions or work product swayed by the possibility of increased revenue or, in the other direction, of not getting paid. Psychologists and their clients should establish compensation and billing arrangements in writing as early as possible in the professional relationship (Standard 6.04, Fees and Financial Arrangements).

The strength of the judicial system derives from society's expectation that the decisions rendered by the court are just. To that end, society anticipates that expert witnesses involved in serving the court will perform their duties objectively. Practices that have the potential to negatively affect objectivity, and by extension justice, must be carefully considered by psychologists. The manner in which the psychologist's fees are arranged is one factor that has the potential to significantly interfere with, or appear to interfere with, objectivity. When a psychologist's fees are contingent upon the outcome of a legal case, the psychologist is vulnerable to intentionally or unintentionally producing a report or testimony that favors the retaining party. Thus, SGFP Guideline 5.02, Fee Arrangements, states the following:

> . . . Forensic practitioners seek to avoid undue influence that might result from financial compensation or other gains. Because of the threat to impartiality presented by the acceptance of contingent fees and associated legal prohibitions, forensic practitioners strive to avoid providing professional services on the basis of contingent fees. Letters of protection, financial guarantees, and other security for payment of fees in the future are not considered contingent fees unless payment is dependent on the outcome of the matter. (p. 12)

It can be argued that contingency fees pose no greater threat to objectivity than does retention by any party with a stake in the outcome of an adversarial proceeding. Although some attorneys appreciate an objective expert opinion, even when it does not support their position—and attorneys may articulate just that position—the expert is well aware that sometimes attorneys are seeking an opinion that does support their case. If the psychologist's opinion does not support the retaining attorney's case, the attorney may attempt to "massage" the opinion into shape. The psychologist who holds firm to the data is sharply aware that the attorney may be lost as a referral source. Thus, it could be argued that psychologists who are retained by one side in a legal case, regardless of how they choose to bill for their services, are subject to financially based threats to objectivity.

Although it is true that the potential for biased reporting exists for all forensic experts, those whose fees are directly contingent upon a certain outcome face a greater threat to objectivity and a clearer appearance of compromised objectivity. The provision of an opinion for which payment is contingent upon the outcome of the case is inappropriate. Thus, cases should not be undertaken on a contingency fee basis, except possibly when one is working as a nontestifying expert in trial consultation.

The nature of trial consultation, in which a psychologist is retained by an attorney to assist in preparing the case against the other side, may raise an exception to the proscription against contingency fees. In this role, the psychologist, like the retaining attorney, assumes a position for one party. The role is not to directly provide opinions to the trier of fact. If the trial consultant's aim is to provide an objective review of the data and to assist the retaining attorney by clarifying mental health issues in the case, it may be that a trial consultant, like any other expert, is advocating for correct use of psychological data and not necessarily for a "win" (Connell, 2019). However, if the goal is to use the data explicitly in a way that will assist the attorney to prevail in the case, the role is not one of neutrality (Heilbrun, 2001). In this context, the manner in which the psychologist is paid may not alter the service provided. Because impartiality is not a requirement of the consultant role, it cannot be affected by contingency fees. Thus, it could be viewed as ethically acceptable for the nontestifying consulting psychologist, like the attorney, to choose to accept payment for services contingent upon the outcome of the case.

Another potential financial arrangement that may provide the psychologist with incentive to deviate from ethical practice is charging higher fees for testimony than for other forensic services (Heilbrun, 2001). Although the added stress and inconvenience that can be associated with testimony may seem to justify increased payment, the higher fees may be viewed as providing motivation to perform one's services with the end result of increasing the likelihood that one may be asked to testify. One such example would be omitting an important piece of information from a report and then informing the attorney of the omission and the need to elicit the information during testimony. The psychologist who wishes to avoid the appearance of ethically questionable practice is advised to avoid charging higher fees for testimony.

In contrast, for a number of reasons, it is reasonable and acceptable to charge higher rates for forensic services than for routine clinical services. Forensic practice demands maintaining familiarity with current research in a broad range of areas, and intimate familiarity with not only the instruments one commonly uses but all of the instruments that might be used in the kind of examination under consideration. Additionally, many forensic practice areas require considerable added infrastructure to manage the complex and demanding scheduling issues that can arise in this area of practice. Court subpoenas and other matters beyond one's control can cause last minute scheduling changes. Travel is often required for forensic interviews, depositions, and court testimony, and it takes time and resources to arrange travel. Additionally, forensic practice requires the management and retention of extremely large data sets.

Ethically acceptable financial arrangements include setting fixed rates for a given service, which may be required in some states, and, when billing an hourly rate, doing so in a manner that is consistent across various forensic services provided. Hourly rates tend to be preferable over fixed rates, when the option is available, because no two forensic cases are exactly the same and when a case requires more document review, more interview time, or more complex testing than the usual case for a service area, there is a danger the practitioner receiving a flat fee for the service may struggle to maintain a positive or constructive attitude toward the demands of the case.

CASE 1: HANDLING REFERRALS IN PERSONAL INJURY LITIGATION

Case Facts

A personal injury attorney contacts a psychologist who has experience working with people who have been involved in car accidents. The attorney explains that her 63-year-old client was involved in a motor vehicle accident a month ago and, in her opinion, has posttraumatic stress disorder (PTSD). She is making the referral for psychological treatment because her client lives alone, has no close relatives, and does not know how to access the services he needs. The attorney explains that the patient's no-fault car insurance will be the payment source. She offers to fax the police report and ambulance and ER records, and she requests an appointment for her client. The psychologist, feeling a little uncomfortable about the proposed fee arrangement, nevertheless accepts the referral and provides an appointment time for the patient to be seen. After hanging up, the psychologist reflects on the nature of the referral.

Case Analysis

In analyzing the case, we use the seven-step structured, systematic ethical decision-making model (CORE OPT) as described in detail in the Introduction to this volume.

Clarify the Ethical Issue

The psychologist accepted a referral from an attorney without exploring his possible role in the litigation. The psychologist asked no questions about the attorney's expectations and conveyed no information regarding his practices with respect to patients who are involved in litigation. The psychologist did not clarify with the attorney who would be the psychologist's client. The ostensible reason for the referral was for treatment, with the attorney assisting in the referral only because the individual lacked the resources to make his own arrangements for treatment. The referral is presented as being for clinical, not forensic, purposes.

Identify Obligations Owed to Stakeholders

This apparent clinical referral occurred within the context of civil litigation. The attorney, while possibly interested in the psychological welfare of her client, may have had additional motivations for initiating psychological treatment. The attorney seemed to have made the diagnosis of PTSD and was sending records that the psychologist had not requested and may or may not have found necessary. The psychologist, in musing about this referral, considered that the attorney would likely be making requests of him once his initial assessment was performed and treatment was underway. He wondered if he should have addressed these expectations proactively—before accepting the referral. As he views it, his obligation is to the patient's psychological well-being and the provision of quality psychological care.

Utilize Ethical and Legal Resources

The psychologist has a responsibility to assist an appropriate patient (beneficence). At the same time, he also must avoid harming the patient (nonmaleficence), which may occur through entering into multiple, potentially conflicting, roles without thoroughly clarifying expectations with the referring attorney and the patient (APA General Principle A: Beneficence and Nonmaleficence; Standard 3.05, Multiple Relationships; Standard 3.07; Standard 3.10, Informed Consent). The psychologist has ethical and legal obligations to bill the appropriate party for services provided (APA General Principle C: Integrity; APA General Principle D: Justice; Standard 6.04, Fees and Financial Arrangements). If the symptoms experienced by the patient predate or are otherwise not related to the accident, it would be fraudulent to bill the no-fault carrier. The psychologist had a responsibility to discuss with the attorney during the initial contact any factors that may affect the attorney's decision to use the psychologist's services or the psychologist's decision to accept the referral.

The blurring of roles is one of the most frequent bases for ethics complaints against psychologists in custody cases (Heilbrun, 2001). In such cases, the role conflict or conflation often involves a treating therapist who steps into a forensic role by making recommendations regarding custody or access without having completed a full forensic assessment of the parties. In addition to role clarity problems in forensic matters, maintaining multiple roles can have a negative effect in a therapeutic relationship. When a clinician is asked to monitor treatment progress and report the findings to an outside authority, for example, the clinician may have difficulty maintaining the trust of the patient (Barsky, 2012) and the patient may be less than forthcoming with the therapist. In forensic contexts, role clarification is critically important for all parties, particularly because the assumptions generally held about psychological treatment, such as the confidential and helping nature of the relationship, generally do not apply. Professional guidelines describe the dangers of assuming multiple roles (SGFP Guideline 4.02, Multiple Relationships; SGFP Guideline 4.02.01, Therapeutic-Forensic Role Conflicts). No laws of that state were found that applied to clarification of roles.

Examine Personal Beliefs and Values

This psychologist believes that any individual reporting symptoms that seem to be consistent with PTSD has the right to access his services. He is generally not concerned about where the referral comes from; however, the nature of this referral was somewhat different for him in that the attorney seemed to have proposed a diagnosis and was sending records that the psychologist typically did not request. Because he had not been retained by the attorney, he preferred to be open to, and accepting of, the patient's experiences. Based upon his understanding, if the patient reported that the symptoms emerged or worsened following the automobile accident, then the no-fault carrier would be the appropriate payor.

Consider Options, Solutions, and Consequences

The psychologist, feeling somewhat uneasy about the referral, considered four options. First, he considered refusing the referral and possibly suggesting alternative treatment providers. The only adverse consequence for this option was the loss of business. Second, he considered accepting the referral and not worrying about any unexplored expectations at this time. The negative consequence that he identified for this option involved disappointment and frustration for the attorney or patient, if the expectations of either of them were for something other than clinical care. There was also the possibility that the patient's lawsuit could suffer. Third, he considered calling the attorney back to obtain further clarification about the attorney's expectations of the nature of his involvement in the matter. Other than taking a bit of time, he identified no drawback for this option. Fourth, he considered contacting a colleague to seek consultation. He also identified no drawback for this option, although he preferred not to bother a colleague.

Put Plan Into Practice

The psychologist did not believe that declining the referral or referring the patient to someone else was necessary. He believed that he could work out the potential conflicts and still provide the patient with appropriate treatment. However, having reflected on the relevant values and ethical guidelines, he believed that the attorney's expectations should be addressed in some way before treating the patient. He thought that a reasonable option would be to call the attorney to clarify expectations, but he also thought that it might be more appropriate to discuss expectations with the patient, without further involving the attorney. However, he wanted to know what others would do, so he chose to call an experienced colleague first.

Take Stock, Evaluate the Outcome, and Revise as Needed

The colleague suggested that the most ethically appropriate course of action would be to call the referring attorney prior to seeing the patient in order to clarify expectations. Indeed, when the psychologist called the attorney, the attorney stated that although the patient's mental health was the first priority, she would be asking for periodic reports on the patient's accident-related psychiatric disability and treatment. The psychologist responded that although he appreciated the referral, he could not promise such reports, as he had not yet met with the patient and had no idea about the patient's psychiatric status or his interest in having that information shared with anyone. The attorney, seemingly losing patience, indicated that she had a number of such clients and was looking for someone to whom she could refer them. She further told the psychologist that although she was hoping that it could be this psychologist, such referrals would be made only if he was "sensitive to litigation issues." The psychologist stated that he would be glad to have the additional referrals, but he maintained his position—an unwillingness to commit prematurely to periodic reports. The attorney said she would send her client elsewhere and terminated the conversation. After the conversation, where he learned that the attorney was determined to select a clinician based on the clinician's willingness to endorse her position, the psychologist was satisfied that he had made the right decision.

CONCLUSION

The manner in which the psychologist handles the referral provides the ethical foundation for the services that will be provided as well as for the relationship with the referral source. Clarifying the expectations, roles and relationships, and fee arrangements are key aspects of the referral process—each with ethical implications. Sensitivity to potential biases and other threats to objectivity, as well as to one's professional competence for the case at hand, serve the forensic practitioner well. Sometimes during the course of a lengthy legal proceeding, one or more party may forget about or fail to respect the specific parameters of the originally established agreements. These issues can, and should, be revisited as needed during the case.

3

Collection and Review of Information

One of the cardinal differences between most forensic and clinical evaluations is the nature and extent of the background information and third-party data that is sought and reviewed prior to the rendering of an opinion or the provision of a report (Heilbrun, Grisso, & Goldstein, 2009; Heilbrun, Warren, & Picarello, 2003; Melton et al., 2018). The examiner needs to develop a broad and thorough foundation that will effectively serve as the basis for the final forensic opinions; information obtained from records and collateral sources helps establish that foundation. In this chapter, we address the foundation for strong and defensible forensic opinions from an ethics perspective. We review the multiple data source model, which helps the examiner develop reasonable opinions, and the need for appropriate review of records, acquisition of third-party information, the methods of obtaining that information (including social media), and the importance of impartiality and accuracy of information.

Thorough review of background information allows the forensic psychologist to support opinions with a degree of confidence that may not be attainable in many clinical contexts. The fundamental values relevant to the collection and review of collateral information are the examinee's right to privacy and the judicial system's right to have expert opinion derived from all information relevant to the formulation of that opinion. These values translate into the ethical principles of respect for autonomy and justice. The potential for conflict

http://dx.doi.org/10.1037/0000164-004
Ethical Practice in Forensic Psychology, Second Edition: A Guide for Mental Health Professionals,
by S. S. Bush, M. Connell, and R. L. Denney

between these values is lessened in many forensic evaluation contexts because the examinee who has raised his or her mental functioning as a legal issue has waived the right to privacy with regard to background information that may be relevant to mental functioning.

There are exceptions to the situation described above, where examinees have not waived their rights to privacy. This can arise in situations where the court develops a concern regarding the mental health of a defendant and raises, *sua sponte,*[1] a request for evaluation; or when, in family law matters, the court seeks information regarding the mental health of a party whose capacity to parent has been challenged, or alternatively when a child has alleged abuse and the court orders an evaluation of the child. Occasions arise, then, when the forensic practitioner must be concerned about the potential intrusion into or violation of a vulnerable party's rights as well as society's interest in autonomy, beneficence, and justice. The goal is to avoid malfeasance.

An interesting case pertaining to this issue in the context of a criminal defendant's competency to proceed arose some time ago in New York. The case of *Hirschfeld v. Stone* (*Hirschfeld;* 2000) arose from a class action civil suit brought by criminal defendants who had been adjudicated as incompetent and sent for restoration treatment; the defendants claimed their personal information was inappropriately disclosed during the case. The defendants' psychiatric and medical treatment information, including sexual orientation, HIV, hepatitis, family history of violence, substance abuse, and mental illness were included in their competency reports at the end of the treatment. Those reports were then filed in a public manner, rather than being sealed. The court held that examiners should only include personal information about a defendant that is directly relevant to the issue of concern to the court. Clearly, lawyers representing the defendants can easily resolve this potential concern by requesting the court to seal any such reports; however, the forensic examiner should remain aware of protecting a defendant's constitutional right to privacy.

The *Hirschfeld* case is not broadly authoritative, but it raises an issue examiners should consider. Making the issue more complicated, at least within the federal system, is 18 U.S.C. § 4247 (General Provisions for Chapter, 2017), which directs that in addition to the clinical and ultimate issue opinions, forensic examiners include the defendant's history and present symptoms, as well as a description of psychiatric, psychological, and medical tests that were employed with any results. Balancing the examinee's rights to privacy and the need for thorough examination is ultimately the court's responsibility, but ethical forensic examiners should remain mindful of this tension and only disclose in their reports truly pertinent information. For a further discussion of the practical implications created by the *Hirschfeld* case, see Poythress and Feld (2002).

---

[1] Upon the court's own authority without either party's motion.

BASES FOR OPINIONS

Ethical psychologists "base the opinions contained in their recommendations, reports, and diagnostic or evaluative statements, including forensic testimony, on information and techniques sufficient to substantiate their findings" (American Psychological Association [APA], 2017a; *Ethical Principles of Psychologists and Code of Conduct* [APA Ethics Code] Standard 9.01a, Bases for Assessments) and document the sources of information upon which their conclusions rest (Standard 6.01, Documentation of Professional and Scientific Work and Maintenance of Records). In addition, as stated in the *Specialty Guidelines for Forensic Psychology* (SGFP; APA, 2013), in forensic contexts psychologists examine the issue from perspectives that differ from those of the referring party and seek and consider information that might rule out plausible rival hypotheses when making determinations (SGFP Guideline 9.01, Use of Appropriate Methods).

The background information obtained "should be guided by relevance to the forensic issues and validity of the different sources" (Heilbrun, 2001, p. 107). The use of a multisource, multimethod assessment strategy to gather and review reliable and relevant information is a valuable approach to competent forensic assessment (Denney 2012a, 2012b; Heilbrun, 2001; Heilbrun et al., 2003; McLearen, Pietz, & Denney, 2004; Melton et al., 2018). It is important for forensic examiners to incorporate methods to assess the validity of their findings, whether subjective report or objective test performance, given the nature of the forensic setting. Related to the validity of obtained results is the determination of exaggerated cognitive dysfunction and exaggerated self-reported somatic, cognitive, or emotional disturbance, as well as defensive presentations where examinees deny emotional dysfunction. Because forensic examinees may distort their presentations, Melton and colleagues (2018) provided the following recommendation:

> Given the significant potential for deception and the implications of the validity of their findings, mental health professionals should have a low threshold for suspecting less-than-candid responding. At the same time, given the limitations of science . . . and the weight that labels used to describe response styles (e.g., "malingerer," "faker") carry with legal decisionmakers, the examiner should make sure that conclusions about an examinee's response style have a sound foundation. Thus the forensic examiner should combine a low threshold for suspecting dissimulation with a cautious stance about reaching conclusions on that issue. (pp. 57–58)

Sources of information should provide incremental validity; that is, each piece of information, if it is relevant, contributes to form a full and accurate understanding of the examinee. Inaccurate information or information that is obtained from a source that lacks credibility, if given too much weight, lessens the accuracy of the evaluation findings. The use of multiple sources of information helps to provide (a) independent corroboration of essential aspects of the examinee's history; (b) essential information about past mental states that may be relevant to forensic questions; and (c) observational data from a variety of contexts, thus increasing the likelihood that they are representative.

Figure 3.1 reveals the common sources of information relevant to a criminal forensic evaluation of past mental state. This multiple data-source model was initially applied to criminal forensic examinations (Denney & Wynkoop, 2000) and also adapted to personal injury assessments (McLearen et al., 2004). Boxes represent information obtained from self-report and collateral sources across different points in time. Lines between boxes should represent reasonable consistency, which then leads to a clinical diagnosis. Each of these lines of information should come together to make a reasonably consistent picture that makes sense for the clinical condition(s) presumed to exist. As demonstrated in Figure 3.1, corroborative information is critical when it comes to determining mental status at a particular time in the past.

The *Daubert v. Merrell Dow Pharmaceuticals, Inc.* (*Daubert*; 1993) decision, like Rule 702 of the Federal Rules of Evidence (House of Representatives, Committee on the Judiciary, 2018), emphasized relevance and reliability of evidence as the most important criteria for acceptance of scientific evidence in federal court. Information that is considered legally relevant is that which directly relates to the psycholegal issue, such as a criminal defendant's mental state at the time of an offense, an individual's capacity to create a will, or the capacity of a suspect to voluntarily confess to a crime. Forensic examiners should consider the assessment methods used during the examination in light of *Daubert* and FRE 702 guidance. For psychological findings to be helpful to the trier of fact, the information upon which the examination rests must be relevant and informative to the ultimate issue in question (Melton et al., 2018).

Review of Records

The collection and review of relevant records is an essential aspect of a thorough forensic evaluation (Heilbrun et al., 2009; Melton et al., 2018). For example, documentation of a plaintiff's preaccident level of functioning, as found in school, work, or military records, is valuable in order to establish a baseline against which postaccident behavior can be compared (McLearen et al., 2004). Records pertaining to postaccident injury and functioning, such as medical records, are necessary for establishing injury severity and subsequent signs and symptoms of impairment and disability (L. Miller, Sadoff, & Dattilio, 2011).

Comparison of preaccident and postaccident records helps establish whether functioning at the time of the evaluation represents a change. As part of a multisource, multimethod assessment strategy, information obtained from records can be used to confirm or contradict the plaintiff's self-report. In rare instances, reviewing some types of written information has the risk of biasing the examiner (Glancy et al., 2015). Medical records of other professionals have the potential to affect one's own professional judgment. For example, neurological reports at times conclude with diagnoses of neurological disorders based

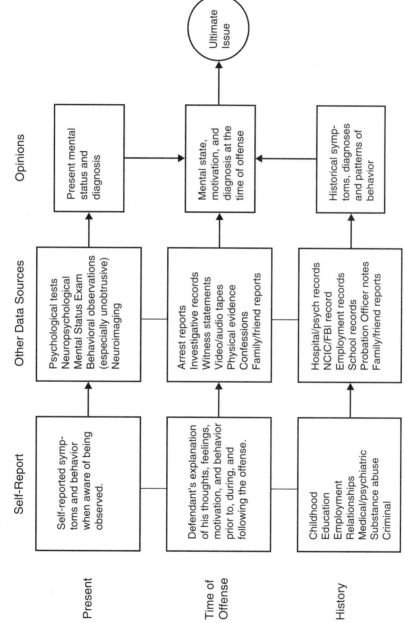

FIGURE 3.1. Multiple Data Source Model

NCIC = National Crime Information Center; FBI = Federal Bureau of Investigation. From "Criminal Responsibility Evaluations," by D. Mrad, 1996, *Issues in Forensic Assessment Symposium*, Federal Bureau of Prisons, Atlanta, GA. Copyright 1996 by David Mrad. Adapted with permission.

solely on patient self-report, despite normal examination findings. Similarly, the parent who is attempting to gain an upper hand in a contested custody matter may prompt the creation of both psychotherapeutic and medical records documenting alleged symptoms of abuse or neglect of the child by falsely reporting symptoms or events. The unsuspecting nonforensic health services professional is less likely to maintain suspended judgment and seek corroboration, but may instead, in the interest of risk management, or out of naiveté or simple expediency, document a diagnostic impression based upon examinee self-report alone. In addition, reports of negative psychiatric histories may be misleading. Potentially inaccurate diagnoses or history, accepted as fact and incorporated into reports, are then perpetuated by other professionals. Savvy forensic examiners must remain aware of the above issues and seek to minimize their impact on examination conclusions.

Experienced forensic examiners understand that some referral sources "cherry pick" records to be provided to the examiner in a "bad faith" effort to bias the examiner's opinions (Schatman & Thoman, 2014). When potentially informative records appear to be missing or incomplete, the examiner should make known the omission to the retaining party and request the complete records. If such records remain unavailable, the examiner should note in the report that additional information appeared to be missing, could have been informative, and was pursued, and that the final results and opinions could be revised, if the missing material later became available for review and supported reconsideration of the conclusions.

Third-Party Information

The use of data from collateral sources increases both the reliability of the overall information obtained and the face validity of the data (Heilbrun et al., 2009; Melton et al., 2018). Information from individuals in a position to observe or interact with the examinee often provides important information to help confirm or refute information obtained through self-report. As stated in SGFP Guideline 9.02, Use of Multiple Sources of Information,

> Forensic practitioners ordinarily avoid relying solely on one source of data, and corroborate important data whenever feasible. . . . When relying upon data that have not been corroborated, forensic practitioners seek to make known the uncorroborated status of the data, any associated strengths and limitations, and the reasons for relying upon the data.

The nature of the examinee's current abilities, symptoms, and their stability or change over time is often critically significant. Information from third parties may come from unstructured or structured interviews and/or standardized questionnaires that clarify the nature and stability of the examinee's behavior.

Just as examinee self-report may be subject to distortion, the information provided by collateral sources may not be accurate. Inaccurate information may also be provided by collateral sources because of bias, a lack of expertise regarding the behaviors in question, suggestibility, and memory loss (Heilbrun, 2001). Examiners can proactively reduce the potential for inaccuracy through the manner in which interview procedures and questions are selected and designed (e.g., Heilbrun, 2001, pp. 174–175, for specific examples). Information obtained from third parties should be verified by additional sources to the extent possible. Collateral sources are often able or willing to convey more during a personal contact than through written documentation. For example, consider the case of a 58-year-old married man who sustained a very minor work-related head injury. During an evaluation 8 months after his injury, he stated that he had not been able to read since his injury. He gave consent for contact with a number of individuals, including his wife. During the course of a telephone interview, his wife related that they both began each morning by reading the newspaper, aspects of which they typically discussed. Such information can be extremely valuable when making a determination regarding the validity of the examinee's statements and responses.

It is important to obtain informed consent from the collateral sources of information, in addition to that provided by the examinee. Consistent with ethical principles of respect for autonomy, nonmaleficence, and justice, individuals serving as collateral sources of information are typically entitled know (a) the limits to confidentiality of their communications, (b) the psychologist's need to cite them as the source of the information provided, (c) the potential range of foreseeable consequences of the evaluation, (d) potential foreseeable consequences of the information that they are providing, and (e) the fact that their communication is voluntary (Standard 3.10, Informed Consent; SGFP Guideline 6.04, Communication With Collateral Sources of Information).

The accuracy of the information provided by the collateral source, like that provided by the examinee, is subject to bias. In the above scenario, imagine that the examinee's wife had supported his invalid contention that he could no longer read. The evaluator relying upon that third-party information as incrementally increasing the validity of the findings would be making an error that would reduce the accuracy and utility of the assessment. Use of the multisource, multimethod strategy by a psychologist with a critical approach to all information obtained helps to increase the likelihood that the psychologist's conclusions accurately capture the examinee's status relevant to the legal issue under investigation.

Obtaining Information

The timing of the collection of collateral information may vary depending upon the context of the evaluation. In some contexts, such as capital sentencing cases in which psychological evaluations are performed to assess competency to be executed, a wide range of sources may be considered for interview (Zapf, Boccaccini, & Brodsky, 2003), including "line and medical correctional staff, other death row inmates, chaplains, appellate counsel, and persons having had recent visitation or phone interactions with the defendant" (Cunningham, in press). In some cases, records may be obtained prior to meeting with the examinee. In those instances, the content of the records may help to determine the nature and scope of the expected evaluation. In other cases, it is only through the initial meeting with the examinee that the examiner can determine what specific additional information would appear to be of potential value. Consent and contact information can often come directly from the examinee in those cases.

The psychologist may encounter difficulty obtaining collateral information because of resistance on the part of the examinee to consent, or resistance of the third party to provide the information. Limited access to the information may spring out of good intentions of the resistant third party. For example, in an attempt to safeguard health care information, providers may claim that the Health Insurance Portability and Accountability Act prohibits the release of certain records and that the requested records exceed what is "minimally necessary." In other instances, a key collateral source of information may prove difficult to reach. The extent to which psychologists should strive to satisfy due diligence in the pursuit of information deemed to hold potential value is difficult to define. The psychologist is advised to make multiple attempts and to clearly document the process. When a critical piece of data is not obtainable, it may become necessary to halt, temporarily or altogether, the completion of the evaluation. Once an effort has been initiated to obtain data, it is difficult to make the case that the data, should they prove difficult to obtain, were not really essential to the evaluation.

Social Media Information

An interesting new source for collateral information includes the Internet. In 2005, Grote provided an early illustrative example of using the internet during a forensic examination and provided a discussion of the risks and benefits of that course of action. Since that time, the issue of mental health professionals using the internet to acquire information about the people they evaluate or treat has gained considerable traction, although most of that literature deals with the clinical setting. Forensic psychiatry has addressed the issue substantively since 2006 (Glancy et al., 2015; Metzner & Ash, 2010; Neimark, Hurford, & DiGiacomo, 2006; Recupero, 2008, 2010). A significant percentage of forensic examiners do search the internet for such collateral information (Pirelli, Hartigan, & Zapf, 2018; Pirelli, Otto, & Estoup, 2016). Although there are no clear guidelines for psychologists yet established on the issue, forensic psychiatry has addressed it within their forensic practice guidelines (Glancy et al., 2015):

> Internet searches regarding the evaluee can also provide useful information. Social networking sites and other Internet social forums may contain information about the evaluee that conflicts with data provided by the evaluee or others, warranting further examination to contextualize this apparent conflict. An evaluee's online persona may constitute impression management or posturing, as people often behave or present themselves differently online than in person. It is also possible that the online information is more accurate than what the evaluee is telling the police and experts. (Glancy et al., 2015, p. S10)

A number of issues are worth considering in making the determination of whether, and to what extent, the psychologist would choose to investigate the background of an examinee through social media. Although the conclusion may depend on the professional context, it appears the issue is generally accepted in the broader field of forensic assessment. It could be argued that it is not only appropriate, but necessary, for the psychologist to make use of publicly-available information in order to provide a fully informed opinion. However, examiners should also remember the information available online may have been created by others specifically to place the examinee in a negative light, as may occur in hotly contested custody cases. If the examiner decides to explore what is available online, the psychologist should proceed with caution and with the understanding that it may be difficult to know with certainty who created the information, when it was created, and for what purpose it was created.

It is also necessary to cite sources for such information. If such information is to be sought, the examiner may wish to notify the examinee beforehand. The decision of whether to pursue the examinee's consent in this context is complicated by the fact that if consent is denied, the psychologist may have less access to certain aspects of the examinee's background than does the general public (Grote, 2005). Additionally, depending on the nature of the evaluation, the examinee may not have the right to withhold consent. SGFP Guideline 8.03, Acquiring Collateral and Third Party Information, includes this statement: "Forensic practitioners strive to access information or records from collateral sources with the consent of the relevant attorney or the relevant party, or when otherwise authorized by law or court order." Given the complexities of the legal situation, it is worthwhile to make the referral source aware of the wish to obtain such information before pursuing it. It may be that the information has already been gathered and can be provided to the examiner by the referral source, or that the referral source has access to investigators who can gather such data. Or if not, the referral source may be able to assist in resolving the question of consent. One can also include within the informed consent or notification of purpose discussion and documents a description of general approaches to information gathering, including internet searches.

It is not uncommon for third-party information to also come from video surveillance that is provided by the referring party (e.g., in the case of independent psychological examination at the request of a disability insurance carrier). In some cases, the nature of the claimed disability may be so clearly countered by the demonstrable facts that the case does not proceed to the independent examination stage. Occasionally in cases that involve psychological independent examination, such obviously counterfactual data are available. However, for many of the cases in which independent psychological examination is requested, the surveillance data are less revealing, and experts are called upon to integrate the information in the examination and weigh its contribution to the clinical and forensic formulations. Sometimes that information comes before the opinion is formulated, and sometimes it only comes as the expert sits on the witness stand (L. Miller et al., 2011). In our view, there is no ethical concern about psychologists reviewing such information and incorporating that which is trustworthy and relevant in their analyses. In fact, the American Academy of Psychiatry and the Law Practice Guideline for Forensic Assessment (Glancy et al., 2015) includes "undercover investigation reports or videotapes" as useful records in such evaluations.

CASE 2: BACKGROUND INFORMATION IN A CRIMINAL CASE

The following case illustrates challenges that can be encountered when working under time pressure.

Case Facts

A prosecuting attorney refers a criminal defendant charged with bank robbery to a psychologist for an evaluation of the defendant's sanity at the time of the alleged offense—8 months prior to the date of the referral. The attorney highlighted the fact that during the arrest, once the Miranda warnings were read to the defendant, he stopped talking and asked for an attorney. This behavior, the attorney believed, revealed "clear awareness of his right to remain silent." The obtained investigative material included the arrest documentation, which described the defendant as talkative and speaking in a rational but nervous manner when apprehended by the police; police interrogation summaries, which revealed that the defendant was silent after he was told of his rights; and surveillance camera photos, which clearly documented the examinee robbing the bank.

During the clinical interview, the defendant presented as oriented and rational, although he displayed indications of at least mild suspiciousness such as hypervigilance and hesitancy to discuss matters in detail with the examiner. He denied hallucinations and no delusions were elicited. He noted he had been in the state psychiatric hospital on more than one occasion with a diagnosis of schizoaffective disorder and had, in fact, been released one month prior to the bank robbery. Following his release from the psychiatric hospital, he had been living at home with his elderly mother. He did not believe he had a mental disorder but described a long history of methamphetamine use. When asked about the robbery, he said he robbed the bank because "that was where the money was," and he needed more money to buy methamphetamine.

The evaluator contacted the district attorney and informed the prosecutor that she needed the records of prior state psychiatric hospitalizations to perform the evaluation. The attorney said that obtaining such material would take considerable time, and that he was dealing with a strict timeline on this case. The district attorney said he needed the report very quickly to stay within legal guidelines. The psychologist was torn between her commitment to conducting an adequate evaluation based on sufficient background information and her desire to satisfy the time demands of the referral source. Ultimately, she agreed to provide the report without the benefit of the requested records.

Case Analysis

In analyzing the case, we use the seven-step structured, systematic ethical decision-making model (CORE OPT) as described in detail in the Introduction to this volume.

Clarify the Ethical Issue

The psychologist provided an opinion regarding a criminal defendant's past mental state without completing a reasonably thorough review of background information relevant to the determination. It was more than appropriate to review investigative material, since this information is often the best source for reconstructing mental states during the time of a crime, but additional highly relevant information was potentially available. That information would likely have clarified the nature of the man's mental illness, but even more importantly helped present a picture of his mental status 1 month before the robbery. The psychologist recognized that such information was needed and, in fact, requested it; but, ultimately the psychologist provided an expert opinion without it and thus rendered an opinion based on insufficient data. She based much of her forensic opinion on three factors: the defendant's current mental state; his descriptions of what happened on the day of the robbery; and the investigative information pertaining to the robber (e.g., witness statements).

Identify Obligations Owed to Stakeholders

The psychologist insufficiently attended to the fact that she had been retained as a partisan expert (Standard 3.07, Third-Party Requests for Services). Although she might have been right in assuming that the referring attorney would not intentionally withhold information from her, she should have also recognized the strong situational press for her to provide an opinion favorable to the referring side, in this instance, the government. The context of the evaluation added weight to the pressure exerted by the prosecutor—the psychologist perceived the entire legal system to be frustrated awaiting her report. Such pressure weighed heavily in her decision to provide an opinion absent necessary records.

Utilize Ethical and Legal Resources

The psychologist has a responsibility to provide forensic services consistent with the highest standards of the profession (SGFP Guideline 2.01, Scope of Competence). The multisource, multimethod model of forensic evaluation requires reliance on as much relevant information from varied sources as is reasonably available. Failure to obtain and consider pertinent information, as occurred in this case, may result in substantial harm to the defendant and society and is inconsistent with the principle of nonmaleficence (APA General Principle A: Beneficence and Nonmaleficence; Standard 3.04, Avoiding Harm).

The psychologist recognized her need to review records from psychiatric hospitalizations, particularly the most recent hospitalization, as this would give a clearer indication of the defendant's mental state just prior to the robbery (Standard 9.01, Bases for Assessment), but she felt considerable time pressure from her referral source. It is incumbent upon forensic evaluators to resist the pressure to perform an incomplete examination. "Forensic practitioners seek to provide opinions and testimony that are sufficiently based upon adequate scientific foundation, and reliable and valid principles and methods that have been applied appropriately to the facts of the case" (SGFP Guideline 2.05, Knowledge of the Scientific Foundation for Opinions and Testimony). When events outside the control of the forensic practitioner limit the scope of the examination, the examiner should make the potential effect of that event known to the referral source and document the extent it potentially impacted the validity of the final opinion.

The psychologist realized that she could benefit from consultation with a colleague. She called two senior forensic psychologists that she had recently met at a workshop to discuss the impact of not having those hospital records.

Examine Personal Beliefs and Values

At the time of entry into forensic work, the psychologist began to examine her personal views about the criminal justice system and the various parties in legal proceedings. In the context of this particular case, she again examined her views regarding the mentally ill, those who abuse substances, and those who perform criminal acts, specifically bank robbery. She believed that she maintained no biases for, or against, any of the parties. She believed that she was able to remain fair in evaluating information gained from the multi-source, multimethod model and to provide balanced, reasonable testimony when called to do so (SGFP Guideline 2.07, Considering the Impact of Personal Beliefs and Experience).

Consider Options, Solutions, and Consequences

After reviewing the relevant ethical and legal references and consulting with colleagues, the psychologist considered two courses of action: (a) tell the district attorney that she could not provide an opinion without the hospital records; or (b) write a report, indicating that the results were "preliminary" and pointing out the missing portion of her formulation and the potential impact that information might have on her opinion.

One of the colleagues she had consulted had informed her that writing a report prematurely to satisfy the urgency of the referral source may indeed reflect prosecutorial bias, and that raised the concern that such bias might affect her opinions. Based on that frank feedback, she engaged in renewed self-examination of her values.

Put Plan Into Practice

Given the pressure to produce a report that might be helpful to the court, the forensic evaluator decided to write a "preliminary" report, which outlined her evaluation methods, results, and opinions. This report also disclosed the fact there was information not reviewed that, once available for review, might prove quite important in the clinical and forensic opinion formulations. She believed that by making her report preliminary and disclosing the limits of her expert opinion, she was complying with the aspirational goal set forth in the SGFP Guidelines (see 1.01, Integrity; 1.02, Impartiality and Fairness; 2.05, Knowledge of the Scientific Foundation for Opinions and Testimony; 3.03, Communication; 9.02, Use of Multiple Sources of Information) suggesting that the forensic psychologist should limit expert opinions when the scope of the evaluation (i.e., scientific foundation) is not fully adequate to provide that opinion. It could be argued, however, that reaching a preliminary opinion without all of the necessary data is precisely a failure to achieve this goal. Even though the report is designated "preliminary," it clearly reflects the bias or leaning of the evaluator, who may have a hard time convincing others that she remained receptive to the forthcoming information, particularly if that information did not result in a change of stance.

Take Stock, Evaluate the Outcome, and Revise as Needed

The forensic evaluator provided the preliminary opinion in written form to the district attorney as requested. Later, during testimony, she reiterated the limitations of her opinion given the limited informational sources. The judge then provided additional time for her to complete a more thorough evaluation, which included a review of the medical records and an interview of the defendant's mother. The psychologist, upon incorporating the additional information, provided an addendum to her findings and was then able to testify with more certainty regarding her clinical and forensic conclusions.

In retrospect, she realized there really had been no need to provide a preliminary report and that it would probably have been preferable not to do so. She realized that the greater potential for harm came from providing a preliminary report with less than fully substantiated conclusions. When later discussing the outcome with one of the colleagues whom she had consulted, she was informed that she had been vulnerable to a legitimate criticism by the defense attorney and factfinder and was fortunate to have escaped such an aggressive and effective cross-examination on the point. Although the psychologist's involvement in this case was concluded, at least for the time being, the psychologist was convinced of the importance of avoiding being pressured into prematurely offering opinions in the future.

CONCLUSION

Competent forensic practitioners understand that forensic evaluations, while typically involving interviews of examinees and administration of standardized assessment measures, require consideration of additional data sources. Essential information is obtained from records, observations, and interviews of collateral sources. A multisource, multimethod assessment strategy enables forensic practitioners to obtain the information needed to advise triers of fact on ultimate forensic issues. Collateral information should be sought to test reasonable rival hypotheses. All parties are best served when conclusions are rendered only after such information has been obtained and considered. Pressure from a retaining party to provide a preliminary report should be resisted, in part through educating the party about the limitations and risks of providing opinions based on incomplete information. If a premature opinion cannot be avoided, the confidence placed in the opinion should be tempered with notation of the specific implications of not having all relevant information. Collateral sources of information should be identified as early as possible, and the information should be diligently sought to ensure a comprehensive, multisource, multimethod assessment resulting in a strong and defensible set of opinions or conclusions.

4

The Evaluation

The forensic evaluation typically involves gathering information, through a variety of means, about the clinical characteristics of the examinee that are relevant to the forensic issues of concern (Heilbrun, 2001; Melton et al., 2018). In this chapter, we highlight the examiner–examinee relationship, including the issue of informed consent and the limits of confidentiality. We then address methodology, with an emphasis on incorporating a multisource and multimethod process, and end the chapter with a discussion about third-party observers.

THE EXAMINER–EXAMINEE RELATIONSHIP

The nature of the relationship between the psychologist and the examinee, and the manner in which the relationship is established, have significant implications for the validity of the information that is obtained and the value of the psychological opinion for the court. As part of the process of informing the examinee of the purpose and nature of the forensic evaluation, the psychologist has an ethical obligation to inform the examinee that a relationship based on a presumption of helpfulness does not exist (Bush, Barth, et al., 2005). Despite the absence of this traditional doctor–patient relationship, the forensic examiner does have ethical obligations to the examinee: The examinee should be told and understand the nature and limitations of confidentiality, feedback, and treatment. An examination of these elements of the evaluation process follows.

http://dx.doi.org/10.1037/0000164-005
Ethical Practice in Forensic Psychology, Second Edition: A Guide for Mental Health Professionals, by S. S. Bush, M. Connell, and R. L. Denney

INFORMED CONSENT, ASSENT, AND NOTIFICATION OF PURPOSE

The right of the examinee to understand the nature and purpose of the evaluation is based on the fundamental right of individuals to freedom of choice. Freedom of choice underlies the ethical principle of respect for autonomy. To the extent that the examinee's ability to understand the information is limited due to intelligence, cognitive impairment, psychiatric state, or some other condition, surrogate decision making may be required. When the legal system has already limited the examinee's rights, the only choice for the examinee may be to undergo the evaluation or experience a negative consequence. The need to impart to the examinee or the surrogate decision-maker information about the evaluation—through the process of informed consent or assent—is established by statute and case law in most jurisdictions, as well as by standards and codes governing professional practice, and, thus, appears to be an established principle of mental health assessment (Heilbrun, 2001; Melton et al., 2018).

Individuals to be examined or evaluated by a forensic psychologist have a fundamental right to understand the evaluation process and its potential implications (American Psychological Association [APA], 2017a; *Ethical Principles of Psychologists and Code of Conduct* [APA Ethics Code] Standard 3.10, Informed Consent; Standard 9.03, Informed Consent in Assessments; Standards for Educational and Psychological Testing [SEPT] Standard 8.4 [American Educational Research Association, American Psychological Association, & National Council on Measurement in Education, 2014]).

> Informed Consent denotes the knowledgeable, voluntary, and competent agreement by a person to a proposed course of conduct after the forensic practitioner has communicated adequate information and explanation about the material risks and benefits of, and reasonably available alternatives to, the proposed course of conduct. (*Specialty Guidelines for Forensic Psychology* [SGFP], Appendix B, Definitions and Terminology [APA, 2013])

Prior to performing a clinical interview or administering psychological tests, the examiner should seek to establish with the examinee a reasonable understanding of the purpose and nature of the evaluation, including limits on confidentiality, reporting of results, and possible uses of the findings. Depending on the context in which the evaluation is performed, the psychologist must obtain informed consent or assent from the examinee or a legal representative or, in the context of court-ordered evaluations, provide notification of the purpose of the evaluation (Standard 3.10; Standard 9.03; SGFP Guidelines, Section 6, Informed Consent, Notification, and Assent).

SGFP Guideline 6.03, Communication with Forensic Examinees, states that information to be provided should include the following:

> anticipated use of the examination; who will have access to the information; associated limitations on privacy, confidentiality, and privilege including who is authorized to release or access the information contained in the forensic practitioner's records; the voluntary or involuntary nature of participation, including potential consequences of participation or nonparticipation, if known; and, if the cost of the service is the responsibility of the examinee, the anticipated cost.

The psychologist must define the parameters of the service to be provided and clarify the examinee's expectations. The information must be tailored to the specific legal context. With the exception of court-ordered examinations, the examinee has the right to provide partial consent; that is, to consent only to some aspects of the evaluation and reporting process. When partial consent is offered, the psychologist may wish to explore and address the examinee's concerns, but the psychologist ultimately determines whether to conduct the evaluation in the face of such limitations.

Mandated Examination and Refusal

When psychological services have been ordered by the court and there is no meaningful choice for the examinee about participation, psychologists provide *notification of purpose*. Such notification includes informing the examinee of the purpose and nature of the evaluation, as well as the limits of confidentiality (Standard 3.10c; SGFP Guideline 6.03.02, Persons Ordered or Mandated to Undergo Examination or Treatment). If the examinee is unwilling to proceed after thorough notification has been provided, it is often quite helpful to facilitate communication between the examinee and his or her legal representative. The concerns of the examinee can often be resolved through education from the lawyer. Even if this effort does not resolve the examinee's concerns, it goes a long way toward communicating proper concern for the examinee and respect for the examinee's rights. Additionally, building adequate situationally appropriate rapport with the examinee may make it more likely that the examinee will cooperate with the examination. Such situations are not uncommon in court-ordered evaluations.

If the examinee has been ordered by the court to participate but does not wish to participate, even after consulting with counsel, the forensic practitioner can notify the retaining party of the examinee's unwillingness to proceed or conduct the examination to the extent possible (Standards 3.10 and 9.03).

Mandated Forensic Assessment With Unrepresented Individuals

Regarding forensic examinees not represented by counsel, special care should be exercised to guard the rights of the examinee who may be unable to act instrumentally. SGFP Guideline 6.03.04, Evaluation of Persons Not Represented by Counsel states that

> Because of the significant rights that may be at issue in a legal proceeding, forensic practitioners carefully consider the appropriateness of conducting a forensic evaluation of an individual who is not represented by counsel. Forensic practitioners may consider conducting such evaluations or delaying the evaluation so as to provide the examinee with the opportunity to consult with counsel.

Note that, in criminal forensic contexts, there is SCOTUS (Supreme Court of the United States) case law against referral for psychological evaluations in the absence of legal representation for the examinee (e.g., *Estelle v. Smith*, 1981).

Maximizing the Potential for Enlightened Consent

To maximize the potential for understanding, the psychologist should provide information in language that is reasonably understandable to the examinee (Standard 3.10(a); Standard 9.03(b); SEPT Standard 8.4, Comment); that is, the language should generally be appropriate to the language fluency, developmental level, and cognitive capacity of the examinee. The psychologist must ensure that the examinee *understands* the information that has been provided about the nature and purpose of the evaluation (American Bar Association, 2016). To verify that the information was understood, the psychologist should question the examinee about the concepts conveyed. Questions that require the examinee to paraphrase the examiner's wording or apply it to the examinee's specific context or to hypothetical contexts may be of value in determining the examinee's level of understanding (Heilbrun, 2001). The information should be repeated as needed to facilitate understanding. In addition, the most salient aspects of information should be reviewed at the beginning of each separate evaluation session. Guidelines and measures for assessing capacity to consent to treatment (e.g., Appelbaum & Grisso, 1995; Grisso, 2003; Grisso & Appelbaum, 1998a, 1998b; Moye et al., 2007) may also apply in forensic settings (Heilbrun, 2001).

When Understanding Has Not Been Gained or Has Been Lost

When the examinee appears to lack the capacity to provide informed consent, the psychologist provides notice to the legal representative (Guideline 6.03.03), provides the examinee with an appropriate explanation, and seeks the examinee's *assent* (Standard 3.10b). Assent, according to the SGFP Guidelines (see Appendix B, Definitions and Terminology)

> refers to the agreement, approval, or permission, especially regarding verbal or nonverbal conduct, that is reasonably intended and interpreted as expressing willingness, even in the absence of unmistakable consent. Forensic practitioners attempt to secure assent when consent and informed consent cannot be obtained or when, because of mental state, the examinee may not be able to consent.

Specifically, SGFP Guideline 6.03.03 identifies that these considerations are offered "for examinees adjudicated or presumed by law to lack the capacity to provide informed consent for the anticipated forensic service." Citing the content of Standard 3.10b and SGFP Guideline 6.03.03 further addresses this cohort of examinees:

> For examinees whom the forensic practitioner has concluded lack capacity to provide informed consent to a proposed, non-court-ordered service, but who have not been adjudicated as lacking such capacity, the forensic practitioner strives to take reasonable steps to protect their rights and welfare.

The Guideline further states, "in such cases, the forensic practitioner may consider suspending the proposed service or notifying the examinee's attorney or the retaining party." In mandated examinations, some form of competency is usually at issue. Forensic psychologists should proceed thoughtfully, facilitating contact between the examinee and his/her attorney to try to resolve the examinee's questions or concerns when possible. This respects the examinee's autonomy and makes the examination process flow more smoothly. There are times when an examination can still occur over the protests of an examinee—when the examination is court ordered and the examinee has legal counsel. Typically, such examinations relate to competency to proceed. In such instances, notification of purpose suffices, and the report outlines the limitations of the examination and any limitations to the final opinions.

When information related to informed consent or notification of purpose does not seem to have been fully understood, the psychologist must determine if the understanding obtained is sufficient to continue with the examination. Consultation with the examinee's attorney may help to clarify whether it is in the best interests of the examinee and the court for the examination to proceed. Depending on the context, the consent of a surrogate decision-maker may be required. The steps in this process should be clearly documented (Standard 3.10d).

Obtaining Assent of Minors

Jurisdictional statutes define the age at which one is legally able to make decisions independently, although the age may differ within jurisdictions depending upon the issue being decided. Typically, individuals under 18 years of age are considered minors with respect to providing authorization for psychological services. As a result, authorization from one holding the legal right to consent to the evaluation on behalf of the minor is usually required. Such authorization may be provided by a custodial parent, court order, or other legal surrogate decision-maker, such as an attorney, depending on the circumstances (Heilbrun, 2001).

In addition to this informed consent process with the minor's legal decision-maker, the cooperation and assent of the minor should be sought. Minors who are, by virtue of age, presumed by law to lack the capacity to provide informed consent for examination are provided information in language they can understand. The forensic psychologist explains in age-appropriate language the nature of the evaluation, the purpose, the people to whom the results will be conveyed, and the examiner's role. The examiner explains who gave permission for the examination and provides an opportunity for the minor to ask questions; if necessary and when possible, the minor should be given the opportunity to consult with the legal representative or guardian (SGFP Guidelines 6.01 and 6.03). The forensic psychologist seeks the examinee's assent in addition to gaining appropriate permission from a legally authorized person, as permitted or required by law (Standards 3.10 and 9.03).

Limits of Confidentiality

A primary difference between forensic and clinical psychological services is the nature of confidentiality. With some exceptions, communication between treatment provider and recipient in a clinical context is protected. The APA Ethics Code states that protecting confidential information is a primary obligation of psychologists (see Standard 4.01, Maintaining Confidentiality). In contrast, communications made in a forensic context are generally subject to review by others and, in many instances, may become a matter of public record. Forensic psychologists must discuss all reasonably foreseeable disclosures with the potential examinee or his/her legal representative as part of the consent/notification process (Standard, 4.02(a), Discussing the Limits of Confidentiality). SGFP Guideline 8 cautions that "forensic practitioners recognize their ethical obligations to maintain the confidentiality of information relating to a client or retaining party, except insofar as disclosure is consented to by the client or retaining party, or required or permitted by law" (Privacy, Confidentiality, and Privilege). However, when information is sought,

> forensic practitioners are encouraged to recognize the importance of complying with properly noticed and served subpoenas or court orders directing release of information, or other legally proper consent from duly authorized persons, unless there is a legally valid reason to offer an objection. (SGFP Guideline 8.01, Release of Information)

It is appropriate to notify the examinee, through counsel if necessary, that the information has been requested so that the examinee can intervene legally if he/she wishes to do so. If the forensic practitioner is in doubt about the validity of a subpoena or request for information, it is advisable to seek legal assistance or to formally notify the drafter of the subpoena or order to gain clarification (SGFP Guideline 8.01). Some demands for information provide a place for designating that all information requested has been provided or the nature of information not provided, with an explanation.

Feedback

In many clinical settings and in some forensic contexts, psychologists provide examinees with feedback about the results of the evaluation. However, in many forensic contexts, feedback is not to be provided to the examinee directly, and this is clearly explained at the outset (Standard 9.10, Explaining Assessment Results). When feedback is permissible, the guidelines address the provision of examination feedback in a manner consistent with the APA Ethics Code, suggesting that "forensic practitioners take reasonable steps to explain assessment results to the examinee or a designated representative in language the _____ can understand" (SGFP Guideline 10.05, Provision of Assessment Feedback). SGFP Guideline 10.05 recognizes that professional and legal standards may govern the disclosure of test data or results, interpretation of data, and the underlying bases for conclusions and suggests that forensic practitioners practice in a way consistent with those professional and legal standards. SGFP Guideline 8.02, Access to Information, recognizes that examinees may request access to their records and advises the following:

> If requested, forensic practitioners seek to provide the retaining party access to, and a meaningful explanation of, all information that is in their records for the matter at hand, consistent with the relevant law, applicable codes of ethics and

professional standards, and institutional rules and regulations. Forensic examinees typically are not provided access to the forensic practitioner's records without the consent of the retaining party. Access to records by anyone other than the retaining party is governed by legal process, usually subpoena or court order, or by explicit consent of the retaining party.

There may be tensions between competing ethical principles, state and federal provisions for access to one's health information, and the needs of the legal system, along with lack of clarification regarding whether forensic examinations are excepted from health information because they are done for legal purposes. The forensic examiner may engage in a case-specific analysis to determine the best way to respond to a request by the examinee to obtain file data.

PROCEDURES AND MEASURES

Forensic practitioners have at their disposal a variety of informal and psychometric methods for assessing constructs of interests (e.g., cognitive abilities, emotional states, personality traits). Indeed, there has been a substantial increase in the development and use of psychological assessment measures in forensic settings in recent decades (Edens & Boccaccini, 2017). Choosing appropriate methods is an essential component of the process of gaining an understanding of the examinee and educating triers of fact. The APA Ethics Code requires that psychologists limit their expressed opinions to information and techniques sufficient to substantiate their findings (Standard 9.01a, Bases for Assessment). Determining which techniques are sufficient may be challenging in some cases, and there is room for difference of opinion, given the complexities of cases, the range of assessment instruments available for consideration, and circumstances that might affect access to relevant materials or collateral resources.

The assumptions, roles, and alliances inherent in forensic practice necessitate the use of a comprehensive evaluation methodology consisting of systematic incorporation of multiple data sources (Denney, 2012a, 2012b; Heilbrun, Grisso, & Goldstein, 2009; McLearen, Pietz, & Denney, 2004; Melton et al., 2018; Packer & Grisso, 2011). Typically, the forensic psychological evaluation consists of the following procedures: review of records, interviews with collateral sources of information, behavioral observations, interview(s) of the examinee, and psychological testing. For review of records and interviews with collateral sources, see previous sections of this chapter; the focus of this section is on behavioral observations, interview(s) of the examinee, and psychological testing.

Behavioral Observations

Behavioral observations may occur within and beyond the evaluation room, depending on the psychological questions being asked and the hypotheses being considered. Additionally, the examiner may observe the examinee's behavior directly or obtain, through interviews or records, descriptions of behavioral observations made by others. Observations that occur across settings on multiple occasions may help to maximize the reliability of the information obtained from the behaviors being observed. A multisource, multimethod approach increases the likelihood of making accurate assessment of consistencies between behavior and self-report (Shapiro, 1999). Establishing a pattern of consistency adds confidence to the diagnostic formulation or helps reveal disingenuous claims. There is face validity in behavioral observations made by the examiner and behavioral descriptions garnered from records, such as jail records, school behavioral records, and employment records, for the issue before the court. Such data may carry considerable weight with the trier of fact, even though they lack the scientific rigor of other types of data (Grisso, 2003).

In certain circumstances, meaningful information can be gained through surreptitious observation made by the examiner or others. In settings such as correctional centers and hospitals, observations made of the examinee when the examinee is not aware of the observation are often readily available from correctional officers and nursing staff. Even in the private practice setting, the examiner may note examinee behavior during the arrival to and departure from the office, such as walking unassisted or independently driving, which may be inconsistent with the examinee's claims of disability. However, consistent with the principle of respect for autonomy, the examinee has a right to be informed during the consent process that data from such observations may be obtained and considered.

Investigative information in criminal cases often includes audio and video recordings of defendant behavior at the time of an alleged offense, and it is competent practice to incorporate that information in the formulation of past mental states (Denney, 2012b; Denney & Wynkoop, 2000). It is also not unusual for examiners to receive video surveillance of plaintiffs in personal injury cases or insurance disability cases. Using such information in clinical evaluations may seem inappropriate to some providers, but in forensic mental health evaluations, by contrast, reliance upon a variety of data sources is the standard of practice (SGFP Guideline 9.02, Use of Multiple Sources of Information), and litigants are informed at the outset that corroboration of claims will be sought.

The forensic evaluator strives to ensure that any such material obtained and reviewed is admissible in a court of law. To review, and, therefore, potentially rely upon, material that was illegally obtained may render the evaluator's findings and conclusions inadmissible. For that reason, it is prudent to ask that all information provided be scrutinized by the retaining attorney (or, when the evaluation is being performed by court order or agreement of the parties, such as might occur in an assessment concerning contested parenting issues, by all attorneys to the matter) to be sure that it is appropriate for review. It is also essential to maintain copies of any such material reviewed so that the data upon which conclusions were based can be provided, if necessary, in response to challenges (SGFP Guidelines 10.05, 10.06, and 10.07 address maintenance and provision of all data relied upon in forming opinions).

An evaluation of a criminal defendant in the correctional environment under court order establishes limitations on examinee privacy. One forensic case study illustrated the potentially rich data accessible through review of recorded telephone conversations made during the evaluation that gave explicit descriptions of exaggerating deficits (see Wynkoop & Denney, 1999). The fact that the psychologist relied upon the recordings in the evaluation was reviewed by the U.S. District Court Judge overseeing the case; that judge held that the use of the recordings was not a violation of the defendant's right to privacy. The Judge reasoned that because the defendant was housed in a correctional facility for the evaluation and was specifically warned that his behavior during the evaluation period was not private, in addition to the fact that placards were placed next to the inmate phones indicating they were subject to review, there were no constitutional concerns. In the authors' view, the facts of this case also relieved the psychologist of any ethical concerns about reviewing surreptitious telephone conversations (Wynkoop & Denney, 1999).

Interviews

Face-to-face or in-person interviews with the examinee are typically an essential aspect of the evaluation process. The examinee's thoughts, feelings, and memories are often fundamental to the forensic issue at hand. However, the subjective nature of the examinee's experience and the potential for bias may reduce the reliability of information obtained directly from the examinee (Otgaar & Baker, 2018). Sbordone, Rogers, Thomas, and de Armas (2003) summarized the literature on the accuracy of criminal defendants' autobiographical memory, stating that the primary problem with "utilizing a defendant's recollection of what occurred during the alleged crime is that their memory of this event is likely to change over time" (p. 479). Such change tends to be in the direction of decreasing their culpability. Similarly, Bieliauskas (1999) cautioned,

> It is important to be careful in obtaining the history of a patient directly from the patient himself or from relatives and friends. On the face of it, these individuals should know the patient's situation best. . . . However, it is also the case that the veracity of interview information is open to question in forensic evaluation. (p. 125)

Williams, Lees-Haley, and Djanogly (1999) reviewed the empirical research in personal injury evaluations and concluded that when a great deal may be at stake and pressures may exist to cause the litigant to try to affect the outcome of the assessment, there is significant risk for distortion in symptom presentation. They advised practitioners working in this area to adopt a more analytical, data-oriented attitude toward examinee self-report when conducting forensic examinations than they might in working with people in more traditional clinical settings.

Children's capacity to accurately recall events, benign or traumatic, has been vastly researched, and effective interview protocols have been recommended for forensic evaluators to follow to ensure that the most accurate and detailed possible information is gathered without contamination (Ceci & Bruck, 1995; Ceci & Hembrooke, 1998; Chrobak & Zaragoza, 2013; Gudjonsson, Sveinsdottir, Sigurdsson, & Jonsdottir, 2010; La Rooy et al., 2015; Poole & Lamb, 1998; Saywitz & Snyder, 1996; Vagni, Maiorano, Pajardi, & Gudjonsson, 2015). In general, child interviews require an appreciation for the capacities of children to understand complex constructs and to express notions about time, source attribution, and causal relationships. Children may respond to interview characteristics differently from adults and are somewhat more vulnerable to influences that may shape the nature or accuracy of their recollections. Good data can be gathered from children by interviewers trained to do so, but the contours of this arena are not necessarily intuitively obvious, and specialized training is essential.

Because forensic examinees have a significant stake in the outcome of the assessment, interviews with others are an important part of most forensic assessments. Heilbrun (2003) noted that use of multiple data sources of information for each area being assessed is a principle of forensic mental health assessment. Collateral interviews add richness and depth to a forensic assessment and are important in providing information that may be less biased than self-report. Third-party sources increase the examiner's certainty as opinions are formulated; divergent data generates new hypotheses to be explored, while convergent data increases reliability of findings (Heilbrun, Warren, & Picarello, 2003).

Psychological Testing

One of the strengths of psychological testing, as part of a psychodiagnostic evaluation, is the introduction of standardized measurement of cognitive and emotional functioning and personality organization, as contrasted to reliance on clinical judgment alone. Many commonly used psychological measures were not developed for forensic purposes, however, and do not have relevant normative data, although an increasing number of forensic measures is becoming available. Standard 9.02b, Use of Assessments, states, "Psychologists use assessment instruments whose validity and reliability have been established for use with members of the population tested. When such validity or reliability has not been established, psychologists describe the strengths and limitations of test results and interpretation."

The selection of psychological measures depends on multiple factors, including (a) the purpose of the evaluation, (b) the available normative data and the relevance of the norms to the examinee's demographics and known or suspected psychopathology, (c) other examinee characteristics such as sensory or motor impairments or lack of English fluency, (d) the evaluation setting, (e) the examinee's prior experience with psychological measures, and (f) the availability of prior test results (Bush & Morgan, 2017). SGFP Guideline 10.02, Selection and Use of Assessment Procedures, advises psychologists to use assessment procedures in the manner and for the purposes that are appropriate given available research or other evidence that they are useful and appropriate for the circumstances. Further,

> Forensic practitioners use assessment instruments whose validity and reliability have been established for use with members of the population assessed. When such validity and reliability have not been established, forensic practitioners consider and describe the strengths and limitations of their findings (SGFP Guideline 10.02, p. 15)

The SEPT Standard 10 (Psychological Testing and Assessment) addresses this issue as follows: "Many tests measure constructs that are generally relevant to the legal issues even though norms specific to the judicial or governmental context may not be available" (p. 162). However, the SEPT also explain that when normative data or validity studies are lacking for the purposes of a given examination, the interpretation of the results should be qualified and presented as hypotheses rather than firm conclusions.

When selecting psychometric measures from among the available options, forensic psychologists must recognize the uniqueness of the population from which the examinee comes (Standard 9.02, Use of Assessments; SGFP Guideline 10.02). Forensic examiners are not required to limit test selection to those developed and standardized on forensic populations but must be cognizant that a particular forensic setting may include an atypical population—a population that was underrepresented in the standardization sample. Obvious examples of examinee characteristics to consider include age, education, race, and nationality, but other less obvious factors, such as lower levels of intellectual functioning or lower socioeconomic status, can be factors to consider in some forensic settings.

The results of tests or indices that have been developed with one forensic population may not generalize to different forensic populations. Such tests or indices may require validation with different forensic populations before being broadly utilized. Forensic examiners should select technically sound measures that are appropriate for the situation (International Test Commission, 2013).

Forensic examiners need to proceed with caution when extrapolating results of general clinical assessment instruments to specific legal questions. When such extrapolation occurs, forensic examiners should consider qualifying or presenting their interpretations as hypotheses rather than conclusions. When qualifying one's interpretations, it is not sufficient to merely state that "caution" was used in the test interpretation. The examiner should not only alert the reader to a lower level of confidence in the findings but should specifically state the manner in which deviations from standardized testing conditions or normative samples may have impacted the test results or interpretation. For example, in a parenting assessment in which the parent and child have been separated, the examiner using a parenting satisfaction scale should not only indicate in the report that the instrument was normed for intact families but should also note that measures of parental attachment may not be applicable to the current situation, because the items making up the scales query the examinee about time spent with the child.

A similar concern is that the psychometric properties of some forensic measures normed with research populations do not adequately translate into "real world" applications (Edens & Boccaccini, 2017). Although many forensic practitioners rely almost exclusively on the psychometric properties reported in the test's technical manuals to support their use and interpretation of the tests, "it is unwise to assume—without cross-validation findings from field research—that reliability and validity findings from research-based normative samples apply to real-world forensic evaluation contexts" (Edens & Boccaccini, 2017, p. 600). SCOTUS has considered fairly recently the issue of psychometric properties of measures used in forensic mental health assessment. In *Hall v. Florida* (2014), SCOTUS considered the reliability, particularly the standard error of measurement, of psychological instruments (i.e., intelligence tests) when adjudicating criminal justice issues, specifically whether the defendant in a capital punishment case could be accurately diagnosed with an intellectual disability that would preclude him from being eligible for execution, according to *Atkins v. Virginia* (2002). Thus, forensic practitioners should be able to defend their selection, use, and interpretation of the assessment measures that are employed in a given case, understanding that test manuals are commonly not the sole, and often not the best, source of information about a test's psychometric properties and normative data.

In general, the responsibility lies with the examiner to select procedures sufficient to address the forensic psychological issues bearing on the legal question, to utilize those procedures appropriately, and to describe in detail any limitations or reservations regarding conclusions. Otto, Buffington-Vollum, and Edens (2003) posed a series of questions that examiners should consider when deciding the issue of testing in custody evaluation, although the considerations also apply to psychological testing in other evaluation contexts. Exhibit 4.1 provides questions to consider when selecting psychological tests.

EXHIBIT 4.1

Considerations for Selecting Psychological Tests

1. Is the test commercially published?
2. Is a comprehensive test manual available?
3. Are adequate levels of reliability demonstrated?
4. Have adequate levels of validity been demonstrated?
5. Is the test valid for the purpose for which it will be used?
6. Has the instrument been peer-reviewed?[a]
7. Do I possess the qualifications necessary to use this instrument?
8. Does the test require an unacceptable level of inference from the construct it assesses to the psycholegal question(s) of relevance?

Note. [a]We add the caveat that although it may seem apparent, the reviews of the instrument must be reasonably positive. From *Handbook of Psychology: Forensic Psychology* (Vol. 11, p. 188), by A. M. Goldstein (Ed.), 2003, Hoboken, NJ: Wiley. Copyright 2003 by Wiley. Adapted with permission.

Survey data regarding instruments commonly used by forensic psychologists may also guide the examiner, although, of course, just because an instrument is commonly used does not mean that it is the appropriate instrument for the psycholegal issue that drives an assessment. A number of researchers have surveyed forensic practitioners and published the frequency with which instruments are used in various contexts as well as other useful information on instrument selection. R. P. Archer, Buffington-Vollum, Stredney, and Handel (2006) surveyed forensic psychologists regarding instrument selection in both adult and child forensic issues. Lally (2003) queried forensic psychologists to determine frequency of instruments used in various assessment types including mental state at the time of the offense, risk for violence, risk for sexual violence, competency to stand trial, competency to waive Miranda Rights, and evaluations of malingering. Quinnell and Bow (2001) and Keilin and Bloom (1986) surveyed evaluators regarding the procedures used, including instruments administered, in child custody evaluations. LaDuke, Barr, Brodale, and Rabin (2018) surveyed forensic neuropsychologists regarding their test usage. Martin, Schroeder, and Odland (2015) conducted a survey of neuropsychologists' practices in assessing for malingering and then later compared that data to a survey of experts in validity testing (Schroeder, Martin, & Odland, 2016). Additionally, Ryba, Cooper, and Zapf (2003) surveyed psychologists regarding test usage in assessing juvenile competence to stand trial evaluations. Some of these data are dated and certainly there are evolutions in available instruments as well as in usage. It is beyond the scope of this writing to provide a list of "acceptable" instruments to be used in a forensic setting. Where there is controversy regarding an instrument or a class of instruments, the forensic examiner should be aware of arguments for and against their use in forensic work. Regarding projective instruments, for example, there may be good reason to forego their use when interpretation is a matter of subjective judgment.

> The use of projective tests (e.g., Draw-A-Person, Thematic Apperception Test, Children's Apperception Test, and Rorschach) can open the psychologist to severe cross-examination. Psychologists who use these tests need to be sure that they know them well enough to justify them as valid for some meaningful purpose in this situation. (Knapp, Younggren, VandeCreek, Harris, and Martin, 2013, p. 102)

Symptom and Performance Validity Assessment

Forensic examinees have considerable incentive to present in a manner favorable to their cause. Such incentive can lead to misrepresentation of background information, misleading behavioral presentations, under- or overreporting of symptoms, and/or suboptimal performance on cognitive or other ability (e.g., motor) tests. As a result, forensic evaluations must include assessment of the validity of the examinee's symptoms, presentation, and test-taking effort to determine whether the examinee may be engaging in impression management. Efforts to determine the accuracy of reported symptoms or problems is known as *symptom validity assessment*; efforts to establish whether adequate effort was generated on cognitive or other ability tests is known as *performance validity assessment*; and efforts to establish the accuracy of reported biographical information has been referred to as *response validity assessment* (Bush, Heilbronner, & Ruff, 2014; Larrabee, 2012). In the official position statement of the Association for Scientific Advancement in Psychological Injury and Law on psychological assessment of symptom and performance validity, response bias, and malingering, Bush et al. (2014) stated that "the assessment of validity as part of forensic psychological evaluations is essential" and noted "the importance of adopting a comprehensive, impartial, and scientific approach to validity assessment" (p. 197).

Psychometric instruments, such as personality inventories, can promote evidence-based diagnostic decision making, but they depend on genuine responding, rather than denial or minimization of symptoms and common fallibilities or exaggeration or fabrication of problems. Valid test results allow the forensic psychologist to make inferences regarding constructs of interest with a certain degree of confidence, whereas invalid results limit such confidence. Although such issues are important in clinical evaluations, they may be even weightier in forensic assessments. The tremendous incentives encountered in forensic contexts increase the likelihood that an examinee will approach the evaluation with the impression management in mind. Therefore,

> forensic practitioners consider and seek to make known that forensic examination results can be affected by factors unique to, or differentially present in, forensic contexts including response style, voluntariness of participation, and situational stress associated with involvement in forensic or legal matters. (SGFP Guideline 10.02, Selection and Use of Assessment Procedures)

Even with those individuals for whom standardized testing is not appropriate (e.g., due to severe behavioral problems, apparent severe cognitive impairment, acute psychosis), the validity of the individual's presentation should be assessed through other evaluation methods, such as behavioral observations, interviews of collateral sources, and review of records. Such evaluation methods may reveal inconsistencies that suggest fabrication or exaggeration of symptoms. Invalid symptom manifestation can reflect irrelevant or uncooperative behavior or feelings of justification, entitlement, frustration, neediness, greed, or manipulation (Iverson & Slick, 2003).

In forensic assessments in which the litigant has a vested interest in appearing virtuous or normal, the litigant may deny existing symptoms and present as "too good to be true." Litigants in contested parenting matters or fitness-for-duty assessment, for example, demonstrate a higher degree of defensive responding or other efforts at distortion (E. M. Archer, Hagan, Mason, Handel, & Archer, 2012; Bagby, Nicholson, Buis, Radovanovic, & Fidler, 1999; Bathurst, Gottfried, & Gottfried, 1997; Erickson, Lilienfeld, & Vitacco, 2007; Hynan, 2013, 2014; Posthuma & Harper, 1998; Siegel, 1996; Siegel, Bow, & Gottlieb, 2012; Siegel & Langford, 1998; Young, 2014). Although the assessment of potential minimization of symptoms is essential in some evaluation contexts, the assessment of exaggerated or feigned symptoms has been emphasized in the psychological literature in recent years and is the focus of the remainder of this section.

Ethical Misconduct in Validity Assessment

With validity assessment, forensic psychologists may stray, unintentionally or intentionally, into areas of questionable ethical conduct. Unintentional ethical misconduct may result from insufficient competence in forensic practice or assessment; for example, the psychologist may fail to employ some measure of impression management when the nature of the evaluation calls for it. Standard 9.01(a), Bases for Assessments, states, "Psychologists base the opinions contained in their recommendations, reports, and diagnostic or evaluative statements, including forensic testimony, on information and techniques sufficient to substantiate their findings." Psychologists bear the burden of justifying their selection of tools for evaluation, and the absence of empirically based, multimethod approach to validity assessment in forensic examinations may be difficult to justify, or may draw into question the adequacy of the assessment to substantiate the opinions offered. Given the continually evolving nature of validity assessment research and test development, it is incumbent upon the forensic practitioner to maintain current knowledge of the research and instrumentation relevant to the practice area (Standard 2.03, Maintaining Competence; Standard 9.08, Obsolete Tests and Outdated Test Results).

In addition to inadvertent ethical misconduct related to competence, differences in symptom and performance validity measurement selection, administration, interpretation, and use can lead to the appearance of intentional manipulation by the examiner to serve a specific purpose. Test selection may at times be guided, deliberately or unintentionally, by the examiner's wish to develop a certain result. Not all validity assessment measures have equivalent sensitivity. An examiner wishing to give the appearance of assessing validity, but also to avoid detecting malingering or some other form of invalid presentation, may select tests that have relatively poor sensitivity. The examiner may also administer the fewest number of measures that he or she believes can be justified. In contrast, an examiner wishing to demonstrate invalid symptom manifestation or performance may administer many validity assessment measures in the hope that at least some scores will fall in the range indicative of impression management. Psychologists engaging in either of these patterns of test selection give the appearance of intentional misconduct. In addition, examiners who differentially select the number and type of validity assessment measures depending on which side has retained them may have a particularly difficult time defending allegations of biased test selection.

The manner in which validity tests are administered may also be inappropriately manipulated to support a given position. For example, certain very simple measures of effort appear to assess memory (e.g., the Rey 15-Item Memory Test), and recommended instructions require the examiner to describe the measures as being difficult (Lezak, Howieson, Bigler, & Tranel, 2012).

However, the extent to which the difficulty level is emphasized has the potential to influence the examinee's performance. Such manipulation of outcome may be difficult to detect. It is the ethical obligation of the forensic practitioner to use instruments fairly.

Interpreting validity assessment test scores or patterns of scores, within the context of overall findings, poses perhaps the greatest opportunity for misunderstanding and abuse of tests. Some professional guidelines are available to inform examiners about validity assessment in general (e.g., Bush et al., 2014; Bush, Ruff, et al., 2005; Heilbronner et al., 2009); however, such resources cannot inform examiners about exactly what meaning to attribute to test scores or patterns of scores in a case-specific circumstance, leaving the biased examiner to exploit this ambiguity in the interpretation process. For example, consider the following excerpts from a hypothetical neuropsychological report.

> The evaluation was initiated by a referral from the examinee's attorney in the context of a disability claim and civil litigation 6 months after a work-related accident.
>
> A 60-year-old woman tripped and fell at work, hitting her knee and head. There was a brief loss of consciousness and a 24-hour period of posttraumatic amnesia. Her first memories consisted of medical interventions by hospital staff while on the neurology service. A CT scan of the brain was negative. The examinee was discharged home to her husband's care 2 days after admission. . . . The examinee is a poor historian due to retrograde memory problems. She reported that she lost all memory from her childhood on. She reported that she only knows the information that she does know because her husband and childhood friends have reminded her of certain details.
>
> The report included the following statements regarding performance validity: "Rapport was excellent and the examinee appeared to try her best. Thus, the results of the evaluation were considered to be a valid representation of the examinee's cognitive, behavioral, and psychological functioning."
>
> Later in the report, the examiner wrote, "The results of symptom validity testing were equivocal. While some results were within normal limits and others were below established cut-offs, none were significantly below chance."
>
> The only performance validity test listed was the Rey 15-Item Memory Test, and the score was not reported. Despite reporting invalid performance on "some" performance validity tests, the psychologist did not list those tests or their scores and ultimately diagnosed impairments and their cause, localized cerebral dysfunction, and made the following determination regarding disability:

> The examinee presents with a variety of cognitive, behavioral, and psychological problems that emerged following a head injury that she sustained at work. The results of this preliminary examination suggest that some neurologic functions have been compromised by injury to the brain, with impairment of neurobehavioral and neurocognitive status resulting from damage to dorsolateral, orbital, and mesial prefrontal systems. The symptom picture and documented deficits are indicative of a totally disabling injury.

In the discussion section, the psychologist attempted to explain away the examinee's suboptimal performance on validity testing.

A complicating factor in this examinee's case is her variable performance on measures of performance validity. . . . Her performance in this area is equivocal, which makes interpretation of her cognitive abilities difficult. . . . Consideration has been given to the possibility that she has exaggerated her deficits. However, the pattern of findings is not consistent with exaggeration or fabrication of symptoms. The examinee has consistently and vociferously emphasized her wish to return to her job. Despite the income received from Workers' Compensation, her financial situation has been negatively affected by her inability to work since her accident, creating a hardship for the examinee and her family. . . . A more likely explanation for her variable performance on measures of performance validity may be found in her severe attention problems. For those performance validity tests on which her performance fell below expectations for individuals with brain injuries, her performance was not below chance, which would be more reflective of malingering. Thus, the examinee's variable performance on effort tests appears to reflect her severe difficulties with attention.

The examiner considered her own potential for self-bias:

Throughout the evaluation process, primary threats to examiner objectivity that may bias the interpretation of neuropsychological data were considered, and a strong commitment to objectivity was maintained. As a result, this evaluation is considered to have been thorough and impartial.

The psychologist's justification of her test interpretation reflects professional incompetence, a striking lack of objectivity, or both. Additionally, references to multiple performance validity measures when only one was listed may indicate an unintentional error of omission or intentional neglect of test results that were unfavorable to the examinee. Finally, it is not up to current professional standards to only view performance validity test results falling below random as indicative of invalid task engagement.

There may be legitimate difference of professional opinion regarding use of validity assessment measures. As a result, it may be difficult to determine, in individual cases, whether a practice reflects the best interests of justice or the best interest of the examiner's referral source, to the extent that those positions differ. Psychologists must determine for each case the appropriate selection, use, and meaning of indicators of validity in order to ensure the validity of examination findings. This thoughtful approach may ensure that the evaluation most effectively addresses the psycholegal question in a relevant and reliable way.

Blau (1998) noted that "the validity and reliability of expert opinion as to the presence or absence of malingering is a complex issue. . . . Testimony regarding malingering brings the expert close to being the Thirteenth Juror" (p. 19). To err by diagnosing malingering, when an alternative explanation for symptom invalidity may be present, "is essentially to accuse an individual of a potentially criminal act (e.g., fraud, perjury), while possibly also denying needed clinical services (e.g., treatment of depression)" (Sweet, 1999, p. 262). Therefore, psychologists have an affirmative obligation to conduct thorough and objective evaluation of symptom and performance validity, and to consider and document all potential explanations for invalid symptom reporting or manifestation. Thoughtful reporting of results of the validity of test responses takes into account a range of possibilities and appropriately limits the generalizations that can fairly be drawn from the validity assessment results. This consideration should include an understanding of specificity and sensitivity of instruments and the likely base rate of poor task engagement within the examination context—factors that contribute to confidence in one's conclusions about potential malingering (Larrabee, 2012). Use of probabilistic language (e.g., possible, probable, definite) based on established criteria (Greve, Ord, Bianchini, & Curtis, 2009; Slick & Sherman, 2013) improves descriptions of invalid presentations.

Examiner Deception

To some extent, deception is required of the examiner in validity assessment. As part of the informed consent process, psychologists typically describe the methods and procedures that will be used during the evaluation. Some psychologists may choose to provide general information regarding the general categories of assessment measures to be used or capacities to be assessed, including symptom and performance validity. For example, they might explain that measures will be used to assess the examinee's effort to do well, and even discuss the importance of being forthcoming and doing one's best, while others may mention this factor briefly or not at all. Whatever tack is determined to be appropriate in disclosing this aspect of the forensic assessment, the evaluator should apply it consistently, providing the same information regardless of which party has requested the evaluation.

Psychologists may give general information suggesting that among the tests are measures of response style or validity, but they do not inform examinees that a specific measure (or index embedded in a specific measure) assesses the validity of their responding. Such information would invalidate the validity assessment measure. By allowing the examinee to believe that validity measures are actually measuring another psychological construct (e.g., memory, psychosis), psychologists use deception to detect deception. The current standard of practice appears to support informing examinees, in the informed consent or notification of purpose process, that their effort and honesty will be assessed. However, the measures used and often their specific instructions rely on deception for their effectiveness. Measures that appear to assess cognitive ability and are described as measures of a certain cognitive ability, such as memory, may actually be measures of the validity of cognitive symptoms. Such deception on the part of the psychologist departs from the goal of obtaining fully informed consent. The ethical tension created by these competing aims—transparency in the examination process and collection of valid and reliable information—must be resolved by each evaluator. Because the examinee may be later evaluated by another forensic psychologist and, in the interest of safeguarding testing procedures more generally, it would be unwise to disclose, at the conclusion of testing, which instruments were utilized for validity assessment purposes. Nonetheless, consistent with SGFP Guideline 11.03, Disclosing Sources of Information and Bases of Opinions, the examiner is encouraged to note the sources of information relied upon in forming a particular conclusion, opinion, or other professional product. The treatment of these instruments that rely on naiveté of the test taker to be effective, in an age when information is easy to find, is challenging, and the skilled examiner may need to have multiple measures of impression management at the ready.

In the context of discussing testimony, Heilbrun (2001) stated that "there is no place for deception in forensic mental health assessment" (p. 274). Although the APA Ethics Code addresses the use of deception in research (Standard 8.07, Deception in Research), it does not specifically address deception in assessment. Consistent with APA General Principle C: Integrity, psychologists seek to practice in a truthful manner; however, there may be instances in which deception may be justified in order to benefit consumers of psychological services and the interests of justice. In such instances, psychologists must be mindful of the possible effects of deception on the sense of trust or the emotional state of the examinee or others involved in the case, and they should attempt to minimize potential adverse effects of such deception (Bush, 2005b). Having provided general information related to the inclusion of measures/indices of response validity during the informed consent process, the examiner has, in our opinion, met the obligation to honestly inform, and to properly obtain informed consent from, the examinee.

Adopting New Tests

New assessment instruments and revised versions of prior measures periodically become available and may improve the ability of forensic practitioners to quantitatively assess constructs of interest. When the forensic psychologist contemplates adopting a new instrument for use, there are a number of important considerations. The APA Ethics Code (Standard 9.02, Use of Assessments) instructs psychologists to use test instruments and assessment techniques consistent with research on or evidence of their usefulness and appropriateness for the manner in which they are to be used. Further, the psychologist is cautioned to refrain from using tests that are obsolete and not useful for the purposes for which they are being considered (Standard 9.08, Obsolete Tests and Outdated Test Results).

Most psychological tests and measures undergo periodic revision intended to improve psychometric properties, normative data, relevance of stimuli, and ease of administration. In addition, new tests are developed to evaluate psychological constructs. However, practitioners may be reluctant to move from a familiar and well-researched instrument to a newly released edition or measure. A primary concern is whether the newer version or measure will assess the constructs of interest in a specific population better than the prior measure.

Questions sometimes arise concerning how long it may be appropriate to continue using an instrument beyond the date of release of a revised version or when it is appropriate to replace an older test with a new test purporting to measure the same or overlapping constructs. The availability of a newer version of a test does not automatically render prior versions of the test obsolete for purposes that are empirically supported (Bush et al., 2018; International Test Commission, 2015). The continued use of a prior version of a test, when it is empirically supported, is consistent with ethical practice. A forensic psychologist may elect to continue using a well-researched instrument until its updated version or a new test has published evidence of improved utility for making diagnostic and related decisions. It is important to be able to justify decisions regarding test selection. Empirical scientific evidence and usefulness of the measures for a given examinee should drive such decisions; the cost or the effort required to upgrade or replace the instruments would not be adequate justification. Ultimately, it is the responsibility of the forensic psychologist to determine which tests are most appropriate for the needs of a given examinee and referral question and to be able to support their decisions with empirical evidence and sound clinical judgment (Bush et al., 2018).

Technology

The use of information technology and telecommunications is increasingly part of psychological practice. Examples include (a) websites that offer information about one's services and sometimes provide materials such as intake forms; (b) use of text messages or emails for scheduling appointments, providing intake forms, and otherwise interacting with examinees; (c) use of the Internet for collecting collateral information; (d) computerized test administration, scoring, interpretation, and report writing; (e) electronic record maintenance; and (f) electronic billing. The use of computerized assessment has many advantages (Bauer et al., 2012; J. B. Miller & Barr, 2017), especially for those who provide services away from the office and need to have a full arsenal of instruments at hand wherever they may be working. Ease of online scoring and of ready access to test records are further advantages. For forensic psychologists, telepsychology applications such as online assessment have the potential to extend forensic services to examinees who otherwise might not have access to the services or who may have to undergo considerable hardship to reach a qualified forensic practitioner.

Despite the advantages of merging psychological assessment with information technology, such advances pose unique ethical challenges (Bush, Naugle, & Johnson-Greene, 2002; Bush & Schatz, 2017), with very little specific guidance provided by the APA Ethics Code. To help remedy the limitations of the APA Ethics Code, The *Guidelines for the Practice of Telepsychology* (APA, 2013; see also Campbell, Millán, & Martin, 2018) provide clarification of the ethical and professional issues and responsibilities by establishing eight guidelines in the following general areas: (a) Competence of the Psychologist; (b) Standards of Care in the Delivery of Telepsychology Services; (c) Informed Consent; (d) Confidentiality of Data and Information; (e) Security and Transmission of Data and Information, Disposal of Data and Information and Technologies; (f) Testing and Assessment; and (g) Interjurisdictional Practice.

Although these guidelines are informative and beneficial for practitioners, additional empirical investigation is needed to address technological applications of forensic psychological services, such as whether (a) meaningful data is lost when face-to-face interviews are replaced with online video interviews, (b) it is necessary and proper to maintain recordings of online interviews, and (c) compromises might be made in instrument selection to accommodate the psychologist's wish to restrict testing to online instruments. Forensic psychology will inevitably continue to move toward increased technological applications to address professional needs. As this process continues, a commitment to establishing, maintaining, and improving ethical practices, including working within the boundaries of one's technological competence, facilitate and enhance the services that are provided to forensic examinees and triers of fact.

LEGAL CONSIDERATIONS IN METHODS SELECTION

Forensic psychologists select the methods and procedures they determine to be most appropriate to address the psycholegal question at hand. Such selection decisions are guided not only by the psychometric merits of the instrument or procedure, but also by the admissibility standards established by the court; it is the court serves as gatekeeper for determining whether the psychologist's testimony will be allowed. To assist with the determination of admissibility of forensic psychological evidence, the court historically relied on the standard of "general acceptance." That standard was established in *Frye v. United States* (1923), when the Court ruled that the methods and procedures upon which psychological determinations are made "must be sufficiently established to have gained general acceptance in the particular field" (p. 1014).

In 1993, the case of *Daubert v. Merrell Dow Pharmaceuticals, Inc.* (*Daubert*) refined the standard of admissibility of expert testimony in federal jurisdictions by articulating that methods and procedures must not only have achieved general acceptance in the field to which they belong, but also must be relevant to issues at hand and must have demonstrated scientific reliability and validity in contributing to the conclusions of the expert. *Daubert*'s focus on testability, falsifiability, reliability, validity, and error rates of the basis underlying scientific expert testimony was ultimately determined to be less important than the "relevance and reliability" of the testimony (Shapiro, 2012). A number of other cases, including *Kumho Tire Company v. Carmichael* (*Kumho*) (1999), have also dealt with issues of admissibility of expert testimony. *Kumho* extended the analysis to nonscientific expert testimony. In 2000, the Federal Rules of Evidence 702 and 703, which address expert testimony, were amended to reinforce the importance of "relevance and reliability" and noted that the judge, as gatekeeper, determines whether the expert testimony is based on sufficient evidence that is relevant to the case at hand (Shapiro, 2012).

After noting that there is a misunderstanding among psychologists about the function of the *Daubert* factors, Shapiro (2012) concluded,

> Clearly, Courts do not generally use these in assessing the reliability of social science or behavioral science evidence and are generally more concerned with relevance, reliability and whether the proposed testimony is of assistance to the trier of fact, along with whether or not the expert is sufficiently qualified. (p. 207)

Nonetheless, forensic practitioners may be asked by attorneys during pre-trial evidentiary hearings to articulate the falsifiability, error rate, and general acceptance of a technique on which they have relied. Regardless of whether these are factors the court really needs to consider in admissibility determinations, attorneys continue to put opposing experts through the paces to attempt to have their testimony excluded.

The *Daubert* analysis extends beyond the measures employed to include the nature of the reasoning upon which the expert's conclusions rest; both must be grounded in scientific method. Thus, forensic psychologists should be prepared to defend their choices of methods and procedures and the reasoning that flowed from data collection to the opinion offered in court—a defense based upon both general acceptance and scientific merit. The forensic expert must be prepared to illuminate the path that led from data to opinion, even if the court does not demand it; failure to do so falls below the standard of practice (Grisso, 2003; Heilbrun, 2001). Whether admissibility is governed by *Frye*, *Daubert*, or some other standard, and whether there are challenges raised regarding admissibility of the testimony to be offered, psychologists practicing in forensic contexts limit opinions to those supported by data collected through procedures recognized in the field as legitimate.

MANDATED MEASURES

The psychologist maintains responsibility for conducting an examination adequate to answer the referral questions. It is the psychologist's responsibility to determine the procedures that comprise an adequate examination in each case. Retaining parties may make requests for psychologists to administer specific tests. If the psychologist believes that different, or additional, measures should be used than those requested, an attempt should be made to explain the reasoning behind the preferred measures and seek to establish an understanding with the retaining party of the importance of the psychologist making such test selection based upon professional expertise (Bush, Barth, et al., 2005). If the retaining party indicates that the measures preferred by the psychologist are "allowable" but will not be reimbursed, the psychologist must determine how to proceed in an ethically appropriate manner. Possible courses of action include administering the additional tests pro bono or refusing to perform the examination. The psychologist is ethically obligated to document in the report any restrictions placed on selection of methods and procedures. The psychologist maintains responsibility for instrument or technique selection and should accept, modify, or reject recommendations based on their appropriateness for a given examination (Bush, Barth, et al., 2005). The National Academy of Neuropsychology produced a position statement that specifically clarifies that it is the responsibility of the neuropsychological examiner, rather than other parties in a legal matter, to select the assessment methods that are to be used (Fazio et al., 2018). Surely this principle applies to other areas of forensic psychology as well.

There may be instances in which the psychologist is asked to provide the retaining party or the examinee's counsel with a list of the examination measures in advance of the examination. To minimize the possibility of successful coaching of the examinee, the psychologist may elect to provide general information. Such information might include a description of the cognitive or psychological domains to be assessed, such as intelligence, achievement, personality, or impression management, or a list of all measures at one's disposal, without stating specifically which measures will be selected for the evaluation in question (Bush, Barth, et al., 2005).

THIRD-PARTY OBSERVERS

Interest in observing forensic psychological evaluations for other than training purposes is to ensure that the examinee receives an appropriate and competently performed evaluation and to ensure that the examinee is not asked legally objectionable questions. Thus, in personal injury litigation, it is often the plaintiff's attorney who has an interest in observing an evaluation conducted by a psychologist who has been retained by the defense. In criminal settings, the defense attorney may request observation of an evaluation performed by the prosecution's expert. In examinations of children or alleged victims of emotionally laden incidents, plaintiff's counsel or the victim advocate may request the presence of an observer to prevent the examiner from further traumatizing the examinee. Although motives of ensuring adequacy of the psychological evaluation and protecting the examinee's legal rights may justify requests to have counsel or other designees present during testing, potential threats to the evaluation's validity and test security must be considered.

Effects on Performance

Empirical evidence demonstrates that allowing observation of cognitive testing affects the examinee's performance (Constantinou, Ashendorf, & McCaffrey, 2002, 2005; Duff & Fisher, 2005; Gavett, Lynch, & McCaffrey, 2005; Gavett &

McCaffrey, 2007; Horwitz & McCaffrey, 2008; Howe & McCaffrey, 2010; Lewandowski et al., 2016; McCaffrey, 2005; Yantz & McCaffrey, 2009). The social psychology literature has demonstrated that people perform differently when being observed (Guerin, 1986). This phenomenon, referred to both as *social facilitation* and as *reactivity*, refers to a change in one's behavior when and because it is under observation (Russell, Russell, & Midwinter, 1992). Observation has been found to facilitate performance on easy tasks and inhibit performance on more difficult tasks (Green, 1983). In addition, studies of the effects of observers on psychological test results have revealed that examinees perform differently when observers are present.

Specifically, performance on measures of attention, processing speed, and verbal fluency was found to be negatively affected when a significant other observed test administration, whereas motor and cognitive flexibility results were not significantly affected (Kehrer, Sanchez, Habif, Rosenbaum, & Townes, 2000). Similarly, performance on a measure of delayed memory was negatively impacted by a third-party observer, whereas motor performance was not (Lynch, 1997). Yantz and McCaffrey (2005) found that even the presence of a supervisor adversely affects performance on memory tests. These authors also found that the presence of a parent affects the validity of a child's performance on neuropsychological testing and concluded, "no neuropsychological assessment should be assumed to be valid if administered in the presence of a parent" (Yantz & McCaffrey, 2009). They advised that efforts to help reduce a child's test-taking anxiety should occur prior to testing, so that the child is comfortable when testing begins.

Further, the effects of third-party observers on test results extend to the use of recording devices. Audio recording has been found to negatively affect verbal learning and recall but not motor performance (Constantinou, Ashendorf, & McCaffrey, 2002), and video recording was found to negatively affect immediate and delayed memory performance but not motor performance or recognition memory (Constantinou & McCaffrey, 2003). Thus, research studies indicate that both direct observation and indirect observation via recording devices may have an effect on psychological test performance. Such influences pose a threat to the validity and reliability of subsequent interpretation of test results.

The adverse effects of the presence of an observer are not limited to testing. The APA Committee on Psychological Tests and Assessment (2007) noted that

> because some examinees may be less likely to share personal information if the examinee believes that others are observing or could observe the examinee's actual statements or behavior (e.g., Sattler, 1998), the validity of non-standardized or non-test assessment procedures such as interviews or observations may also be affected by the perceived or actual presence of a third party. (p. 2)

Experience has revealed that the presence of an attorney or an attorney's representative can be quite disruptive to the flow of the interview, can be a hurdle to the development of rapport with the examinee, and can inhibit the examinee's responding. Attorneys have also disrupted interviews conducted via live video feeds (Denney, 2005b). Consequently, some forensic examiners choose not to allow a third party to be present in person or via live video feed when interviewing examinees.

Ethical Requirements and Professional Guidelines

The APA Ethics Code (Standard 9.02a, Use of Assessments) requires psychologists to use assessment techniques and instruments "in a manner and for purposes that are appropriate in light of the research on or evidence of the usefulness and proper application of the techniques." Allowing a third party to be present during cognitive testing represents a deviation from standardized administration and will have unknown effects on a given examinee and the validity of the examinee's test data. Test publishers specifically state that, with few exceptions, only the examinee and examiner should be present during the evaluation (e.g., NCS Pearson, Inc., 2009; Reynolds & Kamphaus, 2003). In those instances in which nonstandard test administration occurs, psychologists must "indicate any significant limitation of their interpretations" (Standard 9.06, Interpreting Assessment Results). Based on the research related to observation of testing, the implication of Standards 9.02a and 9.06 is that psychologists who allow observation of evaluations must indicate that such observation likely had an effect on the information obtained and that, if memory testing was performed, such observation likely had a negative effect on the results. The extent and nature of observer effects on any individual case are unknowable, and this should be indicated as well. In addition to the necessity of following standardized testing procedures, the APA Ethics Code mandates that psychologists maintain test security (Standard 9.11, Maintaining Test Security); this standard is violated when nonpsychologists observe test administration.

The position of the National Academy of Neuropsychology (2000) on third-party observers is that "neuropsychologists should strive to minimize all influences that may compromise accuracy of assessment and should make every effort to exclude observers from the evaluation" (p. 380). The American Academy of Clinical Neuropsychology (AACN; 2001) makes a distinction between involved observers (e.g., an attorney) and uninvolved observers (e.g., psychology students and other health care professionals). The position of AACN (2001) is that "it is not permissible for involved 3rd parties to be physically or electronically present during the course of an evaluation assessment of a plaintiff examinee with the exception of those situations noted below" (p. 434). Exceptions include adults with extreme behavioral disturbances and children. The APA Committee on Psychological Tests and Assessment (2007) noted that "the inclusion of a third party in psychological evaluations raises complex and sometimes paradoxical issues," (p. 3) and that "the overall goal of any situation surrounding the formal psychological evaluation of an individual is to maximize the assessment conditions to complete the most valid and fair evaluation in order to obtain the best data possible" (p. 4).

The SGFP Guidelines provide the following guidance regarding the matter (SGFP Guideline 10.06, Documentation and Compilation of Data Considered):

> When contemplating third party observation or audio/video-recording of examinations forensic practitioners strive to consider any law that may control such matters, the need for transparency and documentation, and the potential impact of observation or recording on the validity of the examination and test security. (p. 16)

A primary responsibility of psychologists when providing assessment services is to limit construct-irrelevant barriers to the attainment of valid assessment results, thereby reducing measurement error (American Educational Research Association, APA, & National Council on Measurement in Education, 2014); third-party observation is a significant construct-irrelevant barrier.

Laws

Jurisdictional laws may require that, in some contexts, examinees be allowed to record the evaluation and/or have an observer present. For example, the New York State Workers' Compensation Board *Statement of Rights and Obligations, Independent Medical Examinations* (Section 137 WCL) states that "the claimant has the right to videotape or otherwise record the examination" and "has the right to be accompanied during the exam by an individual/individuals of his/her choosing." Similarly, the Florida Supreme Court, in *U.S. Security Insurance Co. v. Cimino* (2000), concluded that when an independent medical examination (IME) is necessary for either party: (a) the parties' relationship is clearly adversarial, (b) the doctor performing the IME should be treated as the requesting party's expert witness, and (c) for the protection of the examinee, the presence of a third party (attorney, court reporter, or recording device) is not precluded. The burden falls on the retaining party to establish why an observer should be excluded.

Despite laws granting examinees the right to have an observer present, psychologists have the right to refuse to perform an evaluation under such circumstances and should particularly consider exercising that right when cognitive testing is performed. In those employment contexts in which psychologists are required to evaluate examinees with a third-party present, psychologists should strive to reduce the impact of the observation and to change the policy by educating those involved in making such decisions and participating in the observation.

Essential Use of Third Parties

In some instances, observers serve an important function in facilitating the psychological evaluation. For example, interpreters may be needed when the examiner is not fluent in the language of the examinee. When interpreters are needed, psychologists must first assess the potential biases or other influences of proposed interpreters. Interpreters who may have a stake in the outcome of the evaluation should be avoided. Once an appropriate interpreter has been selected, the examiner must

> obtain informed consent from the client/patient to use that interpreter, ensure that confidentiality of test results and test security are maintained, and include in their recommendations, reports, and diagnostic or evaluative statements, including forensic testimony, discussion of any limitations on the data obtained. (Standard 9.03c, Informed Consent in Assessments)

The use of interpreters in forensic assessment is more fully explored later in this chapter.

In addition to the use of interpreters, the presence of a third party may be indicated when evaluating persons who have substantial behavioral problems or when the purpose of the evaluation is to assess the interaction between two or more people. In forensic practice with children, the request sometimes arises for a child's therapist to accompany the child in an interview or evaluation session to accommodate the child's need for a trusted ally in the room. Although there may be merit in allowing therapist attendance, the potential contamination of the therapist's presence on the child's presentation should be carefully weighed. The therapist is an advocate for the child, and possibly for a particular view of history constructed through their therapy sessions together, potentially regarding the very issues cogent to the evaluation. If the therapist is present, the child may feel compelled to stay true to the version of history constructed through the therapist's interpretative work. A mutually agreed upon neutral third party, such as a guardian ad litem (i.e., appointed by the court), a former babysitter, or a neighbor, might be a more benign alternative, but any such accommodation should also be considered in the context of research demonstrating that even parental presence can impact the child's performance to an unacceptable degree (Yantz & McCaffrey, 2009).

Recommendations Regarding Observers

The issue of allowing a third party into the examination session is complicated. Persuasive arguments are offered both for and against such presence. When considering allowing third parties into the psychological evaluation setting, forensic psychologists are cautioned to carefully consider the potential effects of the third party on the validity of the data and on test security. For the reasons previously described, efforts should be made to resist having a third party present during forensic psychological evaluations. It is particularly important to avoid having a third party present during psychological testing. Parties requesting observation of an evaluation, whether the proposed observation is direct or indirect, should be educated about the potential effects of the observation on the conclusions drawn, and should also be warned that any potential effects must be reported. Similarly, retaining parties should be informed of the manner in which the psychological results, opinions, and testimony will be weakened if a third party is present during the evaluation; armed with such information, they can assist in advocating for exclusion of third parties.

When observers are permitted during a psychological evaluation, the situation should be structured to minimize the intrusion, with clear ground rules established before the examinee is present. The APA Committee on Psychological Tests and Assessment (2007) suggested some potentially useful ground rules, including the following:

1. Seat the observer behind the examinee and ensure the observer consents not to speak or otherwise influence the examinee during the assessment, or seat the observer behind a one-way mirror.

2. Recommend audio recording or video recording as a less intrusive option than having an individual present to observe; audio recording is less intrusive than video recording. In case of recording; take steps to limit the availability of such recordings to only those who are directly involved in the litigation and consider seeking a protective order from the judge obligating all parties to maintain test security and to destroy the recordings at the conclusion of legal proceedings.

3. Document and assist in clarifying the reasons for which observation was ultimately permitted.

4. Inform the examinee that the results of the evaluation may be altered by the observation process when seeking the examinee's consent to be observed.

5. Document in the report the potential limitations wrought by the presence of the observer.

Because of competing ethical and legal requirements and certain practical demands, this issue of allowing third parties to be present during forensic psychological evaluations is extremely complex and subject to debate among psychologists. What is clear is that having a third party be present, in person or electronically, during cognitive testing affects the validity of the test data and therefore may skew the forensic opinions offered by the practitioner. Deviations from standardized procedures and from ethical guidelines should be carefully considered, the advantages and disadvantages weighed, and the likely impact described in the report.

DIVERSITY CONSIDERATIONS

Psychological functioning is influenced by one's sociocultural background. Despite commonalties that exist among members of the same races, ethnic backgrounds, and cultures, considerable intragroup differences exist (Manly & Jacobs, 2002). Therefore, forensic psychological evaluations should include a thorough exploration of the examinee's unique racial and ethnic identity and cultural background. Failure to consider factors such as race, nationality, place of birth, immigration status, the level at which the culture of origin is maintained, perception of health care institutions and professionals, cultural factors in family roles and interactions, and importance of religious influences to the examinee may result in significant misunderstanding of the examinee and an increased potential for error in psycholegal opinions (DeJesus-Zayas, Buigas, & Denney, 2012). In addition, some of the traits and abilities assessed by psychologists may differ from those that are valued by members of different cultures, and the expression of certain traits and abilities may differ (DeJesus-Zayas et al., 2012; Iverson & Slick, 2003; Manly & Jacobs, 2002; Peery, Byrd, & Strutt, 2017). Furthermore, failure by examiners to consider their own feelings toward, and understanding of, members of different groups may also contribute to misunderstanding of the examinee's psychological functioning.

Diversity considerations are not limited to race and ethnicity. Differences in sexual orientation, gender identity, economic status, religion, disability status, and other aspects of diversity can be very important to consider in the forensic psychological evaluations. APA General Principle D: Justice states that all individuals are entitled to access to and benefit from psychological services of equal quality. Psychologists must be proactive in ensuring that biases and limitations of competence do not interfere with the provision of their services. Standard 2.01, Boundaries of Competence, subsection (b), requires sensitivity to the impact of culture, disability, and other diversity factors on one's professional competency. Knapp and VandeCreek (2003) stated, "It is not an ethical violation to provide less optimal treatment to members of . . . any groups; it is only a violation if the knowledge that is lacking is essential for providing services" (p. 303).

Standard 9.02b requires psychologists to use assessment instruments that have established validity and reliability for use with members of the population that the examinee represents. In the absence of such validity or reliability, psychologists must describe the strengths and limitations of the test results and interpretation. Subsection (c) states that psychologists should use measures that are appropriate given the examinee's language preference and competence, unless use of an alternative language is relevant to the examination. SGFP Guideline 10.02, Selection and Use of Assessment Procedures, provides essentially the same guidance.

However, some of the psychometric challenges faced in the assessment of racial or ethnic minorities are potentially insurmountable (Iverson & Slick, 2003). Neither conceptual nor metric equivalence has been established for many tests, including nonverbal tests, administered to ethnic minorities. Standard 9.06, Interpreting Assessment Results, requires psychologists to "take into account" the various factors that may affect the accuracy of their interpretations. However, due to the number of potentially invalidating factors, "in some situations, it is impossible to determine if the interpretations made by psychologists under these circumstances could be valid" (Iverson & Slick, 2003, p. 2078).

Standard 9.03, Informed Consent in Assessments, addresses, in three subsections, informed consent in assessments relevant to cultural diversity.

Section (c) describes the need for psychologists to obtain informed consent before using the services of an interpreter. Determinations regarding the need for and selection of interpreters are challenging, and universal conclusions are not feasible. What can be stated with confidence is that interpreters should (a) be sufficiently fluent in both the examinee's primary language and culture and the language and content of the test to be able to translate the test instructions and explain the examinee's responses, (b) follow standardized procedures (SEPT, 3.14). To be fully informed, the examinee and/or designated representatives should be told that the interpretation and translation may result in a degree of imprecision in the test results, and the degree of imprecision will be greater the more divergent the dialect or regional variation of the language of the interpreter and the examinee. Standard 9.03(c) notes that it is the responsibility of psychologists to ensure that their interpreters follow requirements to maintain confidentiality of test results and maintain test security. The APA Ethics Code emphasizes the need to state the limitations of one's interpretations and opinions, and culture, ethnicity, or use of interpreters all potentially call for limiting statements (Standard 9.06, Interpreting Assessment Results).

SGFP Guideline 10.03, Appreciation of Individual Differences, cautions forensic practitioners to strive to identify any significant strengths and limitations of their procedures and interpretations. It is not sufficient to state that test results were interpreted "with caution." The potential impact of linguistic and cultural factors must be described with as much specificity as possible. When measures are used that have not been standardized on the population of which the examinee is a member, interpretations should include a statement that the test results may misrepresent the examinee's true psychological state. When cognitive tests lacking adequate standardization with the specific population have been administered, the possible underrepresentation of the examinee's true ability should be stated.

In addition to cultural issues related to psychological testing, cultural diversity issues may affect the interview process and data collected from examinees and collateral data sources. Authors have described the unique considerations that may be relevant in interviewing collateral contacts, particularly the defendant's family members, in forensic evaluations of capital defendants for sentencing (Cunningham & Reidy, 2001; DeMatteo, Murrie, Anumba, & Keesler, 2011). Subcultural variations in speaking to outsiders about private family matters, in revealing history of domestic violence or substance abuse, shame about poverty, and other such factors may cause the family members to be incapable of providing accurate information, particularly if given only one opportunity to do so. Special effort may be required to ensure that the collateral contact understands the importance of providing an accurate picture of (a) the background from which the defendant came, (b) being forthcoming about the defendant's early symptoms of difficulty and the relative availability or absence of effective tools for intervention, (c) the history of chemical dependency that may have influenced the defendant's behavior, and (d) other such issues that may be reflexively denied or hidden. Multiple interviews, occurring over time and in the home or neighborhood of the collateral contact, may be necessary in order to overcome resistances borne of cultural issues. The uniqueness of these kinds of assessment and the potential gravity of the outcome warrant special consideration of cultural variations and particular emphasis on the possible limitations of the psychological techniques employed (Cunningham & Reidy, 2001).

Ethical challenges in the consideration of ethnic and cultural diversity pose considerable difficulty for psychologists, as these considerations cut across practice settings, age ranges, and psychopathological conditions. These challenges are faced not only by psychologists representing dominant U.S. demographics but also by those psychologists who are members of the minority groups with whom they work, as many psychological measures were not developed with such variations in mind and were not standardized on diverse groups or specific populations (Bush, 2005a). Sustained attention and effort on the part of the psychologist are required in order to obtain valid evaluation results from members of ethnic or racial groups that differ from those upon which the psychological measures used were developed and normed. However, with awareness of potential ethical pitfalls and ways to avoid them, forensic psychologists can make appropriate referrals, seek assistance in translation or in cultural contours at play, and make appropriate statements about assessment results (DeJesus-Zayas et al., 2012).

RECORD OR PEER REVIEWS

The majority of this chapter has focused on the psychological evaluation of individuals; however, psychologists practicing in forensic contexts may also be asked to make determinations about cases based solely on an examination of records. These record or peer reviews often take one of two forms. First, psychologists may be asked to render opinions about the work product (e.g., methods used and conclusions drawn about an examinee) of colleagues, opinions that may impact the lives of those evaluated by colleagues. Second, psychologists may be asked to render opinions about individuals involved in a forensic matter based on review of records, without having personally evaluated the individuals. Psychologists who perform, or are considering performing, such reviews should understand the relevant ethical standards and guidelines, including the APA Ethics Code and Guidelines.

The APA Ethics Code directly addresses the issue of record review and similar consultation. "When psychologists conduct a record review or provide consultation or supervision and an individual examination is not warranted or necessary for the opinion, psychologists explain this and the sources of information on which they based their conclusions and recommendations" (Standard 9.01c, Bases for Assessments). Thus, the APA Ethics Code deems it to be consistent with ethical practice to rely on record review alone, in the appropriate context; when that occurs, the psychologist needs to be clear in representing the information upon which opinions are based.

The SGFP guidelines offer essentially the same guidance. SGFP Guideline 9.03, Opinions Regarding Persons Not Examined, was drafted with the anticipation that forensic work may at times involve record review, consultation, or supervision that does not warrant an individual examination. SGFP Guideline 9.03 cautions psychologists to follow Standard 9.01, Bases for Assessments, to limit written or oral commentary about the psychological characteristics of an individual to only those opinions for which the forensic examiner has sufficient information or data to form an adequate foundation. SGFP Guideline 9.03 suggests making reasonable efforts to obtain data and documenting those efforts, and when it is not feasible to examine the individual about whom an opinion is being offered, striving to "make clear the impact of such limitations on the reliability and validity of their professional products, opinions, or testimony." In that case, "forensic practitioners seek to identify the sources of information on which they are basing their opinions and recommendations, including any substantial limitations to their opinions and recommendations." Thus, there is consistency between the APA Ethics Code and the Guidelines. Nonetheless, this issue may be a focus of cross-examination when testimony is offered based on file review or without benefit of direct examination. Ultimately, when a skilled objection is put forth, the court may arbitrate whether to allow such testimony or may provide instructions to the factfinder on the weight to give testimony based on records review alone.

CASE 3: CUSTODY EVALUATION

The following case provides a sample of ethical challenges in court-mandated child custody evaluations.

Case Facts

The custody evaluation of a family comprised of two parents and their children was court mandated, and preliminary information provided by the court support staff noted that the mother was a psychiatrist and the father was an engineer. In meeting with each parent for initial discussions regarding the evaluation, it became apparent that the mother was familiar with psychological testing in general and that both parents were sophisticated consumers of services, likely to have ready access to information about forensic psychological assessment.

The evaluator wanted to gather data using multiple reliable methods, but it appeared that psychological testing might yield little reliable material, regarding the mother specifically, under these circumstances. Uncertain whether to proceed with the standard approach that she understood to be the most efficacious evaluation protocol, based on experience and training, or whether to try to find alternative methods of measuring relevant domains, the evaluator undertook an analysis of the ethical contours of the situation.

Case Analysis

Using the mnemonic CORE OPT (Bush, Allen, & Molinari, 2017), the evaluator sought to clarify the ethical issue; identify the obligations owed to stakeholders; utilize ethical and legal resources; examine personal beliefs and values; consider options, solutions, and consequences; and put a plan into practice. Then, she would take stock, evaluate the outcome, and revise as needed.

Clarify the Ethical Issue

The primary ethical issue was identified as a need to use a fair and just approach to the assessment that would not necessarily advantage one parent over the other. As part of obtaining informed consent, the evaluator intended to inform these people, whose evaluations were court ordered, of the nature of the anticipated services and to document this notification and the assent of the parties. If the evaluator decided to forego the standard psychological testing she ordinarily utilized and rely exclusively on document review, interviews, and collateral contacts, she recognized that this would limit the multisource or multimethod assessment recognized as important in a forensic examination; yet she was not at all confident that testing would increase the reliability of her opinions.

A secondary ethical issue was the possibility that the evaluator would over-identify with the mother, a psychiatrist, or assume the mother had greater parental insight or sensitivity because of her training. The evaluator felt a keen need to examine whether this factor would impair her objectivity in any way in performing her duties. She was sensitive to the father's fears that the mother would have an unfair advantage.

Identify Obligations Owed to Stakeholders

The evaluator considered her obligations to the stakeholders. These included each parent and the children whose lives would be significantly affected by the court's ultimate determination of parenting time and responsibility. Further, the court was clearly a stakeholder; the judge had ordered the evaluations in order to obtain relevant and reliable information to include in the calculation of an appropriate determination of the children's best interest. It was by no fault of either parent that there was a significant difference in their levels of sophistication regarding psychological testing, and yet both parents could be affected, deleteriously or positively, by one or another assessment protocol. Notably, the father had raised the concern during the preliminary session, saying he recognized that his estranged wife was likely to do very well on any psychological testing, because she understood the nature and construction of the instruments and would know how to "throw" them. There were two considerations at play, the actual fairness of the evaluator's protocol and the appearance of fairness. Even if the foreknowledge of testing did not advantage the mother, the father might feel that she had a significant advantage in the process.

Utilize Ethical and Legal Resources

The evaluator consulted the resources available for consultation, including the APA Ethics Code and the SGFP Guidelines, her professional liability attorney consultant, the attorney consultant made available to her by the certifying organization that granted her board certification in forensic psychology, and two trusted colleagues with whom she regularly consulted about difficult professional matters. A review of pertinent sections of the APA Ethics Code reminded the evaluator that her work must be based on established scientific and professional knowledge of her discipline (Standard 2.04, Bases for Scientific and Professional Judgments). Standard 3.10, Informed Consent, was the evaluator's guide in informing the parties at the outset that multiple sources and methods would be employed. Finally, the evaluator examined whether she might grant special respect to the mother as an allied professional (Standard 3.06, Conflict of Interest). She felt confident that her view of the mother's training would not impair her objectivity, competence, or effectiveness in performing her function as a custody evaluator. She determined that the very fact she had considered this as an area of concern in the first place reflected the exercise of appropriate caution and consideration, and sensitivity to the father's fears that the mother would have an unfair advantage.

The guidelines point to the importance of multiple data sources in forensic examinations (SGFP Guideline 9.02, Use of Multiple Sources of Information). However, the guidelines also highlight the concerns held by the evaluator regarding the need, in interpreting assessment results, to take into account the test-taking abilities and other characteristics of the person being assessed that might affect judgments or reduce the accuracy of interpretations (SGFP Guideline 10.03, Appreciation of Individual Differences, citing Standard 9.06, Interpreting Assessment Results).

The forensic evaluator called on trusted colleagues to consider with them the alternatives she was considering. The advice and counsel she received highlighted the importance of using the same methods of assessment for each parent, using the methods that the evaluator regularly used in such assessments, and including a discussion of the potential impact of the mother's foreknowledge in her interpretations and report. Her colleagues pointed out that even though the mother had knowledge about the structure of the test scales, she nevertheless could be quite honest and forthcoming in answering questions. Further, through the multiple data sources, including interviews with each parent, the children, and collateral sources of information, a contradictory presentation of her functioning would very likely stand out if she did attempt to manage the impression she was making by the answers she provided. Finally, the discussion with her colleagues refined the evaluator's appreciation for the assessment of impression management included in the protocol she regularly employed.

Examine Personal Beliefs and Values

The evaluator next examined her personal beliefs and explored the possibility that she felt threatened or intimidated by the mother's training in a related field. In actuality, she was not sure how much training or experience the mother had with psychological testing, and certainly she recognized that her own training and experience was quite solid. She did not perceive herself to feel intimidated and felt confident she could perform the evaluation as competently as she generally did.

Consider Options, Solutions, and Consequences

Options available were identified to include (a) omitting all testing from both parents' assessments, (b) omitting testing from the mother's assessment but including it in the father's assessment, or (c) using less well-known instruments to measure the domains of interest in the hope that the mother would be less likely to be familiar with those instruments. The multimethod data collection she regularly utilized included psychological testing, and eliminating that data source seemed too extreme a solution. Similarly, using less well-known instruments, which lacked the research database of the instruments she usually relied on, seemed to be a compromise that, while it might reduce risk of the mother being familiar with them, was not fully justified. It did not seem that this option would increase the father's sense of the fairness of the evaluation, because he would likely be unaware of the differential exposure the mother might have had to each instrument. And certainly there was little to recommend the option to administer the familiar battery to the father and some less well-established battery to the mother. The likely consequences of not proceeding with the assessment procedures that the evaluator ordinarily employed in custody evaluations were that insufficient data would be generated to support her decision making, an unjust legal determination could result, and one or more parents and/or the children could be harmed.

Put Plan Into Practice

The psychologist used her typical assessment methods and procedures, being particularly mindful of the potential for impression management on behalf of the mother because of her possible familiarity with some assessment measures.

Take Stock, Evaluate the Outcome, and Revise as Needed

As it turned out, the testing was quite productive of important considerations, both for the mother and for the father. As the evaluator reflected later, in taking stock and assessing whether her decisions were the right ones, she recognized that a great deal of important data might have been lost had she opted to limit or change her testing protocol in this case. The rich material coincided with or underscored several important factors and strengthened the evaluator's findings. She included a paragraph in her report to the court discussing the mother's background and familiarity with psychological testing, and the father's expressed fear that she would be advantaged. In testimony this issue was explored at some length, and the evaluator found that she could confidently respond to challenges about how she had reasoned the appropriate methods to employ and about the impact of the findings from testing.

CONCLUSION

The forensic evaluation is the mainstay of most work performed by forensic psychologists. It forms the basis for opinions offered in consultation and testimony. Although guidelines and standards provide a framework for determining the correct course of action in many aspects of assessment, forensic psychologists nevertheless may be faced with areas of ambiguity. For example, determining the appropriateness of an online search for data regarding an examinee, determining whether a supplanted test must be "retired" from usage, or facing pressure from counsel or a court to alter one's examination paradigm can be challenges for which no easy answer is found in standards and guidelines. Just as a multisource and multimethod process of data collection advances the formation of evidence-based forensic opinions, a structured approach to ethical decision making that involves use of multiple resources and consideration of an empirical evidence base promotes sound ethical determinations regarding forensic psychological assessment.

5

Documentation of Findings and Opinions

Documentation is the primary vehicle for preserving and conveying forensic evaluation findings and opinions to attorneys, triers of fact, and other decision-makers, with discussion and testimony being additional possible means of conveying the information. The manner in which the forensic practitioner's evaluation results and conclusions are documented has implications for their usefulness, and the nature and maintenance of the records are governed by ethical and legal requirements. This chapter describes ethical considerations in the documentation of psychological findings and forensic opinions. Specific issues that are covered include (a) forensic psychological records; (b) scope of interpretation, (c) monitoring self-bias, (d) forensic reports, (e) requests for raw test data and test materials, and (f) feedback about the findings of the evaluation. A personal injury case illustration is also provided, illustrating the dangers of neglecting steps in the CORE OPT model (see Chapter 1, this volume, and Table 1.2) and of not maintaining a personal and professional commitment to ethical practice.

FORENSIC PSYCHOLOGICAL RECORDS

Consumers of forensic psychological services have a right to expect and receive competent services. For services to reflect competence, the opinions offered must arise from "information and techniques sufficient to substantiate

http://dx.doi.org/10.1037/0000164-006
Ethical Practice in Forensic Psychology, Second Edition: A Guide for Mental Health Professionals,
by S. S. Bush, M. Connell, and R. L. Denney

their findings" (American Psychological Association [APA], 2017a; *Ethical Principles of Psychologists and Code of Conduct*; APA Ethics Code, Standard 9.01a, Use of Appropriate Methods). The law requires that expert opinions, including the methods of data collection and reasoning upon which they are based, derive from techniques generally acceptable within the professional community (*Frye v. United States*, 1923) and sufficiently grounded to withstand scientific scrutiny (*Daubert v. Merrell Dow Pharmaceuticals, Inc.*, 1993). It is generally the documentation of one's work that allows a reviewer to determine whether the evaluation performed was relevant, reliable, and valid.

To enable review, psychologists have an ethical obligation to appropriately document and maintain records of their work (Standard 6.01, Documentation of Professional and Scientific Work and Maintenance of Records), and the documentation must be accurate (Standard 5.01b, Avoidance of False or Deceptive Statements). To address questions about which materials are considered "documentation," the *Specialty Guidelines for Forensic Psychology* (SGFP; APA, 2013) Guideline 10.06, Documentation and Compilation of Data Considered, states,

> This documentation includes, but is not limited to, letters and consultations; notes, recordings, and transcriptions; assessment and test data, scoring reports and interpretations; and all other records in any form or medium that were created or exchanged in connection with a matter.

Although practitioners may not naturally consider electronic communications with others to be part of the record, information obtained, expressed, or exchanged via email or text messages or stored as voicemail may be subject to discovery and review and should be preserved along with other case data.

SGFP Guideline 10.06 states, "Forensic practitioners are encouraged to recognize the importance of documenting all data they consider with enough detail and quality to allow for reasonable judicial scrutiny and adequate discovery by all parties." However, determining the nature of documentation that is "sufficient to withstand scrutiny in an adjudicative forum" and "the best documentation possible" may be a difficult task. Documentation linked to a competent evaluation and of sufficient detail to allow an independent peer reviewer to arrive at similar conclusions or clearly identify how the conclusions in a report or testimony were reached would most likely withstand adjudicative scrutiny.

Documentation throughout the process of forensic evaluation or treatment is necessary to ensure that competent services are provided and to assist the legal decision-maker. Following the provision of services, the availability of the documentation for reviewers helps to establish that competent services were provided. In addition, such documentation protects examinees, the public, and the psychologist (APA, 2007; Barsky, 2012). The foreknowledge by forensic psychologists that their records may be reviewed provides considerable incentive to ensure that all facets of the evaluation process are performed in a manner that reflects highest professional standards. Thus, maintaining appropriate records is consistent with the general ethical principles of beneficence, nonmaleficence, and justice, and is an underpinning of competent forensic psychological services to which consumers have a fundamental right.

SCOPE OF INTERPRETATION

The integration of scientific data and reasoning is important for relevant and reliable psychological decision making. Psychological conclusions of value to the trier of fact tend to be based on a combination of individualized (ideographic) and group referenced (nomothetic) approaches to data interpretation. Information specific to the examinee is collected and compared to the performance of one or more groups of interest. Cognitive, psychopathologic, or behavioral data that differ from the comparison groups must be understood in terms of the individual's unique life circumstances, with an emphasis on variables that are known to affect such performance. Opinions based on reasoning that lack either the ideographic or nomothetic approach are weaker than when based on the combined approach. Standard 2.04, Bases for Scientific and Professional Judgments, states, "Psychologists' work is based upon established scientific and professional knowledge of the discipline." An opinion that is not grounded in objective data and scientific principles may be insufficient to meet the requirements of this standard.

Legal decision making tends to be dichotomous in nature, with referral sources and triers of fact preferring definitive statements regarding diagnosis, proximal cause, and other determinations relevant to the forensic issues at hand. Requests or demands for definitive statements tend to conflict with the more probabilistic statements that are generally acceptable to clinicians and to clinical referral sources. There is risk in offering definitive statements in forensic contexts that would traditionally have been offered as statements of possibility in clinical contexts. Such statements may be seen as inaccurate or misleading, in violation of Standard 5.01, Avoidance of False or Deceptive Statements, and counter to SGFP Guideline 11.01, Accuracy, Fairness, and Avoidance of Deception. It is important for the psychologist, having conducted a thorough evaluation, to assert opinions as strongly as the data merits, but to also describe the limitations of those opinions. Opinions reported "with a reasonable degree of psychological certainty" allow for the expression of confident opinions while maintaining an acknowledged margin for potential error.

Psychological capacities are a component of many legal questions, such as criminal responsibility, civil commitment, multiple legal competencies, and custodial arrangements, and psychologists are often retained to evaluate and comment on psychological issues pertaining to such questions. However, there are occasions when the psychologist's opinion regarding the legal question itself is requested. There is vigorous debate on this issue within the forensic community (Packer & Grisso, 2011; Pivovarova, 2017). There is no federal prohibition against answering the legal question, often referred to as the "ultimate issue," and Federal Rule of Evidence (FRE) 704 (House of Representatives, Committee on the Judiciary, 2018), with a specific exception regarding criminal responsibility opinions provided in front of a jury, explicitly permits it. In fact, 18 U.S.C. § 4247(c)(4) (General Provisions for Chapter, 2017) requires the ultimate issue opinion within court-ordered forensic mental health reports performed in the criminal setting. Additionally, most U.S. states permit or require forensic experts to offer opinions about ultimate issues. However, Heilbrun (2001) stated that the ultimate legal opinion is generally not the appropriate focus for forensic mental health evaluations. Melton et al. (2018) noted that when forensic practitioners venture to opine on the ultimate issue before the court, they risk overstepping the bounds of competency by opining about issues outside their areas of expertise or unsupportable by the data. Additionally, Grisso (2003) said, "An expert opinion that answers the ultimate legal question is not an 'expert' opinion, but a personal value judgment" (p. 477). Having reviewed the very limited empirical literature on this topic, Pivovarova (2017) concluded that the "findings suggest that there may be no empirical basis for prohibiting ultimate issue opinions by practitioners" (p. 266). An ultimate issue opinion, which includes a description of the supporting evidence, is one piece of information that the trier of fact can consider in making a determination. Refusing to offer such an opinion when asked may frustrate the legal decision-maker who may not put great stock in differentiating the value-laden ultimate opinion from the scientifically derived expert opinion, making it harder for them to understand how the psychological factors of interest interact with the legal matter.

Psychologists who practice in contexts in which it is expected or required that they answer the legal question may make a special effort to temper their opinions, by including cautionary language and caveats regarding the limitations of, and potential influences on, their opinions. The following example may be useful to consider when responding to an ultimate legal question. The forensic psychologist is asked, "How do you think the court should apportion parental responsibility for caregiving for this child?" The psychologist might first briefly hesitate to allow time for objection to be offered. Then the psychologist might preface the response by making an explicit statement about that being the ultimate issue and, therefore, within the province of the trier of fact, and then couch the opinion within that limitation, saying something to the effect of,

> Although that question is, of course, a matter for the court to determine, and the court may have a great deal more information than I do to arrive at that determination, I can offer the following observations and opinions, based on the data that I have collected. It is my opinion that . . .

Psychologists may be retained by attorneys or others to answer specific, rather than general, questions. In such instances, psychologists may wonder to what extent they should document potentially related issues that fall outside the question posed. For example, a psychologist may be asked to determine whether a plaintiff has objective memory deficits subsequent to a motor vehicle collision. If the results of the evaluation reveal no cognitive deficits but are consistent with adjustment-related depression, would it be appropriate for the psychologist to simply state that memory was within normal limits, or is the psychologist also responsible for reporting emotional disturbance? SGFP Guideline 11.02, Differentiating Observations, Inferences, and Conclusions, states, "Forensic practitioners are encouraged to explain the relationship between their expert opinions and the legal issues and facts of the case at hand." SGFP Guideline 11.01 further states,

> When providing reports and other sworn statements or testimony in any form, forensic practitioners strive to present their conclusions, evidence, opinions, or other professional products in a fair manner. Forensic practitioners do not, by either commission or omission, participate in misrepresentation of their evidence, nor do they participate in partisan attempts to avoid, deny, or subvert the presentation of evidence contrary to their own position or opinion.

However, the forensic practitioner is also cautioned not to include data or information extraneous to the legal question at hand (SGFP Guideline 11.04, Comprehensive and Accurate Presentation of Opinions in Reports and Testimony). To answer the hypothetical question posed at the beginning of this paragraph, a thorough and appropriate response would be to describe the adjustment-related depression and the potential impact of such emotional distress on the examinee's subjective sense of concentration or memory problems in daily life.

Although the psycholegal questions investigated by psychologists and documented in reports may be specifically defined by the retaining party, the psychologist's responsibility in many instances extends beyond the narrow scope of the referral question. For example, some referral sources may not fully appreciate the potential psychological issues involved and, thus, may not know how to pose the question they want answered. In addition, the concept of *due diligence* underscores the psychologist's ethical and professional responsibility to address and document substantial medical or psychological problems that are relevant but were not included in the referral question (Bush, Barth, et al., 2005). Bush, Barth, et al. (2005) described the issue this way:

> If failure to document another condition can result in harm to the examinee, the option of nondisclosure may not be ethically viable. If this becomes a point of concern, the neuropsychologist should seek clarification from the retaining party regarding the reason for the limitation posed, present his/her reasoning regarding the presence of a different condition, and consider the judiciousness of accepting cases in which limitations are placed on independence. (p. 1001)

Similarly, even though the court may have narrowly defined a custody evaluation referral, the psychologist would nevertheless need to include in reports any other psychopathology or parenting behavior that would likely impact upon the child's well-being. For example, a psychologist asked to evaluate the potential impact of alleged alcohol abuse of one of the parents upon that parent's ability to provide for the needs of the child would also need to describe issues of depression or anger that may coexist with alcohol abuse and affect the child's well-being, if such a situation was encountered. This does not mean, however, that the evaluator must report extraneous data that, however interesting or outrageous, has nothing to do with the child's best interests. An example might be the admission, on the part of the litigant, of a transgression that occurred one time, many years before. If the litigant has since demonstrated a clear pattern of acting more appropriately with respect to that behavior or issue, and there is no apparent impact of the earlier behavior on current functioning, then it may be inappropriate to include it in the report. It would, nevertheless, be in the evaluator's notes and records and thus be discoverable.

Likewise, psychological evaluations conducted in criminal settings often have quite specific referral questions, such as whether the defendant was insane at the time of the alleged offense or competent to waive the Miranda warning and confess at a particular time in the past. Ordinarily, it is prudent to limit the scope of documented opinions regarding such matters to the referral question, as well as the underlying clinical basis for the opinion. However, when referral questions do not address current competency to proceed, and the evaluator has concern about the defendant's ability to understand the nature and consequences of the proceedings or to assist properly in the defense, the evaluator has an ethical responsibility to raise the question of the defendant's competency (APA General Principle A: Beneficence and Nonmaleficence). Evaluators in the criminal setting have an ethical obligation to safeguard defendants' U.S. Constitutional rights—the 14th Amendment right to *due process* necessitates a defendant's competency to proceed (Denney, 2012a; *Youtsey v. United States*, 1899). Because prosecuting an incompetent defendant violates the defendant's *due process* rights, evaluators must be cognizant of examinee competency and raise the issue when worrisome mental health issues arise that could affect competence to proceed.

The range of issues to be explored and potentially addressed in the report should be anticipated so that the entire range of possibilities can be included when gaining informed consent or providing notification of purpose. The litigant needs to know and have time to consider, for example, that questions may be asked about acting out in adolescence. When there is a sealed record of juvenile adjudication, the litigant may need to have time to consult with counsel regarding rights and responsibilities in responding to the examiner's question. Where an issue is irrelevant, because it has no impact upon the question before the court, it legitimately can be, and generally should be, omitted from the report. However, in global assessment of psychological functioning, such as might be requested in a parenting assessment, virtually no issue can automatically be assumed to be irrelevant, and caution is in order when considering whether to omit a finding.

MONITORING SELF-BIAS

Forensic psychologists must be keenly aware of the internal and external challenges to objectivity in both their data collection and documentation as there are invariably great stakes in the outcome and reasons for each side in the adversarial legal process to view things quite differently. It is essential to strive to maintain independence and autonomy from external pressures and to carefully monitor one's efforts to identify and exclude internal tugs at partisanship. Failure to consider the possibility of self-bias in forensic practice may represent compromised professional integrity.

SGFP Guideline 9.01, Use of Appropriate Methods, states,

> When performing examinations, treatment, consultation, educational activities, or scholarly investigations, forensic practitioners seek to maintain integrity by examining the issue or problem at hand from all reasonable perspectives and seek information that will differentially test plausible rival hypotheses.

Psychologists involved in forensic practice must be sensitive to potential sources of bias and guard against the impact of such biases on their work. Although biases may impact data collection and interpretation, their influence tends to become evident in the practitioner's documentation and testimony.

Financial Incentive

The potential for immediate or future financial gain provides considerable incentive for professionals to obtain and present findings that support the position of the retaining party. Although it may be that some attorneys are interested in objective psychological conclusions, whether or not their positions are supported, it is certain that a substantial number of attorneys only want to receive psychological reports that unequivocally support their position. Psychologists must guard against threats, however subtle, to their objectivity resulting from financial considerations or from the social pressure to be a part of "the team." Boccaccini, Murrie, and colleagues (Boccaccini, Turner, & Murrie, 2008; Murrie, Boccaccini, Johnson, & Janke, 2008) found that forensic psychologists who conducted assessments of future danger among allegedly sexually violent predators for purposes of legal determinations of the need for civil commitment opined in the direction of the retaining party, scoring tests in a way that would support the finding. A subsequent experimental study found that this scoring pattern occurred even when experts were randomly assigned to sides, ruling out the possibility of it being attributable to attorneys being shrewd in selecting only those experts who they believed would be favorable to their side (Murrie, Boccaccini, Guarnera, & Rufino, 2013). This important research confirmed the worst suspicion that practitioners might tend to "dance with whomever brought them," a most distressing finding and one that should serve as a wake-up call to all forensic psychologists. These researchers (Chevalier, Boccaccini, Murrie, & Valora, 2015) found evidence of adversarial allegiance in test score interpretation and "bias blind spots" in how instruments were scored and data were integrated. They found that evaluators could acknowledge the possibility of bias in other evaluators but not in themselves. These findings alert forensic psychologists to the need for continuous monitoring and for assuming bias will creep into work in an adversarial setting.

Inferential Bias

Coexisting with the potential for financially motivated or partisan bias is the susceptibility of psychologists to inferential bias (Deidan & Bush, 2002). The use of general rules (e.g., heuristics) in the inferential process can result in biases (Faust, 1986) and lead to ethical misconduct. Inferential biases include (a) the availability and representative heuristics, (b) fundamental attribution error, (c) anchoring, (d) confirmatory hypothesis testing, and (e) reconstructive memory. Adverse effects of inferential bias for psychologists include misdiagnosis, inappropriate treatments, exacerbation of symptoms, and inaccurate expert opinions. Although these biases may occur in nonforensic psychology practices, the potential for referral sources to repeatedly select practitioners with biases that support their positions may reinforce the bias for the practitioner. Brief descriptions of these five inferential biases follow.

Availability and Representative Heuristics

The availability heuristic (Kahneman & Tversky, 1973) occurs when the psychologist attempts to determine the frequency of occurrence of a particular situation, such as a certain diagnosis. Situations stemming from information that is readily available in the psychologist's memory (e.g., frequently encountered diagnoses) are perceived as being more likely to occur, and the psychologist is unlikely to search for less accessible alternative explanations.

The representative heuristic (Kahneman & Tversky, 1973) involves categorizing information according to how closely it approximates the characteristics of certain groups. For example, psychologists may classify examinees as probable malingerers or unlikely malingerers based on their experience with prior examinees with similar traits, symptoms, injuries, or other characteristics.

Fundamental Attribution Error

Fundamental attribution error is the tendency for individuals involved in a situation to overattribute their behaviors to situational requirements and for observers of the same situation to over attribute the individual's behaviors to stable personal characteristics (Ross, 1977). This dynamic makes it more likely for psychologists to attribute examinee symptoms or issues to character traits, although examinees will be more likely to attribute their symptoms or issues to external factors.

Susceptibility to this type of error may result from education and training paradigms and from philosophical positions that psychologists may adopt as a result of their experiences. Psychologists make judgments about diagnostic conditions based on their professional experiences and their interpretation of the psychological literature. For example, an expert with considerable experience evaluating persons with a history of traumatic brain injury (TBI) may erroneously diagnose TBI-related problems when symptoms have psychiatric etiology, whereas a psychologist experienced in evaluating and treating psychotic disorders may infer psychogenic etiologies for TBI sequelae. Some examiners hold extreme positions with regard to certain diagnoses, to the extent that the specific details related to a certain case may have little impact on the opinions rendered. Applying predetermined or formulaic conclusions to individual cases is inconsistent with ethical practice (Standard 9.06, Interpreting Assessment Results; Standard 3.01, Unfair Discrimination).

Anchoring

Anchoring involves failure to revise initial impressions, beliefs, or preconceptions despite being faced with new, contradictory information. In psychological practice, anchoring may be seen (a) in the formation of preconceptions or opinions from information attained prior to meeting, interviewing, or evaluating an examinee (i.e., prior knowledge); or (b) in the formation of preconceptions or opinions from previous conditions or diagnoses associated with an examinee (i.e., labeling; Cantor & Mischel, 1979). Psychologists' opinions may also become biased by the timing of receipt of information about an examinee, with information obtained first carrying greater weight than information obtained later. Preconceived impressions tend to remain durable; once formed, they are difficult to change. This primacy effect may be somewhat ameliorated by arranging to hear from parties adverse to the source of initial input on the assumption that some "recency bias" might counterbalance the earlier effect.

Confirmatory Hypothesis Testing Bias

Use of a hypothesis-testing approach for gathering background information or selecting tests is useful for pursuing information that is considered to be most relevant to specific referral questions and the unique circumstances of each case. However, pursuing information in such a manner as to selectively influence the information obtained in order to support initial beliefs is known as confirmatory hypothesis testing bias (Snyder & Campbell, 1980). Confirmatory hypothesis testing bias can result in psychologists eliciting incomplete or inaccurate information.

Reconstructive Memory

Filling in gaps in memory or altering memory to make it consistent with current experience is known as reconstructive memory (Wells, 1982). Although reconstructive memory decreases the likelihood that information will be recalled accurately, people nevertheless tend to be overconfident in their memories and their ability to reconstruct events, conversations, or other important events and information after a period of time has lapsed. This type of bias in examiners may be particularly relevant for practice activities that involve evaluation or other psychological services provided for a number of hours across multiple sessions. Delays in completing notes or reports increase the likelihood that some information will be forgotten and later replaced by information that confirms current opinions.

Addressing Self-Bias Proactively

Remaining aware of the potential for bias in formulating opinions is necessary but not sufficient to avoid falling victim to bias. Taking steps to minimize potential sources of bias and their impact on psychological opinions should be considered an integral component of the forensic evaluation (Brodsky, 2013; Martelli, Bush, & Zasler, 2003; Neal, 2017; Sweet & Moulthrop, 1999). Strategies designed to minimize the potential for bias may involve consideration of alternative explanations that may disconfirm initial hypotheses (Arkes, 1981; Arnoult & Anderson, 1988; Neal & Brodsky, 2016), writing explicit arguments for and against proposed opinions (Fischhoff, 1982), and generating self-examination questions when formulating opinions (Sweet & Moulthrop, 1999). To reduce the potential influence of inferential biases, Deidan and Bush (2002) offered multiple recommendations specific to each of the inferential biases discussed above.

FORENSIC REPORTS

The written report is the primary vehicle by which the forensic psychologist communicates opinions about the forensic issues of interest that may assist the legal decision-maker. Although written reports are not required for all forensic services, the vast majority of forensic referrals result in a written report (Melton et al., 2018). Forensic psychological reports tend to differ from clinical reports. Authors of forensic mental health texts describe the elements to be included in forensic reports (e.g., Barsky, 2012; Bartol & Bartol, 2019; Heilbrun, 2001; Karson & Nadkarni, 2013; Melton et al., 2018; Otto, DeMier, & Boccaccini, 2014). Minimally, a forensic report includes the purpose of the evaluation, the methods and procedures employed, the results, and the conclusions. The report should be sufficiently detailed and scientifically based to allow the reader to follow the genesis of the writer's conclusions or opinions (Heilbrun, 2001). Although in some cases the report is the end product of the forensic consultation, in other cases testimony, by deposition or in court, is required, and an organized and well-supported report can serve as the foundation for organized, well-supported testimony (Heilbrun, 2001). In contrast, a poorly written report may be used to discredit and embarrass the practitioner (Melton et al., 2018). Careless errors such as (a) wrongly stating the age or gender of the examinee, (b) cutting and pasting from a template and failing to thoroughly redact material from a prior assessment, (c) failing to list all instruments administered, (d) spelling instrument names incorrectly, and (e) other such errors detract significantly and reduce the examiner's credibility and professionalism in the eyes of the consumer.

SGFP Guideline 11.03, Disclosing Sources of Information and Bases of Opinions, states,

> Forensic practitioners are encouraged to disclose all sources of information obtained in the course of their professional services, and to identify the source of each piece of information that was considered and relied upon in formulating a particular conclusion, opinion, or other professional product.

In addition to listing sources of information used, full disclosure includes acknowledging those resources that may have been of value but were unavailable.

Psychologists may be asked to modify reports with regard to format and/or content. However, any submitted report should be considered final for its purpose. When factual errors are found subsequent to the release of the report or the referral question has not been adequately addressed, the examiner may elect to append the corrected or additional information in an amendment or addendum to the report or create a corrected version of the report. In such instances, the practitioner clearly documents within that report that it is a corrected version and provides the rationale for the change. An amendment or addendum, rather than a revision, may be preferable because it is less likely that confusion will arise about the final opinion, and how it clarifies or adds to any earlier conclusions. The question, "Doctor, just how many reports of yours on this matter are floating around out there?" would be an unpleasant one to face. An amendment or addendum, clearly titled as such, is less vulnerable to such criticism.

A request to modify a report that comes from an invested party and reflects that party's self-interest in the outcome of a case represents a request for the psychologist to become a biased advocate, rather than an objective expert (Bush, Barth, et al., 2005). Such requests should be considered cautiously. There are very few acceptable reasons to modify reports once they have been completed, and any modification must ultimately reflect the beliefs of the psychologist rather than those of any other party.

Reproducing Examinee Statements

In criminal evaluation contexts, reproducing defendants' statements in psychological reports has the potential to violate the defendant's due process rights. This issue clearly arises when evaluating the sanity (mental state at the time of the alleged offense) of a defendant whose competency to proceed has not been established; however, it can also arise during a simple competence examination. When a defendant's competency to proceed is questionable, his or her ability to fully appreciate the limits of confidentiality and right to waive Fifth Amendment rights to silence and avoidance of self-incrimination are also potentially questionable. Within the federal jurisdiction, there are statutory safeguards (FRE 12.2[c][4], House of Representatives, Committee on the Judiciary, 2018) that ostensibly do not allow statements or "fruits" of the statements made to the examiner to be admitted into evidence against a defendant for criminal prosecution (Denney, 2012b); however, counsel for defense understandably tends to remain wary in such situations. When a potentially incompetent defendant discloses self-incriminating information during a competence to proceed examination, it is incumbent on the forensic examiner to limit disclosure of that material within the report to the minimum required to support the clinical and forensic decision making (Denney & Wynkoop, 2000).

To determine whether the defendant has a rational as well as factual understanding of the alleged crime, it is important for the examiner to discuss the defendant's perception of the allegations and his or her recollection of his behaviors at the time of the offense (whether they relate to the allegations or not). Covering this material during interviews allows the examiner to establish that the defendant has recollection sufficient to aid counsel in assisting with a defense and it also investigates the defendant's reasoning related to the alleged offense. Oftentimes it suffices for the examiner to write that the defendant was able to recall events and his behaviors at the time of the alleged offense without disclosing details of those actions. However, when the defendant is mentally ill, those abnormal thoughts or manner of expressing his thoughts at the time may be part of the basis for the diagnostic and forensic formulations and may need to be disclosed in the report. The examiner should seek to limit incriminating details when possible. In instances where the examiner must disclose details because they demonstrate severe mental illness (and/or incompetence), the examiner's ethical dilemma is to determine how to disclose these necessary details while trusting the court to protect the rights of the defendant. One possible way to alleviate some of that concern is to contact the court directly and voice those concerns (in the case of court-ordered or prosecution-referred examination). In defense-referred examinations, the examiner need only discuss the issue with the defendant's counsel to seek how best to proceed.

Evaluating sanity generally requires, among other procedures, interviewing the defendant about the details of the alleged offense to better understand the defendant's intent, motivation, planning, organization, thought process, and general mental status at the time of the offense (in essence, it assumes the behaviors constituting the offense truly occurred). Reproducing a defendant's recollected details of a crime has the potential to further the prosecutorial investigation by providing important clues and "leads" that were previously unknown. As a result, the defendant could inadvertently provide a confession that gives the prosecution additional information to follow up on and use against him or her (FRE 12.2[c]; House of Representatives, Committee on the Judiciary, 2018, notwithstanding). There is little concern when the defendant is clearly competent to decide how much incriminating information he or she wants to provide the evaluator. The issue is also moot when the defendant does not provide incriminating information. However, when the competency of the defendant is clearly questionable or the information the defendant provides is not only incriminating but also an integral factor in the clinical formulation for a diagnosis or ultimate-issue opinion, the psychologist faces the same dilemma outlined above regarding competency examinations— whether to provide incriminating information in the report regarding a questionably competent defendant or not be able to explain the rationale for the forensic opinion. Both situations are ethically onerous. As noted earlier, one effective strategy in dealing with this dilemma is contacting the court directly prior to writing the report to voice the concern (in the case of a court-ordered or prosecution-referred examination) or contact the defense counsel directly in a defense-referred examination.

Court-ordered examinations oftentimes include the requirement to examine both competence to proceed and sanity at the same time. One option to resolve the conundrum of potentially incriminating self-disclosure during sanity-related interviewing is to provide separate documents—a report addressing the defendant's competency and an addendum addressing the defendant's sanity. The main report contains all the standard clinical information leading to a diagnosis, as well as current mental status and competency issues. The addendum contains information relating to the investigative details of the offense, the defendant's explanation and description of the offense, and the forensic opinion regarding sanity. The examiner still needs to remain mindful of limiting inclusion of potentially incriminating self-report in the competency portion of the report, however. This method of report writing works particularly well when responding to court-ordered evaluations, because the report and addendum can be sent to the court with a cover letter explaining that the two topics were separated due to Fifth Amendment issues. This information provides the court with the opportunity to release competency-related material first to resolve questions of the defendant's competency. The addendum can then be released to the defense for consideration of a sanity defense and to the prosecution if the defense intends to pursue a sanity defense. In this manner, the court effectively protects the defendant's constitutional rights, and the forensic examiner avoids an ethical conundrum. The issue is generally less of a concern when the evaluation is requested by the defense, depending on work product rules in that particular jurisdiction (Melton et al., 2018).

Preliminary Reports

It is the practice of some psychologists who perform clinical evaluations and treatment in a forensic context to write a report that is considered, and may be labeled, a preliminary report, with the expectation that a "forensic" report may later be requested and produced. Such reports may list the differences between preliminary-clinical reports and more conclusive-forensic reports in the body of the report. This practice invites the establishment of dual and conflicting roles that occur when transitioning from a clinical examiner to a forensic examiner.

In addition to inviting role conflicts, the use of preliminary reports may be problematic because they are generally offered when not all of the data have been collected, with the caveat that the report will be supplemented when the remaining data are available. The problem with such a practice is that it demonstrates that the evaluator has come to a conclusion of some sort without data that were considered to be important enough to have been sought.

The following sections are taken from a hypothetical "Preliminary Psychological Examination Report":

> *Introduction section.* The purpose of this preliminary psychological evaluation was to examine the patient's psychological functioning from the perspective of her self-reported symptoms, cognitive abilities, emotional state, personality traits, behavioral presentation, disability status, and causality. This evaluation is considered preliminary because (a) not all potentially relevant background information

has been reviewed; (b) self-reported information has not been corroborated by additional, reliable sources; and, (c) psychometric assessment of symptom validity has not been performed; and (d) alternative explanations for reported and observed difficulties have not been thoroughly considered.

Conclusions section. The results of the evaluation are consistent with a posttraumatic stress disorder. The disorder is causally related to the event in question. The nature and extent of psychological deficits is consistent with a total disability. However, the background information reported by the patient was taken at face value and requires verification by additional sources. . . . This evaluation, despite being preliminary, is considered complete and objective.

The lines from this hypothetical report raise questions of appropriateness for a number of reasons. First, the report is labeled "preliminary," suggesting that it is being released prematurely, before the necessary information has been obtained and considered. Despite these limitations, the examiner goes on to address forensic issues, such as causality and disability status, in the absence of information that the examiner acknowledges is important. Finally, the examiner makes the unsupported self-appraisal of objectivity, despite the existence of statements that are consistent with partiality. As noted in Chapter 3, use of preliminary reports should be avoided. Reports that are released should be considered final for the purposes for which they are provided. Requests for preliminary reports can be addressed by educating the requesting party about the limitations and risks of providing opinions based on incomplete information. If a tentative formulation must be provided, the confidence placed in the opinion should be tempered, with notation of the specific implications of not having all relevant information.

TEST SECURITY AND RELEASE OF RAW DATA

The disclosure of raw test data to nonpsychologists, as may be required in forensic practice, presents a unique problem for psychologists (Rapp, Ferber, & Bush, 2008). The problem involves determining how to balance the discovery rules, which provide disclosure of the underlying data parties will rely on at trial, against the psychologist's ethical responsibilities and contractual obligations regarding the test publisher's proprietary testing materials. For litigation purposes, there is a well-established necessity to disclose the sources of information and methods upon which an expert's opinions are based. FRE 705 (House of Representatives, Committee on the Judiciary, 2018) states that "the expert may testify in terms of opinion or inference and give reasons therefore without first testifying to the underlying facts or data, unless the court requires otherwise. The expert may in any event be required to disclose the underlying facts or data on cross-examination." In contrast to the benefits of disclosure in litigation, far reaching negative consequences may flow from wide dissemination of psychological evaluation methods and procedures. As a result, psychologists working in forensic contexts may struggle with how to negotiate the competing legal demands (e.g., copyright law vs. discovery law) and competing legal and ethical requirements.

The APA Ethics Code distinguishes test *materials* from test *data*. "The term *test materials* refers to manuals, instruments, protocols, and test questions or stimuli" (Standard 9.11, Maintaining Test Security). *Test materials* do not include test data (as defined in Standard 9.04a). Standard 9.11 states, "Psychologists make reasonable efforts to maintain the integrity and security of test materials and other assessment techniques consistent with law and contractual obligations, and in a manner that permits adherence to this Ethics Code." Thus, the APA Ethics Code recognizes the importance of safeguarding psychological tests to avoid potential damage that would result to the profession and potential examinees and parties in future cases if such measures were made available to those who were not qualified to use them.

In contrast to *test materials*, *test data* are defined in Standard 9.04a, Release of Test Data, as "raw and scaled scores, client/patient responses to test questions or stimuli, and psychologists' notes and recordings concerning client/patient statements and behavior during an examination." In order to address the problem of physically separating the test data from the test materials, Standard 9.04(a) states, "Those portions of test materials that include client/patient responses are included in the definition of *test data*." Clarification from the APA Ethics Office indicated that once test materials have responses written on them, they "convert" to test data (Behnke, 2003). This position suggests that test materials, which enjoy protection under Standard 9.11, Maintaining Test Security, are no longer test materials and no longer enjoy such protection once they have answers written on them. This same premise apparently applies to test materials that are reproduced by examinees as their responses, such as verbal learning tests and visual reproduction tests.

Despite the efforts of the drafters of the APA Ethics Code to separate test materials and test data, such separation is artificial and impossible for many commonly used tests. For example, with a list learning test, the words that are repeated back by examinees (test data) are exactly the same as the words that were read to them (test materials). The same situation occurs with visual reproduction tests: the examinee's reproduction (if correct) is considered test data and is exactly the same as the stimulus that was shown to the examinee (test materials). Thus, the test data and materials are exactly the same in these instances and cannot be separated as the APA Ethics Code attempts to do. Bush et al. (2010) stated that "test materials and test data deserve equal protection under the general rubric of *test security*" (p. 179).

Regarding release of test data, Standard 9.04(a) states, "Pursuant to a client/patient release, psychologists provide test data to the client/patient or other persons identified in the release." That is, according to the APA Ethics Code, psychologists are to provide test data to anyone that the client/patient specifies. In many forensic contexts, the attorney or court may determine to whom the data are released. Standard 9.04(a) does offer exceptions to the obligatory release at the behest of the client/patient:

> Psychologists may refrain from releasing test data to protect a client/patient or others from substantial harm or misuse or misinterpretation of the data or the test, recognizing that in many instances release of confidential information under these circumstances is regulated by law.

Celia Fisher, PhD, former chair of the APA Ethics Code Task Force, defined *substantial harm* as "reasonably likely to endanger the life or physical safety of the individual or another person or cause equally substantial harm" (Fisher, 2003, p. 12). Fisher cautioned, however, that before refusing to release test data under the "substantial harm" clause in Standard 9.04(a), psychologists should carefully review relevant law.

The misinterpretation or misuse clause may pose greater challenges for psychologists. Psychologists may wonder, "How could data not be misinterpreted or misused in the hands of those not trained to interpret them?" They may further wonder, "How could misinterpretation or misuse not be harmful?" When psychologists have undergone years of education and training to be competent to interpret psychological tests, they may find it unlikely that people who lack such training could interpret those tests appropriately. Bush, Rapp, and Ferber (2010) noted that a client's test answers are meaningless without the psychologist's analysis and, therefore, are likely to be misinterpreted by anyone other than a qualified psychologist.

Psychologists should avail themselves of additional sources of ethical and legal authority that address this issue. The Standards for Educational and Psychological Testing (SEPT; American Educational Research Association, American Psychological Association, & National Council on Measurement in Education, 2014) Cluster 3 (Test Security and Protection of Copyrights) informs test users of their responsibility to protect the security of tests. SEPT Standard 9.21 states, "the rigorous protection of test security is essential, for reasons related to the validity of inferences drawn, protection of intellectual property rights, and the costs associated with developing tests" (p. 147). Additionally, SEPT Standard 9.23 indicates that clinicians should inform patients (i.e., retaining parties in forensic cases) of copyright issues and prohibitions on the disclosure of test items. The SGFP guidelines offer general statements regarding test data. "Forensic practitioners seek to provide information about professional work in a manner consistent with professional and legal standards for the disclosure of test data or results, interpretation of data, and the factual bases for conclusions" (SGFP Guideline 10.05, Provision of Assessment Feedback). The SGFP guidelines do recognize the importance of test security in the context of third party observers (SGFP Guideline 10.06, Documentation and Compilation of Data Considered). When responding to discovery requests and providing sworn testimony, forensic practitioners strive to have readily available for inspection all data which they considered, regardless of whether the data supports their opinion, subject to and consistent with court order, relevant rules of evidence, test security issues, and professional standards (SGFP Guideline 11.01, Accuracy, Fairness, and Avoidance of Deception).

Laws regarding access to medical records must also be considered. Courts are frequently more interested in relevant laws than in psychological ethics. Additionally, laws supersede ethics. Kaufmann (2009) noted,

> Best record release practices recognize the supremacy of the law, and that legal requirements vary with the jurisdiction in which the case is being heard.

Psychologists managing a forensic consulting practice must be aware of jurisdictional law governing their roles, even when the court and the attorneys involved may not. (p. 1140)

There are multiple legal justifications for psychologists to maintain test security. The discovery laws defined by the Federal Rules of Civil Procedure (Fed. R. Civ. P.; House of Representatives, Committee on the Judiciary, 2019) should be considered. According to Fed. R. Civ. P. 26 (House of Representatives, Committee on the Judiciary, 2019), litigants are entitled to have access to "any matter, not privileged, which is relevant to the subject matter involved in the pending action . . ." (Fed. R. Civ. P. 26[b][1]; House of Representatives, Committee on the Judiciary, 2019). However, Fed. R. Civ. P. 26 (c)(7); House of Representatives, Committee on the Judiciary, 2019) allows the court to "make any order which justice requires to protect a party or person." Specifically, this rule empowers the court to "enter an order that a *trade secret or other confidential research, development, or commercial information* **not be disclosed or be disclosed only in a designated way** . . ." [emphasis added]. There is no federal statutory psychologist nondisclosure privilege regarding test data and test materials specifically, although many states recognize the importance of protecting the integrity of psychological tests and appropriate test interpretation.

Psychologists also have contractual obligations regarding intellectual property rights. Federal law grants copyright owners (e.g., test publishers) the exclusive right to copy and distribute copyrighted works (Exclusive Rights in Copyrighted Works, 2017) When psychologists purchase tests and test forms, they agree to comply with federal copyright law.

Statutory laws provide guidelines for psychological practice in general but frequently do not adequately address the activities of psychological specialties such as forensic psychology. In such instances, case law can provide clarification. In *Detroit Edison Co. v. NLRB* (1979), the U.S. Supreme Court determined that psychologists should not release raw data and psychological test materials to nonpsychologists. Additionally, although protective orders may be considered as a means of safeguarding test security in litigation, all of the U.S. Supreme Court justices in this case expressed reservations regarding the effectiveness of protective orders, noting potential problems with both inadvertent and intentional wrongful disclosure by the parties that are allowed access to the records. Courts have held that components of the Minnesota Multiphasic Personality Inventory are protected by copyright law (e.g., *Applied Innovation, Inc. v. Regents of the University of Minnesota*, 1989), and it has been argued that standardized tests, such as those designed to evaluate cognitive and emotional functioning, may be copyrighted as "secure tests" (*Carpenter v. Superior Court*, 2006), similar to the Law School Admission Test (see *Chicago Board of Education v. Substance, Inc.*, 2003 [involving the Chicago Academic Standards Exams]).

In *Ochs v. Ochs* (2002), a New York court determined that the defendant should not have access to the raw psychological test data used by a forensic psychologist in a child custody dispute. Kaufmann (2005) noted that the court emphasized that disclosure of such material leads to a lengthy and expensive critique of the psychologist's methodology rather than the psychologist's conclusions. The court stated that such lengthy examination of neuropsychological evaluation techniques undermines the future effectiveness of the tests, because responses to item by item analysis would read psychometric test items directly into the public record of the court proceeding and that such disclosure should occur only for circumstances such as deficiency, bias, or other error in the report. A U.S. District Court in the District of Columbia ruled in *Chiperas v. Rubin* (1998) that neuropsychological test data should not be disclosed to a psychiatrist who did not have the qualifications and training necessary to understand such data. These cases demonstrate that courts understand the importance of test security.

Finally, the question arises of the obligation to include test data as part of the records that must be released under the Health Insurance Portability and Accountability Act of 1996 (HIPAA). In forensic evaluation contexts, some HIPAA constraints may not be relevant (Connell & Koocher, 2003; Fisher, 2003). HIPAA states that information compiled in anticipation of use in *civil, criminal, and administrative* proceedings is not subject to the same right of review and amendment as is health care information in general. In contrast, Borkosky, Pellett, and Thomas (2014), having considered this issue in detail from multiple perspectives, noted that HIPAA has no exclusion criteria based on type of service, only inclusion criteria for providers, and concluded that "the evidence strongly suggests that, for those forensic mental health practitioners who are *covered entities*, HIPAA does apply to forensic evaluations" (p. 1). Additionally, Fisher (2003) opined that "HIPAA does not recognize the protection of test materials as a legitimate reason to withhold designated record sets appropriately requested by a client/patient" (p. 12). Lamade (2017) advised,

> To understand their HIPAA obligations, forensic practitioners must consider the setting in which they are providing services and determine if they are employed by a HIPAA-covered or exempt entity, as well as clearly define the services they are providing. . . . Applicable rules may be less obvious for practitioners in private practice . . . forensic evaluations are not always subject to HIPAA penumbra . . . forensic therapeutic services, including legally mandated therapy services and treatment provided to those in legal custody, are likely to fall into a gray area. For those who practice in these contexts, consultation with appropriate authorities to address questions and clarify HIPAA requirements can help ensure compliancy. (pp. 84–85)

Scholars continue to describe the application of the HIPAA Privacy Rule as complex, unclear, and difficult to understand, particularly in forensic contexts (e.g., Knapp, VandeCreek, & Fingerhut, 2017). Psychologists whose practices involve hybrid roles consisting of both direct forensic services (e.g., hired by attorneys) and clinical services provided in medicolegal contexts are more likely to be subject to HIPAA requirements. If the HIPAA rule applies for even one patient, then the entire practice is subject to the requirements at that time (Bennett et al., 2006; Knapp et al., 2017).

Fisher (2003) stated, "The extent to which HIPAA, state privacy rules, and Standard 9.04 of the Ethics Code will conflict with test copyright laws will be determined over time" (p. 12). Such clarification was provided by Richard Campanelli, Director of the Office for Civil Rights at the U.S. Department of Health and Human Services, the Office responsible for the administration of HIPAA. Mr. Campanelli stated,

> Any requirement for disclosure of protected health information pursuant to the Privacy Rule is subject to Section 1172(e) of HIPAA, "Protection of Trade Secrets." As such, we confirm that it would not be a violation of the Privacy Rule for a covered entity to refrain from providing access to an individual's protected health information, to the extent that doing so would result in a disclosure of trade secrets. (Pearson Assessments, 2018)

Thus, HIPAA does not prohibit psychologists from withholding test materials and data that incorporates test materials when the disclosure would reveal trade secrets.

The APA Ethics Code (Standard 9.04b, Release of Test Data) permits psychologists to release data, without client/patient consent, in response to a court order or other legal authority. However, psychologists need not automatically release data in such situations without taking steps to safeguard test materials. When conflicts between legal and ethical requirements exist, psychologists should strive to meet the requirements of both demands (Standard 1.02, Conflicts Between Ethics and Law, Regulations, or Other Governing Legal Authority). In cases in which no solution adequately satisfies both demands, psychologists "ultimately must let their own personal conscience guide them" (Iverson & Slick, 2003, p. 2032). They should be cognizant, however, that running afoul of their professional ethics code and/or the law may place them in a difficult situation.

Access to raw test data and materials can be limited to psychologists, or a protective order can be obtained, to maximize test security and minimize the potential for harm, and still conform to discovery rules. In instances in which a psychologist is required by a court to release raw test data or materials to nonpsychologists, the psychologist should make known the relevant concerns, in writing or "on the record," and then follow the directive of the law, which is consistent with the Introduction and Applicability section of the APA Ethics Code. Kois (2017, p. 137) offered specific language that can be used as a warning regarding the appropriate and permissible use of the materials. The warning covers the copyright issues, the importance of not further disseminating the materials, and the need for only appropriately trained professionals to interpret the measures.

Axelrod et al. (2000) and the National Academy of Neuropsychology (2003), emphasizing the importance of maximizing test security in the context of requests for test data or materials, offered specific steps to safeguard test materials. Kaufmann (2009) also provided a stepwise approach to managing the multiple components that comprise this complex issue, and Bush et al. (2010) offered a number of solutions for handling requests for raw test data and emphasized the importance of a proactive approach that involves advance planning and preparation. The steps typically range from providing a narrative report with test scores only; to offering to release the data to a psychologist colleague to a variety of legal options, such as filing a motion to modify or quash the subpoena; to seeking an in camera review (i.e., when the judge reviews evidence outside the presence of others to determine whether it should be provided to other parties) of the data; and to moving for a protective order. The APA Committee on Legal Issues (2006) also provided suggestions for practitioners whose records are subpoenaed. Psychologists releasing raw test data to those not qualified to interpret them, in the absence of a court order, should carefully consider their motivations for departing from the authority of the majority of legal scholars.

CLINICIANS THWARTING DISCLOSURE

In their desire to protect their examinees or clients or to avoid scrutiny of their own work, some practitioners may attempt to prevent disclosure of their records. The following strategies are sometimes used to inappropriately thwart disclosure: keeping minimal records, keeping double sets of records, coding information in their records, doctoring or disposing of records and documents, or outright lying (Barsky, 2012). Each of these actions, regardless of the underlying motivation, represents ethical misconduct, with the exception that psychotherapy notes may indeed be maintained as a separate set of records. Psychotherapy notes, as defined by HIPAA, may be kept separate from other client records, and their disclosure may be withheld except in response to a specific authorization. Maintaining records sufficient to serve the clinical or forensic purposes of the treatment or evaluation is a primary means of avoiding ethical misconduct and of demonstrating a commitment to sound practices. Forensic practitioners in most contexts should anticipate receiving legally valid requests for review or copies of their records with appropriate release authorization, and they should maintain documentation accordingly.

FEEDBACK

Psychologists in clinical settings and in some forensic contexts typically share test results and interpretations with the test taker (Standard 9.10, Explaining Assessment Results; SEPT Standard 9.16). SGFP Guideline 10.05, Provision of Assessment Feedback, states,

> Forensic practitioners take reasonable steps to explain assessment results to the examinee or a designated representative in language they can understand. . . . In those circumstances in which communication about assessment results is precluded, the forensic practitioner explains this to the examinee in advance.

Judicial referrals represent one exception to the ethical and professional requirement to provide feedback. In the context of examinations by psychological experts retained by opposing counsel (e.g., Independent Medical

Examinations), psychologists typically do not provide examinees with feedback regarding results, conclusions, or recommendations. Reports are released to the retaining party and not to examinees or their family members, doctors, lawyers, or other representatives without the permission of the retaining party. Similarly, in court-ordered child custody evaluations, the evaluator may elect to release the report to the court and the attorneys, without giving feedback directly to the parties, and in fact, it is not unusual for the court to direct the manner in which the evaluator's findings will be released. HIPAA does not seem to protect the examinee's right to access and amend psychological records in forensic contexts (Connell & Koocher, 2003; HIPAA, 1996). The examinee should be provided with clear information regarding the extent and nature of the feedback that will be provided, if any, and by whom as well as to whom it will be provided, before the evaluation is begun.

CASE 4: ANTICIPATING INVOLVEMENT IN A PERSONAL INJURY CASE

The following case reveals ethical challenges that can emerge when treatment cases develop a forensic component.

Case Facts

A single 35-year-old accountant sustained a severe brain injury when thrown from his horse while riding on his own property. He recovered fairly well. Although he was able to live independently, persisting cognitive deficits prohibited his return to work. Emotional distress emerged. He began treatment with a psychologist during inpatient rehabilitation and continued psychotherapy on an outpatient basis in her new private practice, paying out of pocket. Treatment covered the patient's accident-related changes as well as longstanding, sensitive family problems. A caring therapeutic relationship developed.

The psychologist kept detailed notes of the therapy as well as test results from early in treatment. A few months into treatment, the patient mentioned that his family was considering a lawsuit against the hospital, although he was unsure of the details. Within a week, the psychologist received a request for her records, accompanied by a signed consent to release, from the attorney representing her patient. She went back through her progress notes and found very sensitive and personal information. She briefly considered what to do.

Case Analysis

Using the mnemonic CORE OPT (Bush, Allen, & Molinari, 2017), the evaluator sought to clarify the ethical issue; consider the obligations owed to stakeholders; utilize ethical and legal resources; examine personal beliefs and values;

consider options, solutions, and consequences; and put a plan into practice. Then, she would take stock, evaluate the outcome, and revise as needed.

Clarify the Ethical Issue

The psychologist did not want to release sensitive patient information. She did not have a strong opinion about releasing raw test data and materials and did not see that as a sensitive issue. She did not want to be called to testify. She was unprepared for a situation that would inevitably arise in a practice in which she evaluated and treated people who were injured in accidents.

Identify Obligations Owed to Stakeholders

The psychologist was treating the patient in her independent practice, with no institutional support and little immediate collegial support. Her primary obligation was to the patient's treatment and his wishes regarding to whom information about him was to be released. She also has an obligation to the legal system, including complying with appropriate requests for records to be used in litigation and otherwise participating in the legal process as required. She had an additional obligation to the profession of psychology to protect tools of the trade (i.e., psychological tests) from widespread dissemination and inappropriate use.

Utilize Ethical and Legal Resources

Multiple ethical, professional, and legal resources were available to the psychologist. A review of these resources, had it occurred, would have revealed the following. Her desire to protect her patient was consistent with the principle of beneficence (General Principle A: Beneficence and Nonmaleficence). Due primarily to a lack of experience in this treatment context, she was unaware of potential courses of action that would best serve her patient, herself, the profession of psychology, and the legal system (Standard 2.01, Boundaries of Competence). Altering and destroying records would violate Standard 6.01, Documentation of Professional and Scientific Work and Maintenance of Records, and producing notes with new and potentially different content would be inconsistent with Standard 5.01, Avoidance of False and Deceptive Statements, and with the law. The psychologist's state laws prohibited destruction of medical records until a specified period after the last service was rendered.

Releasing testing materials and raw test data, when presented with an appropriate signed release, without taking steps to safeguard them, seemed to be inappropriate, according to some sources of ethical authority (Axelrod et al., 2000; National Academy of Neuropsychology Policy and Planning Committee, 2003; see also SEPT Cluster 3, copyright law, and case law). The principle of Justice could be considered applicable to both sides of this issue. Releasing the materials and data would serve the justice system, as well as help her patient's case (Beneficence). However, the potentially adverse consequences of uncontrolled dissemination of test materials and data could include invalidation of the tests, which could potentially deny future examinees their right to access to and benefit from the contributions of psychology, thus potentially harming the public. Further, test developers and publishers who may have spent great effort and cost to bring the tests to market, and who have copyrights, would be damaged by uncontrolled distribution and resultant invalidation of the instruments if she released actual test materials. Such damage to test developers and publishers would have repercussions for psychological practice. When conflicts exist between or within principles, a determination or judgment regarding the potential for the greatest harm and the greatest benefit must be made. The psychologist's state laws were consistent with the release of all records with the patient's consent.

Discussing the potential therapeutic and personal implications of releasing sensitive information with her patient would reflect appreciation of the importance of individual autonomy (APA General Principle E: Respect for People's Rights and Dignity).

Examine Personal Beliefs and Values

The psychologist's primary motivation was the wish to help her patient. She believed that protecting her patient would justify almost any behavior she chose, including the destruction and modification of records. She had never given much thought to the issues surrounding release of data. She was aware that, with signed consent from the patient, the APA Ethics Code not only allowed but essentially required her to release her records, and she gave that issue no further thought.

Consider Options, Solutions, and Consequences

The psychologist briefly considered releasing her current record as it was. She then considered revising her progress notes to eliminate the sensitive personal information that the patient had shared and to focus on accident-related content. She considered making up details to fill in notes in which session content was uncertain or scantily recorded. She briefly considered calling a colleague but could not think of anyone to call. She also considered posting her dilemma on a professional Listserv and asking for advice. She did not consider any of contacting the ethics committee of a professional organization; taking time to weigh the potential advantages and consequences of various courses of action, making notes of the issues being weighed; or discussing the potential ramifications of disclosing sensitive materials and other such issues with her patient.

Put Plan Into Practice

The psychologist rewrote some of her notes, shredding the originals. She then copied and sent to the court the remaining entire record, including the revised notes, test reports, and test data. The psychologist acted without giving much thought, if any, to other possible courses of action. She opted to do what she considered to be in the patient's best interest, without regard for the potential ethical and legal implication.

Take Stock, Evaluate the Outcome, and Revise as Needed

No one ever knew that the psychologist modified and destroyed records. The release of raw test data was supported by her state laws and the APA Ethics Code and, therefore, created no problems. The violation of copyright laws, which would have occurred with the release of test materials, was never alleged. Treatment continued as it had before, although the psychologist anticipated that subsequent notes would be subject to review by others and thus omitted detailed sensitive information. Based on her experience with this patient, she modified her informed consent and note-writing procedures to avoid such problems in the future.

Comment

The psychologist engaged in inappropriate professional behavior by destroying and altering her records, violating ethical and legal requirements in the process. Consultation with a knowledgeable colleague when she found herself in an unfamiliar and uncomfortable situation could have led to an appropriate course of action. For example, an efficient way to have dealt with the issue of sensitive information being in her records was simply to contact the patient, explain to him that she received the request with his consent included, and remind him that there was some sensitive information in her records and clarify whether he really intended for her to share it. Such a discussion would have resolved the issue quickly, if he had confirmed his wish to have the information released. Alternatively, he may have elected to rescind his consent, with the understanding that the possible litigation would be impacted.

In addition to the unethical and illegal altering and destruction of records, releasing testing materials and raw test data to nonpsychologists (e.g., the court) without taking steps to safeguard them or identify an appropriately qualified expert to whom they could be released was a poor choice. Multiple ethical and legal resources address the importance of maintaining test security and the steps that can be taken to do so. Had the psychologist thought through, ideally with an experienced colleague, the potential ethical and legal implications of her options before acting, she would have been in a better position to serve her patient, herself, and the profession of psychology.

This case illustrates that neglecting steps in the decision-making process, such as failing to review relevant resources or consult with colleagues, or a lack of commitment to high standards of ethical practice, can result in inappropriate decisions about ethical (and legal) aspects of practice. Additionally, psychologists can follow the CORE OPT model and still choose to select an inappropriate course of action. Personal integrity and a commitment to high standards of ethical practice are necessary for use of the decision-making model to be effective. Although the psychologist's decision to destroy records went unknown by others in this case, she risked facing severe ethical and legal consequences that could have impacted her ability to continue practicing.

CONCLUSION

Generating and maintaining appropriate documentation is an essential aspect of sound forensic psychology practices. The documentation is the primary method by which practitioners communicate the nature of the services that were provided and the conclusions that were drawn. Appropriately inclusive and accurately detailed documentation serves well examinees, retaining parties, and triers of fact, whereas incomplete, misleading, or illegible documentation is likely to adversely affect the involved parties, including leading to unjust forensic decisions. Forensic practitioners have ethical and legal responsibility to generate and maintain appropriate documentation and to safeguard and release records in manner consistent with psychological ethics, other professional resources, and relevant laws.

6

Testimony and Termination

The psychologist's activities in a forensic matter may change as the status of the case changes, progresses, and nears conclusion. Care must be taken at case transition points to ensure that services already provided do not conflict with or contaminate anticipated activities, and that future activities do not undermine services that were previously provided. Testimony and termination are transition points at which psychologists are well served by clarifying prior understandings with the retaining party, reaffirming a commitment to accuracy, understanding attorney tactics, and anticipating responsibilities associated with the conclusion of the case. This chapter reviews ethical and professional considerations related to roles, accuracy, ultimate legal issues, attorney tactics, and maintenance and disclosure of records in the context of testimony and termination.

ROLE CLARIFICATION

Clarification of the roles that psychologists and clients establish at the outset of professional interactions may be necessary at multiple points during the provision of forensic psychological services. The transition from treatment or evaluation to testimony is one point at which role clarification may be particularly important. Forensic testimony often provides enticement or unintended opportunity for psychologists to engage in two or more roles with a single client or

http://dx.doi.org/10.1037/0000164-007
Ethical Practice in Forensic Psychology, Second Edition: A Guide for Mental Health Professionals,
by S. S. Bush, M. Connell, and R. L. Denney

examinee. Some attorneys and courts have a preference for treating psychologists (versus independent experts) to provide testimony regarding forensic issues and may instruct or entice psychologists to blur role boundaries or to engage in clear dual roles. When asked or required to testify, practitioners should assess the potential for deviation from the role agreed upon at the outset of service provision. When considering adopting dual or multiple roles, psychologists should carefully consider the potential for reduced objectivity and effectiveness and for exploitation or harm to the patient or examinee (S. A. Greenberg & Shuman, 1997, 2007; Heilbrun, 2001; Richards & Wortzel, 2015; Stafford & Sadoff, 2011).

Treating psychologists can be called to testify as either fact witnesses or expert witnesses. Fact witnesses are not paid expert fees; they must limit their testimony to what they know firsthand; and they cannot rely on hearsay information. Fact witnesses also have very little freedom to draw conclusions or provide opinions. Treating psychologists who are called to testify as expert witnesses are also called *percipient experts* (Caudill & Pope, 1995). They are experts because of specialized training and/or experience but were not retained for the purpose of litigation. Treating psychologists do not properly provide ultimate issue opinions, and they must be aware that offering expert testimony about such forensic issues is risky for three primary reasons. First, in treatment contexts, the nature and extent of the background and evaluation data obtained may be insufficient for making forensic determinations, and the manner in which they were obtained may lack the skepticism required for critical review (American Academy of Psychiatry and the Law [AAPL], 2005). Second, the existence of an established treatment relationship reduces the impartiality required for unbiased testimony regarding forensic issues. Treating psychologists tend to be appropriately empathic, wanting the best for their patients; however, this stance is inconsistent with impartiality (S. A. Greenberg & Shuman, 1997, 2007; Richards & Wortzel, 2015). Third, assuming the role of forensic evaluator may interfere with the patient's treatment. For these very types of reasons, the need to generally avoid potentially harmful dual or multiple relationships is an established principle (AAPL, 2005; American Psychological Association [APA], 2013, 2017a; Melton et al., 2018) and should be considered cautiously by treating psychologists when first asked to testify. Knapp, Younggren, VandeCreek, Harris, and Martin (2013), in discussing risk management, went so far as to conclude that treating experts *cannot* provide opinions that go beyond diagnostic and prognostic judgments, even if attorneys attempt to manipulate them into providing such ultimate issue opinions while on the witness stand.

The need to inform the examinee, in a manner that can be understood, of the nature of the psychologist–examinee relationship is fundamental to the informed consent/notification of purpose process. Deviations from the initial mutually agreed upon relationship should generally be avoided. Psychologists are advised to be vigilant to attorneys' efforts, throughout the provision of psychological services, to induce them to take on multiple roles; for example, there may be tendencies for attorneys to ask questions during testimony that would require the psychologist to cross role boundaries.

ACCURACY

Expert testimony is an integral component of forensic psychological services, even though it is required in only a minority of cases. Testimony, as an extension of the written report, should be based upon the integration of relevant research and the information gathered in the conduct of the evaluation. Anchoring conclusions to the data reduces the potential for bias to sway the evaluator when articulating opinions in reports and testimony (Heilbrun, 2001; Otto, DeMier, & Boccaccini, 2014).

Effective expert testimony requires attention to both style and substance of presentation (Heilbrun, 2001; Otto et al., 2014). Effectiveness in style alone, or in substance without style, considerably limits the psychologist's contribution to the court. Although a communication style that resonates with the trier of fact adds considerably to the value of the expert's testimony, psychological ethics traditionally focus solely on the accuracy, rather than style, of communication. *Ethical Principles of Psychologists and Code of Conduct* (APA Ethics Code; 2017a) Standard 5.01, Avoidance of False or Deceptive Statements, states, "Psychologists do not knowingly make public statements that are false, deceptive, or fraudulent." The APA Ethics Code also requires psychologists to base the opinions expressed in their reports and forensic testimony on information and techniques sufficient to substantiate their findings (Standard 2.04, Bases for Scientific and Professional Judgments; Standard 9.01, Bases for Assessments). In addition, the *Specialty Guidelines for Forensic Psychology* (SGFP; APA, 2013) Guideline 11.01, Accuracy, Fairness, and Avoidance of Deception, notes that when testifying, psychologists should not, either actively or passively, engage in partisan distortion or misrepresentation.

THE ULTIMATE LEGAL ISSUE

As was introduced in Chapter 5, controversy exists within forensic psychology about whether experts should offer opinions and testify about the ultimate legal issues before the court (Packer & Grisso, 2011), such as whether (a) a given disorder is causally related to an accident, (b) a criminal defendant had diminished capacity or lacked responsibility at the time an offense was committed, or (c) custody of a child should be awarded to one parent or the other. Those who oppose experts testifying about such issues do so on the grounds that the determination is of a legal or moral nature and, therefore, should be made by the trier of fact. Proponents take the position that the expert simply provides a professional opinion, which the trier of fact can consider or disregard in its decision making.

The Federal Rules of Evidence (FRE) 704 (House of Representatives, Committee on the Judiciary, 2018) permit psychological experts, like other experts, to provide testimony about the ultimate legal issue. Although section (b) was added to FRE 704 in 1984 to prohibit oral opinions about a criminal defendant's mental state at the time of an offense before a jury, many states have not adopted the addition, and some states specifically include language in their statutes that call for experts to provide opinions about this issue (Packer & Grisso, 2011). Although not addressing the question of ultimate issue testimony directly, SGFP Guideline 11.04, Comprehensive and Accurate Presentation of Opinions in Reports and Testimony, states, "The specific substance of forensic reports is determined by the type of psycholegal issue at hand as well as relevant laws or rules in the jurisdiction in which the work is completed." Appropriate testimony requires thoroughness when providing opinions and describing the underlying basis, including data, and reasoning for the opinions. For this reason, it is best practice to clarify this issue with the referral source prior to writing a report, and certainly prior to testimony.

ATTORNEY TACTICS

Retaining attorneys may misrepresent the expert's opinions to the court or may attempt to elicit distorted or inaccurate testimony from the expert on the stand. When this occurs, it may be that the attorney has misunderstood the expert's opinion or it may be a not so subtle attempt to move the opinion closer to what the attorney wishes it to be. This can be avoided in most cases by clear communication with the attorney. When psychologists become aware of such attempts, it is necessary to correct the misinformation. SGFP Guideline 11.01, Accuracy, Fairness, and Avoidance of Deception, and Standard 1.01, Misuse of Psychologists' Work, are relevant in this situation. Standard 1.01 states, "If psychologists learn of misuse or misrepresentation of their work, they take reasonable steps to correct or minimize the misuse or misrepresentation." Similarly, on the stand during direct examination, when the retaining attorney attempts to restate the expert's opinion in some way that reflects a distortion, firmly correcting the misstatement is in order.

Opposing attorneys may inaccurately restate an expert's opinion during cross-examination. In such instances, it may be beneficial to pause before answering, thus allowing the retaining attorney an opportunity to object. If such objection is not forthcoming, the psychologist should restate the correct opinion, as forcefully as is necessary. SGFP Guideline 11.01 provides no restriction to forceful representation of the data and reasoning upon which one's opinion is based as long as the information is presented accurately. During testimony, it is always wise to maintain a professional demeanor and to continue the same demeanor during cross-examination as was on display during direct examination. Forceful presentation of opinion does not require an argumentative or harsh tone.

COMPLETION OF THE CASE

In a specific case, the relationship between the forensic psychologist and the retaining party typically ends when the report has been submitted, testimony has been provided, or payment for services has been received. As part of the contract for services established at the outset of the relationship, the psychologist and the retaining party should agree on the point at which the case will be considered completed; this issue should be revisited when the case appears to be at a close as well. The SGFP Guidelines note that the psychologist has responsibility to complete the agreed upon services, but the forensic psychological services can be terminated prior to completion if the terms of the agreement have been violated by the retaining party (SGFP Guideline 3.04, Termination of Services). Like the initial agreement, premature

> termination of services should be explicit and preferably communicated in writing. Any ambiguity in a practitioner's relationship and responsibility to a client, patient, or examinee can potentially leave unclear the duty of care owed by the practitioner to other parties and give rise to claims of malpractice and abandonment. (Lamade, 2017, p. 80)

In some cases, an examinee may request treatment from the psychologist after the conclusion of the case. S. A. Greenberg and Shuman (1997) noted that ethical concerns exist in "the subsequent provision of therapy by a psychologist or psychiatrist who previously provided a forensic assessment of that litigant" (p. 50). The contrasting position is that if the examination relationship has ended and the forensic action that initiated the examination has been completed, the psychologist may consider providing such treatment. However, the psychologist who, as the former forensic examiner, elects to subsequently provide therapy must be prepared to defend the decision not to refer the examinee to another qualified professional. The primary concern is for the welfare of the potential patient.

There are treatment-related reasons to avoid assuming this secondary role with prior adult forensic examinees, a principle reason being that the more investigative and less empathically resonant posture of the examiner is quite different from that of the treating clinician, and may thus lay a predicate for a nontherapeutic environment (S. A. Greenberg & Shuman, 1997). Additionally, the forensic evaluator who stands to gain financially from recommending ongoing treatment is vulnerable to compromised objectivity when considering such a recommendation. A recommendation that the examinee return to the forensic examiner for therapy would typically represent a conflict of interest.

In child custody cases, the best interests of a child are the priority. The evaluator's role as impartial expert to the court continues, in a sense, until the child reaches the age of majority. For a psychologist to take on a treatment relationship with a party from a prior forensic matter may deprive one of the parties or the court of the advantage to be gained by further access to the impartial and objective opinion of the expert who was originally court-appointed or who did an evaluation by agreement of the parties. The *Guidelines for Child Custody Evaluations in Family Law Proceedings* (Child Custody Evaluation Guidelines; APA, 2010) state that conducting psychotherapy with current or former child custody examinees represents a potentially harmful multiple relationship and that fact is an explainable and understandable reason to avoid providing such treatment (Child Custody Evaluation Guideline 7: Psychologists strive to avoid conflicts of interest and multiple relationships in conducting evaluations). An examination of the forensic evaluator's obligations to the parties and the courts would likely bring into focus the perilous nature of entering into this multiple relationship (Knapp et al., 2013).

In practice, then, it is nearly always ill-advised to accept this second role of psychotherapist following forensic evaluation (Knapp et al., 2013). Nevertheless, in rare situations it may be deemed appropriate for a former forensic examiner to assume a subsequent role as a therapist. For example, a forensic examiner who (a) is found by an adult examinee to possess traits that the examinee considers important for a therapist, and (b) is contacted by the former examinee one or more years following the resolution of the forensic matter (and there is no possibility for appeals or other forensic involvement) may consider assuming a therapist role with the former examinee. However, once that treating relationship has been established, further independent examinations would be prohibited (Bush, Ruff, et al., 2005; Denney, 2005a; Knapp et al., 2013); it would be impossible to assure independence in an examination update or reexamination.

RETENTION OF RECORDS

Psychologists are required to retain records of their professional work, including matters in which reports or testimony have been provided, and to produce that information when appropriate requests are made (APA, 2007; Standard 6.01, Documentation of Professional and Scientific Work and Maintenance of Records; Standard 6.02, Maintenance, Dissemination, and Disposal of Confidential Records of Professional and Scientific Work). In treatment contexts, because patients or their legal representatives have made their psychological status a matter of legal scrutiny, relevant information may no longer have the previous confidentiality protections. Confidentiality requirements should be carefully considered, with requested information provided to authorized parties in a methodical, well-documented fashion.

CASE 5: DISCLOSURE OF TEST RESULTS
USING A CRIMINAL CASE EXAMPLE

The following case involves an evaluation for competency to stand trial.

Case Facts

A forensic psychologist received a referral from a criminal defense attorney to evaluate an individual regarding competency to stand trial. This is his first referral from this attorney. The defense attorney said the defendant received multiple blows to the body and head at the time of his arrest 3 months earlier and now appears to suffer from severe posttraumatic stress; the attorney thinks this currently renders him incompetent to stand trial. The psychologist performed an evaluation that included an interview, record review, personality inventory, and symptom validity assessment. Additionally, the psychologist interviewed the defendant about specific issues and requirements pertaining to his understanding of his legal situation and assessed his ability to assist in his own defense. Evaluation results revealed considerable emotional distress; however, symptom validity was variable. Scores on the validity scales within the personality inventory were within normal limits. In contrast, performance on a free standing symptom validity test (SVT) reflected a tendency to endorse numerous symptoms in an unusual manner, consistent with possible symptom fabrication or exaggeration. The evaluator concluded, however, that the defendant's performance on the SVT was explained by legitimate severe emotional distress. He provided a verbal account of his findings to the defense attorney, reporting that he believed the defendant was not able to assist properly in his defense and, thus, was not competent to stand trial due to severe posttraumatic stress disorder. At the request of defense counsel, he then wrote a preliminary report outlining the evaluation results and opinion. The attorney reviewed the report and noted that it was excellent; however, he recommended that the psychologist streamline the results section slightly to reduce the report length and to better focus the report on the defendant's competence to proceed, which ultimately eliminated the discussion of the stand-alone SVT findings. Although the psychologist noticed this omission, the psychologist viewed it as unimportant because those results were considered reflective of the examinee's severe emotional distress anyway.

During preparation for testimony, the attorney requested the psychologist recount results of the clinical tests, but not "muddy the waters" by discussing the stand-alone SVT results, since the interpretation of the personality inventory results, as reported, reflected emotional distress rather than malingering. The psychologist was concerned about presenting only a portion of the results, but the attorney seemed strongly committed to providing only information that "facilitated the defense strategy." The psychologist wanted to do a good job with this case in order to generate more referrals from this attorney in the future.

Case Analysis

Using the mnemonic CORE OPT (Bush, Allen, & Molinari, 2017), the psychologist sought to clarify the ethical issue; consider the obligations owed to stakeholders; utilize ethical and legal resources; examine personal beliefs and values; consider options, solutions, and consequences; and put a plan into practice. Then, he would take stock, evaluate the outcome, and revise as needed.

Clarify the Ethical Issue

The psychologist was instructed by the attorney not to discuss during testimony the aspects of the test results that might reflect negatively on the criminal defendant because doing so would not "facilitate the defense strategy." The expert agreed with the attorney's representation of the basic thrust of his opinions as they were to be communicated through testimony, but felt uncomfortable not outlining potentially contradictory test results and explaining them. He also realized, in retrospect, that it may have been a mistake to agree to strike that discussion from his report. He was now faced with a dilemma regarding withholding data, on the basis that they were irrelevant and potentially confusing to the trier of fact, when actually such withholding was being requested to advance defense aims. He certainly did not wish to unnecessarily "muddy the water," but he now realized he was concerned about his ethical obligation and may have been unwittingly led down a questionable path by omitting that section in his report.

Identify Obligations Owed to Stakeholders

The legal setting demands that mental health experts answer questions posed by attorneys. Experts do not control the nature of the questions, and there is considerable variability in the amount of "off topic" responding an expert can do. In this instance, the evaluator knew beforehand that the attorney intended to draw forth testimony about the personality inventory, while avoiding testimony about the stand-alone SVT. When prepared regarding the question "Doctor, please tell the court about the manner in which you determined the test results were valid," the expert was asked only to present a portion of the information. Even though testimony is structured by attorney questions, the law requires the witness to tell "the truth, whole truth, and nothing but the truth." Additionally, professional ethics require psychologists to refrain from partisan distortion of their findings. The psychologist was concerned about doing the right thing for the defendant; he did not want to unnecessarily harm the defendant. He was also concerned about his professional relationship with the defense attorney; he was hopeful that he might receive additional cases from this referral source. Thus, the psychologist felt he had obligations to the multiple stakeholders; however, the overarching obligation was to justice, by providing the trier of fact with complete and accurate information about the results of the psychological evaluation.

Utilize Ethical and Legal Resources

The psychologist, in his deliberations about the dilemma, considered biomedical ethical principles and referred to the APA Ethics Code, the SGFP Guidelines, and relevant texts. The psychologist considered the principle of nonmaleficence but had some difficulty discerning which parties would be harmed if he testified either in full or in part. Testifying fully about the invalid SVT results might harm the defendant's case; however, the psychologist considered that his primary obligation was to the truth and justice, not to the defendant or to the defense attorney. The psychologist thought failure to acknowledge the SVT results might be harmful to the justice system and potentially to society, but, most importantly, seemed inconsistent with the principle of Justice. The psychologist found sound guidance within the published sources.

The APA Ethics Code instructs psychologists to avoid false or deceptive statements, including statements in legal proceedings (Standard 5.01, Avoidance of False or Deceptive Statements). Failure to testify about test data that potentially contradict his opinions could be considered deceptive. In addition, psychologists must describe any significant limitations of test data interpretation (Standard 9.06, Interpreting Assessment Results); the examinee's performance on the SVT posed a clear limitation on his interpretation that should have been addressed in reports or testimony.

SGFP Guideline 11.01 reveals that "forensic practitioners make reasonable efforts to ensure that the products of their services, as well as their own public statements and professional reports and testimony, are communicated in ways that promote understanding and avoid deception." Further SGFP Guideline 11.01 points out that

> forensic practitioners do not distort or withhold relevant evidence or opinion in reports or testimony. . . . Forensic psychologists do not, by either commission or omission, participate in a misrepresentation of their evidence, nor do they participate in partisan attempts to avoid, deny or subvert the presentation of evidence contrary to their own position.

In his review of professional literature, the psychologist found a consistent theme reflecting the ethical obligation of psychologists to fully disclose the nature of their findings, not only during testimony but also to include relevant important findings in the report (Grisso, 2003; Heilbrun, 2001; Melton et al., 2018; Otto et al., 2014). He learned it was important to discuss any findings that were contrary to his opinion (e.g., "alternate hypotheses") and provide his explanation for how he weighed that information. That issue certainly included contrary SVT results in a competency to proceed case (Rubenzer, 2018). The psychologist realized the obligation to "fully disclose" would include those evaluation findings that were potentially contradictory to the conclusions reached but were ultimately dismissed or were accounted for in a manner that was consistent with the conclusions reached.

Examine Personal Beliefs and Values

The psychologist takes seriously his legal mandate to "tell the whole truth, and nothing but the truth" during testimony. He believes that just as it is not helpful to leave out important and relevant aspects of the data, it is also not helpful to discuss a laundry list of marginally relevant points. In this instance the psychologist was faced not only with external pressure from the attorney but also internal pressures to serve this referral source well and to appropriately avoid doing something that might *unnecessarily* harm the defendant's case.

Consider Options, Solutions, and Consequences

The psychologist was aware of his unease about limiting his testimony and addressing only the "favorable" symptom validity results. He also realized that he regretted having agreed to excising the information about the SVT results from his report. First, he considered complying with the attorney's request under the reasoning that this was a legal case—the attorney's case at that—so he should just do what she said and not worry about it. To do so, however, he would have to ignore his discomfiture and worry that he was not telling the "whole truth." Second, he considered the option of agreeing to this plan with the attorney but testifying in a forthcoming way when asked about validity issues. He realized this broadsiding of the attorney would be dishonest as well. He wanted to balance doing the right thing with being forthright and reasonable. Third, he considered openly addressing his concerns with the defense attorney prior to testifying. He considered that an honest conversation with the attorney about these issues may reveal that the attorney did not want him to misrepresent his findings or opinion, and that she was probably so focused on defense strategy that she was not thinking through the issues. By following this course of action and standing up for his own principles, he could actually increase the attorney's respect for him. Additionally, the psychologist now believed that a willingness to provide the alternate hypothesis (related to validity issues) and rationale for his conclusions during his testimony would increase his credibility before the judge (Otto et al., 2014); it would also account for and correct the omission in the report.

Put Plan Into Practice

The psychologist determined he simply could not omit the SVT results from his testimony. He also could not mislead the attorney by agreeing to do so and then doing the opposite when testifying. He decided it was more professionally appropriate to demonstrate respect for the attorney and her client by being forthright and direct about the matter. He respected her expertise, but also knew that her professional mandate—*to provide zealous representation*—was not the mandate under which he must practice. He needed to follow his own conscience, the rules of testimony, and his ethical obligations as he now understood them. He told the attorney it was inappropriate for him to omit the SVT results and recommended they take the time during testimony to explain the importance of using multiple measures of symptom validity and integrating the test results and clinical findings in their entirety. He pointed out that including and explaining even potentially negative results would advance his own credibility as a responsible expert. In essence, it also preemptively takes the "wind out of the sails" of an aggressive cross-examination. He also expressed his conviction that he would not be testifying to the "whole" truth if he did not explain these potentially negative test results.

Take Stock, Evaluate the Outcome, and Revise as Needed

After some hesitancy, the defense attorney agreed that full disclosure could potentially increase the psychologist's credibility, and that they could take the time, in testimony, to carefully explain the results. She conceded she did not want him betray his obligation to tell the truth. When he testified and explained the results in their entirety, the testimony went well. After the hearing, the attorney voiced her appreciation for his professionalism and agreed that, by explaining even potentially negative aspects of the results, the principle points of his testimony were made stronger. She said that she hoped to share other cases with him in the future.

CONCLUSION

Testimony offers forensic psychologists opportunities to explain important constructs, methods, and conclusions to forensic decision makers in a manner that is difficult to do solely within a written report. Such testimony commonly represents the culmination and conclusion of the psychologist's involvement in the legal matter. The foundation for successful testimony begins to take shape from the beginning of the interaction with the retaining party, when agreements are established about expectations for the case. Through published and interpersonal resources, psychologists can begin getting a sense of attorney tactics that may pull for professional compromises or the sacrificing of professional ethics and personal values. Advance preparation, including an awareness of relevant ethical guidelines and literature on forensic practice, reduces the likelihood for ethically perilous surprises.

7

Addressing Ethical Misconduct

As the previous chapters illustrate, many factors can contribute to ethically questionable conduct or clear misconduct on the part of psychologists. Some ethical misconduct is intentional and some is unintentional. Forensic practice exposes psychologists' work to greater scrutiny than is typical in other areas of practice. Such critical review by colleagues exposes ethical transgressions, to be certain, but can also unearth genuine disagreements between experts about the appropriateness of a methodology or other action; these disagreements may be reasonably justified or may be petty. This chapter presents ethical and professional issues to be considered when forensic practitioners encounter possible or clearly unethical conduct by colleagues. The chapter includes a systematic framework for addressing perceived ethical misconduct of colleagues, and a family law case is used to illustrate the issues.

Often, psychologists base their conclusions on multiple sources of data, some of which are inconsistent and/or subject to interpretation (Heilbrun, 2001). The inconsistent aspects of the data, if not appropriately addressed by the examiner, can become a source of contention between the examiner and an independent reviewer. Heilbrun (2001) noted that "there are sometimes reasonable alternative explanations or conclusions that would be possible within the context of a single case" (p. 227). Disagreement regarding potential explanations or conclusions can become points of contention, particularly among psychologists who are strongly wedded to a certain perspective regarding the condition being considered. Psychologists are often powerful and persuasive advocates of their positions, and may sometimes stretch the boundaries

http://dx.doi.org/10.1037/0000164-008
Ethical Practice in Forensic Psychology, Second Edition: A Guide for Mental Health Professionals,
by S. S. Bush, M. Connell, and R. L. Denney

of appropriate or justified testimony to make poorly supported partisan statements or may engage in behavior intended to advance their positions.

Financial incentive can also contribute to ethical misconduct. Experts may believe that their livelihood depends upon reaching conclusions harmoniously with the retaining party's wishes. Compared with psychological practice in many health care settings, forensic practice offers the potential for substantially greater income. In clinical settings, income typically is not tied directly or indirectly to the findings of competent examinations. Motivation for increased income may motivate some psychologists practicing in forensic settings to engage in practices that they might not consider in clinical settings. In addition, the adversarial nature of forensic practice may result in strong and, at times, personal feelings toward psychologists retained by the opposing side. Such feelings may bias one's perspective of the work of those colleagues.

FRAMEWORK FOR ADDRESSING PERCEIVED ETHICAL MISCONDUCT

The factors described previously, as well as other aspects of forensic practice, may contribute to psychologists perceiving the work of colleagues to be unethical. Determining an appropriate response to perceived ethical misconduct can be extremely trying for psychologists involved in forensic practice activities. When psychologists perceive the behavior of a colleague to be unethical and consider possible courses of action, there are a variety of issues advisable to consider (see Exhibit 7.1). These sections provide a framework for addressing perceived ethical misconduct of colleagues. This multistep

---

EXHIBIT 7.1

Checklist for Reporting Ethical Violations

- Identify the problem or dilemma.
- Consider the relevant ethical issues.
- Identify and consider applicable laws and regulations.
- Consider the significance of the context and setting.
- Identify the obligations owed to the examinee/patient, referral source, and others.
- Consider the significance of the violation.
- Consider the reliability and persuasiveness of the evidence.
- Consult colleagues or ethics committees.
- Consider the possible courses of action.
- Consider the timing of any action.
- Consider the possible effects of any action or of inaction.
- Consider personal beliefs and values.
- Choose and implement a course of action, if needed.
- Assess the outcome of action or inaction and follow up as needed.
- Document the process.

Note. From *Ethical Issues in Clinical Neuropsychology* (pp. 304–305), by S. S. Bush and M. L. Drexler (Eds.), 2002, Lisse, The Netherlands: Swets & Zeitlinger Publishers. Copyright 2002 by Swets & Zeitlinger B. V. Adapted with permission.

framework is similar to the CORE OPT ethical decision-making model, but there are three primary differences. This framework, although also a structured, systematic approach for addressing a complex problem, focuses on whether, how, and when to address the perceived ethical misconduct of a colleague, rather than guiding one's own practices. Compared with the CORE OPT model, in the present framework, forensic practitioners place more emphasis on (a) consideration of the significance of the perceived ethical violation, (b) the reliability and persuasiveness of the evidence, (c) the timing of any action, and (d) the possible effects of any action or inaction.

Identify the Problem or Dilemma

Psychologists may at times have a sense that something is "wrong" with the professional behavior of a colleague. Clearly identifying the problem or dilemma is the necessary first step in addressing it.

Consider the Relevant Ethical Issues

Psychological practices that may initially appear to be ethically questionable may instead reflect acceptable variations in practice or in the understanding of a psychological issue or condition. Before alleging unethical practice, psychologists should attempt to identify the relevant ethical issues and their specific representation in the *Ethical Principles of Psychologists and Code of Conduct* (American Psychological Association [APA] Ethics Code; APA, 2017a) or other professional guidelines. A lack of mention in the APA Ethics Code of a suspect practice does not necessarily mean that no ethical concern exists. The practice may be questionable when understood in terms of aspirational ethical principles or the guidelines of a particular psychological specialty. In such instances, open and constructive dialogue with the colleague may serve to educate one or both parties regarding a preferred manner of practice. As has been emphasized throughout this book, there are many relevant sources of authority that may guide forensic psychologists in their ethical, professional, legal, and moral decision making. Psychologists who avail themselves of all of these resources tend to be well prepared when attempting to clarify the ethical issues relevant to a colleague's behavior in a specific situation.

Identify and Consider Applicable Laws and Regulations

State licensing laws establish regulations for the practice of psychology. State laws also mandate that particular practices be followed, such as reporting child abuse. Other state and federal laws, legal decisions, and regulations may provide further guidance regarding acceptable practice parameters.

Consider the Significance of the Context and Setting

The importance of considering context and setting when addressing perceived ethical misconduct in forensic psychology cannot be overstated. Relevant factors differ both across and within the primary practice activities and populations served. As a result, there are many parameters for ethical practice. Psychologists judging the appropriateness of colleagues' work must consider that differences in practices may reflect the different demands or allowances of the specific context. At the same time, some ethical issues transcend context and setting and are universally relevant. Practitioners who are unsure of the requirements of a specific setting benefit from consulting with appropriate colleagues.

Consider Obligations Owed to the Examinee, Referral Source, and Others

Early in the process of addressing ethical misconduct, it is necessary to consider the parties to whom obligations are owed. For example, determination of who holds the privilege or owes confidentiality regarding communications may dictate the manner in which the concern is addressed. The purpose and nature of the service provided, the retaining party or referral source, and the context in which the service was provided also have implications for how ethical misconduct is addressed. Understanding the obligations that are owed to various parties helps guide the decision-making process.

Consider the Significance of the Violation

Forensic practitioners employ differing practices in establishing and maintaining professional relationships, obtaining examinee data, interpreting data, managing records, and performing other professional activities. Such differences are not necessarily ethically problematic or indicative of failure to perform forensic psychological services at an acceptable level. Blau (1998) stated, "Variations will undoubtedly occur, but they should stand the tests of being in the client's best interests and falling well within the expectancies and constraints of professional ethics, the law, and standards for the delivery of professional services" (p. 29). In addition, differences in professional practices can serve the constructive function of contributing to the advancement of the field. In contrast, behaviors that fall well beyond the usual and customary standards of practice likely justify further examination and concern. A primary consideration is the severity of the potential misconduct.

Shuman and Greenberg (1998) examined distinctions between the applicability or relevance of ethical rules in the context of admissibility decisions for expert testimony compared to their applicability more broadly. Their observation that ethical rules vary in their significance according to context pertains to the broad topic of addressing perceived ethical misconduct of colleagues. The following distinctions were offered:

> Ethical rules addressing advertising or form of practice, for example, have little bearing on the reliability of the resulting professional's information and therefore, violations of these rules should have little bearing, if any, on admissibility decisions. Ethical rules addressing integrity, objectivity/independence, or

diligence/due care, for example, have a significant impact on the reliability of the resulting professional information and therefore, violations of these rules should have a significant bearing on admissibility decisions. The ethical rules that require psychiatrists and psychologists to avoid conflicting roles . . . are examples of rules that have a significant effect on the reliability of the resulting professional information, and for which unexcused violations should have a significant impact on admissibility decisions. (Shuman & Greenberg, 1998, p. 9)

The degree of potential harmfulness of ethical misconduct determines whether formal or informal resolution is preferred and whether the misconduct is addressed prior to the completion of a legal case or following case resolution.

Consider the Reliability and Persuasiveness of the Evidence

Information and documentation obtained directly by the psychologist are more reliable and persuasive than is information obtained second hand. During adversarial proceedings, information obtained second hand may be intentionally or unintentionally misrepresented due to self-serving motivations of the person providing the information. Forensic practitioners tend to be well served by being critical of information provided by examinees, attorneys, and opposing experts. A reasonable degree of skepticism about the accuracy of such information can lead to a more factual accounting of events. To increase the reliability and persuasiveness of the information, forensic practitioners should attempt to independently establish its accuracy (Heilbrun, Warren, & Picarello, 2003).

Consult Colleagues or Ethics Committees

Consultation with experienced forensic psychology colleagues or ethics committees is fundamental to addressing ethical misconduct. Both local colleagues and those practicing outside of the local area can offer valuable insights and information about an apparently ethically troubling practice of a colleague. They can help to reinforce or dispel initial concerns by facilitating increased understanding of issues at hand. Such consultation may be of value at each step in the decision-making process. It is advisable to request permission from the colleagues or committee representatives to document and cite by source their consultation (Martindale & Gould, 2004), and to ask them to maintain a record of the consultation as well.

Consider Possible Courses of Action

When the behavior of a colleague appears to reflect ethical misconduct, the action to be taken must be carefully considered (Deidan & Bush, 2002; Grote, Lewin, Sweet, & van Gorp, 2000; Martelli, Bush, & Zasler, 2003). As the Introduction and Applicability section of the APA Ethics Code indicates, psychologists in the process of making decisions regarding professional behavior must consider the APA Ethics Code, applicable laws, and psychology board regulations. They may also consider other guidelines that have been endorsed by psychological organizations, the dictates of their own conscience, and advice from colleagues.

Potential actions that psychologists may take to address perceived ethical misconduct include informal resolution which, depending on the nature of the apparent violation and any confidentiality restrictions, is generally the preferred first step in clinical situations (Standard 1.04, Informal Resolution of Ethical Violations). In contrast, in litigation contexts, it is typically inappropriate to contact directly a witness for the opposing side. In cases involving substantial harm or when informal resolution has been ineffective or would be otherwise inappropriate, such as forensic cases, additional or alternative action is required (Standard 1.05, Reporting Ethical Violations). Such action includes filing reports with institutional authorities, ethics committees that have adjudicative authority, or state licensing boards. In all cases, confidentiality restrictions should be considered. The psychologist may benefit from discussing the matter and possible appropriate actions with the retaining party.

Consider the Timing of Any Action

When considering raising an ethical challenge during the course of proceedings, forensic practitioners need to consider the distinction between an aggressive challenge of the expert's opinions and an implication of ethical misconduct. The adversarial process calls for challenging the underlying basis of an expert's opinions, including both the qualifications of the expert to offer the opinion and the methodology used to formulate the opinion. An expert's opinion can be challenged aggressively with no implication that the expert behaved unethically in formulating or offering that opinion. However, the attorney conducting the cross-examination may find it useful to query whether (a) the expert's methodology meets threshold criteria established by psychological ethical standards, and (b) the methodology and opinions offered are in keeping with aspirational principles of the profession and with professional guidelines that inform sound and ethical practice. Having one's professional opinions aggressively challenged during adversarial proceedings may understandably result in strong emotional reactions, prompting one to interpret such challenges as challenges to one's ethics and as potentially unethical personal attacks.

It may be natural to want to sort out and address questions of ethical misconduct immediately. However, the risk of addressing perceived ethical misconduct before the conclusion of a case lies in the possibility of real or perceived specious reporting designed to tarnish the credibility of the other expert (American Academy of Clinical Neuropsychology [AACN], 2003). In addition, the intensity of negative personal feelings toward a colleague and the perceived importance of the ethical issues may dissipate following conclusion of the proceedings. Thus, except for egregious ethical violations, it is often preferable to postpone ethics complaints until the conclusion of any adversarial proceedings that could benefit the complainant (AACN, 2003). Filing ethics complaints as a litigation strategy to remove an opposing expert from a case is clearly unethical (Standard 1.07, Improper Complaints). Nagy (2000) stated, "the ultimate purpose of filing a complaint is to protect some-one from harm, not to 'get even' with another psychologist" (p. 206) or to manipulate the other psychologist in some fashion.

Consider the Possible Effects of any Action or of Inaction

The goal of addressing apparent ethical misconduct is to end or correct the misconduct. Failure to address ethical misconduct, when appropriate client authorization has been given or is not required, may result in continued harm to the recipients of psychological services, to the public, and to the profession of psychology. However, taking such action may have undesirable conse-quences as well. Filing a complaint with an ethics committee or a state psy-chology board may result in a counterfiling, a complaint against the psychologist who made the initial complaint. Filing a complaint may also result in litigation against the complainant for slander or defamation of character. Complaints filed during the case in which the inappropriate behavior occurred may be perceived as an attempt to discredit the opposing expert, thus having the effect of discrediting the complainant and weakening the case of the party that retained the complainant. Although psychologists may have an obligation to report apparent ethical misconduct (Association of State and Provincial Psychology Boards, 2018, section L., subsection 1), consideration of the poten-tial seriousness of the matter, the consequences of such action, and the appro-priate timing is prudent.

Consider Personal Beliefs and Values

Psychologists may have strong feelings about various sections of the APA Ethics Code and about practices that are not specifically addressed by that Code. When such practices are performed in a manner that seems to be inap-propriate, it may be natural to want to react forcefully. Such feelings can serve an important mobilizing function, but they can also skew one's perspec-tive. Situations in which strong personal feelings are experienced may be those in which consultation with colleagues can be particularly beneficial.

In addition to examining personal feelings toward the ethical issues, foren-sic practitioners have an obligation to examine their feelings toward the spe-cific colleague whose work they are reviewing or toward whom allegations of ethical misconduct may be made. The adversarial nature of forensic work can result in contentious relationships with colleagues. Reviews of one's work may be perceived as being, or may actually become, personal attacks. It may be natural for psychologists to want to respond in kind. However, forensic practi-tioners must strive to maintain a distinction between their feelings toward the work of colleagues and the colleagues themselves.

Choose and Implement a Course of Action, if Needed

Determine whether action is necessary; if so, determine the appropriate time to take the action. Then, when the timing is appropriate, implement the course of action.

Assess the Outcome and Follow Up as Needed

Assess the effects of any action or inaction. If the issue was addressed, evaluate the manner in which the colleague or the relevant organization responded. Consider and implement additional or alternative courses of action as needed to bring a satisfactory resolution to the issue.

Document the Process

Detailed documentation of each step in the process is essential to (a) explicate the rationale and procedures underlying decisions to report, or not report, perceived ethical misconduct of colleagues, and (b) help clarify the psychologist's internal process so that the psychologist can use the experience to address future questions of ethical misconduct by colleagues.

CASE 6: REPORTING ETHICAL VIOLATIONS: A FAMILY LAW EXAMPLE

The following case illustrates ethical and professional challenges that can emerge when a colleague's professional behavior is believed to be inappropriate.

Case Facts

A psychologist accepted court appointment to evaluate the mother, father, and 4-year-old daughter in a disputed custody matter following marital dissolution. The psychologist learned that the mother had been taking the child to a privately retained psychologist for "play therapy, to see if something may have happened to her," because she was exhibiting signs of distress following visits with the father. She was reportedly fussy, clingy, and demanding, was having nightmares, and was exhibiting odd behavior toward the mother and her mother's boyfriend. Specifically, she was trying to catch glimpses of her mother's boyfriend's "privates" as he came out of the shower following afternoon swimming at their home, and she was trying to pull her mother's blouse down to expose her breast. Finally, her mother had observed her playing with her "privates" at bath time, and even saw her trying to insert a toy boat in her vagina.

The psychologist who was treating the child in play therapy offered testimony that sexual abuse had occurred to this child, as evidenced by these signs and by her drawings, in play therapy, of her family in which her father was drawn with heavy, shaded lines, and her mother and she were drawn more normally. She also played roughly with the anatomically detailed dolls the therapist had introduced into the play therapy to facilitate discussions with the child of what might have happened to her. In the first six play therapy sessions, the child had insisted nothing had happened to hurt her during visitation with her father, but over time with the therapist, she "opened up, and finally revealed the abuse." She said her dad had touched her "private," when drying her after her bath, when her parents first separated, which was shortly after she had turned 2 years of age. She reported he had not done that since she turned 3 years old.

Based on these findings, the play therapist testified that the child should not visit the father without supervision. She had not evaluated the father or the mother, and her treatment of the child consisted of 13 play therapy sessions. She had met with the mother first individually, for an intake session, and then before and after each session, briefly in the waiting room to hear reports of the child's behavior or to report to the mother what had transpired in therapy. The father's effort to meet with her, when he learned she was treating his child, had been rebuffed; she indicated she did not believe it would be appropriate, as her office was the child's "safe place," and she preferred to protect the boundaries.

The court-appointed psychologist evaluator became aware of this testimony after the judge made a preliminary ruling regarding continued play therapy treatment and supervision of the father's time with the child. In this ruling, the judge, without giving a reason but perhaps because the play therapist's evaluation was insufficient for forensic purposes, rejected the recommendations of the play therapist and ordered continuation of the parents' shared responsibility for, and time with, the child, without supervision. She further ordered that the child not be taken to the play therapist for further sessions. The mother was to undergo some classes and individual didactic sessions to address her growing hostility toward the father, which was exhibited in ways evidenced by other testimony. The court essentially made a finding that the child's best interest would be served by no further exploration of the allegation of sexual abuse, but she deferred disposition of the final parenting plan pending the forensic evaluator's findings.

Case Analysis

This case is considered according to the framework for addressing perceived ethical misconduct of colleagues.

Identify the Problem or Dilemma
The court-appointed psychologist believed that the treating therapist's professional conduct was inappropriate. The primary problem was that the therapist overstepped the bounds of her treating relationship to offer testimony regarding the specific legal question. In doing so, she offered opinions and recommendations that far exceeded the information and data upon which they

were reportedly based. The therapist's training and experience in child therapy, particularly in the context of litigation, also came into question. Faced with unacceptable professional conduct on the part of another psychologist, the court-appointed psychologist considered how best to address the issue, if at all.

Consider the Relevant Ethical Issues

The play therapist's work in the legal arena was not based upon established scientific and professional knowledge of child custody practice (Standard 2.04, Bases for Scientific and Professional Judgments). Guideline 12 of the *Guidelines for Child Custody Evaluations in Family Law Proceedings* (APA, 2010), Section II (Procedural Guidelines: Conducting the Child Custody Evaluation) states,

> When psychologists are not conducting child custody evaluations per se, it may be acceptable to evaluate only one parent, or only the child, or only another professional's assessment methodology, as long as psychologists refrain from comparing the parents or offering opinions or recommendations about the apportionment or decision making, care-taking, or access. (p. 866)

The play therapist, who may well have been a competent practitioner of play therapy in clinical contexts, clearly failed to perform the necessary evaluations or to appropriately limit her testimony in the forensic arena (Standard 2.01, Boundaries of Competence).

Identify and Consider Applicable Laws and Regulations

The ethical and legal resources to be considered included not only the APA Ethics Code but also state board rules of conduct for psychological practice. The administrative rules of practice for psychologists in the state essentially echoed the APA Ethics Code, identifying as substandard practice the offering of a professional opinion without benefit of adequate data.

Consider the Significance of the Context and Setting

The play therapist, working in an agency setting in which the mission of the agency was to provide assessment and treatment of abused children, was clear in testifying that her agency policy was to accept what children alleged at face value, without questioning alternative hypotheses, and then work to ensure the safety of and provide treatment for the child alleging abuse. Within that context and setting, there may have been general support for the care she provided. Within the context of the courtroom, however, in which a higher degree of objectivity, suspended judgment, and convergence of data are sought, the evaluation of the child by the play therapist fell far below the acceptable standard within the forensic context. Questionable treatment competence, however, was not the court-appointed psychologist's primary concern. Although the court-appointed psychologist believed that the "context" of the agency treatment setting might justify the play therapist's advocacy stance in the therapy room, it did not mitigate the egregiousness of the apparent violation regarding making recommendations to the court without adequate data.

Consider Obligations Owed to the Examinee, Referral Source, and Others

The court had already essentially dismissed the testimony and recommendations of the treating therapist. As a result, the child and the family were no longer at risk of ongoing damage from the play therapist and presumably were not permanently harmed by the actions of the therapist in offering unsubstantiated opinion in court. Nonetheless, it could be argued that she harmed the father's reputation and certainly the relationship between the parents, which likely affected the child's future in unforeseen ways. Additionally, the potential for the therapist to perform similarly inappropriate behavior in another case remained. Therefore, the court-appointed psychologist considered her obligations to the legal system and the public. She had an obligation to protect the legal system and society from the potential harm that could be caused by a psychologist practicing beyond her area of expertise and competence. The court-appointed psychologist also had an obligation to the profession of psychology to take action when one of its members tarnished the credibility of the profession in the courtroom, with the family, and beyond.

Consider the Significance of the Violation

The play therapist's behavior had the potential to significantly harm members of the family and their relationships (APA General Principle A: Beneficence and Nonmaleficence; Standard 3.04, Avoiding Harm). Offering misleading information, however unintentional, to the court had the potential to result in an inappropriate custody determination (APA General Principle D: Justice).

Consider the Reliability and Persuasiveness of the Evidence

The court-appointed psychologist believed that she had strong evidence of the professional misconduct. In addition to the potentially less reliable verbal reports of those involved in the case, she received a copy of, and carefully reviewed, the court transcript of the play therapist's testimony.

Consult Colleagues or Ethics Committees

Before consulting with colleagues or filing a report with any authority, the psychologist first addressed the issue of confidentiality. To protect confidentiality of the play therapist's testimony dealing with sensitive material, all communications regarding it were accomplished with sufficient redaction of names and other identifiers to protect the child's privacy. Instead of relying only on the child's initials, for example, Jane Doe initials were used and references to the parents and their workplaces were also redacted.

Upon consultation with colleagues, the psychologist learned that (a) the play therapist had previously been sanctioned by the state board for offering an opinion about the diagnosis of a party without benefit of evaluation or review of prior treatment records, and (b) the play therapist had attended a continuing education workshop conducted by one of the colleagues consulted in this matter within the past year and had received clear instruction about the inappropriateness of making custody or access recommendations without examining one of the parties (handouts for the workshop included Otto, Buffington-Vollum, & Edens, 2003; APA Ethics Code; *Guidelines for Child Custody Evaluations in Family Law Proceedings*; and *Specialty Guidelines for Forensic Psychology*). Colleagues opined that it was the duty of the court-appointed psychologist to report the play therapist's actions to the board and to the APA Ethics Committee.

Consider Possible Courses of Action

Having consulted appropriate authoritative sources, the forensic psychologist was convinced of the following: It was necessary to take some action, whether that be an attempt at an informal resolution or reporting the matter to the state licensing board or the APA Ethics Committee. The state licensing board rules did not require that a complaint be filed. Consultation with the forensic psychologist's own counsel revealed that, without the injured party filing a complaint, it was likely that the matter would not be investigated by the state licensing board. The APA Ethics Code, on the other hand, did support the importance of taking action. Owing to the somewhat less than extreme nature of the apparent wrongdoing, it might be preferable to approach the play therapist directly with the concern before taking the matter further (Standard 1.04, Informal Resolution of Ethical Violations). (Examples of more outrageous professional behavior that would require immediate action might include engaging in a felonious criminal action, such as sexual exploitation of a patient, sexual abuse of a child, extorting money from a patient, filing insurance claims for parties never seen.) The timing, following the culmination of the hearing, was appropriate in that the consultation with the alleged offender would likely not be construed as witness tampering or other attempted manipulation of the case outcome.

Consider the Possible Effects of any Action or of Inaction

The option of speaking with the play therapist directly could have an educational effect. However, because the play therapist had been formally sanctioned in a similar circumstance earlier, the court-appointed psychologist was concerned that an attempt at an informal resolution would not have the intended effect of protecting those who could be harmed from future misconduct. The court-appointed evaluator was confident that failure to act more incisively could only result in further misconduct.

The next option, then, was to file a formal complaint. Although this action could have greater potential to achieve the desire goal of protecting the public, it could also interfere with clients of the agency receiving much-needed clinical services. To make this important decision, the court-appointed evaluator considered a number of factors. In the transparent setting of the courtroom, and in an adversarial proceeding, there was a good opportunity for the allegedly unethical behavior to yield its just due—lessening the credibility of the wrongdoer and invoking, in the end, an outcome unfavorable to the play therapist psychologist's apparent intention. However, that the litigants may have suffered considerably in the process, and the profession of psychology was harmed by the egregious behavior of the play therapist, was almost certain.

The case did not, at this point, involve a civil action against the alleged offender for failure to meet the standard of care. If it had, then the court-appointed psychologist would have had no responsibility to report, in that the standard of practice issue would be decided by the court, and the alleged victim could enjoy some redress. Further, if the play therapist was sued for practicing below the standard of care, the therapist would then have been obligated to report the court action to the state board.

Consider Personal Beliefs and Values

The court-appointed psychologist had strong personal convictions that zealous advocacy of a stance in a forensic arena could interfere with professional objectivity. Perceiving the play therapist to potentially suffer from clouded judgment in the matter at hand, the court-appointed psychologist had to weigh whether impatience with that posture was motivating a state board or ethics complaint. Holding a personal belief that children are often harmed by such intervention, there was a tendency toward outrage that a terrible wrong may have been perpetrated onto the child and the parent if the accusation of sexual abuse was unfounded. It would have been easy to displace some aggressive energy to the process of filing a complaint, and the psychologist gave consideration to this issue.

Choose and Implement a Course of Action, if Needed

The psychologist determined that she had an obligation to report the offense to the state licensing board. There was no reason for the psychologist to attempt to invoke a companion complaint from the allegedly injured party (the father, who was the object of the play therapist's recommendation for supervised visitation), although the state board staff counsel indicated, when the psychologist called to inquire about making a report, that it would be easier to investigate if the report were made directly by an injured party. The court transcript was available to assist the state board in investigating the matter, and the psychologist was able to obtain the transcript and provide a redacted or blinded version of it to the state board to supplement the complaint. A complaint to the APA Ethics Committee was also warranted. The APA Ethics Code (Standard 1.05, Reporting Ethical Violations) states that

> If an apparent ethical violation has substantially harmed or is likely to substantially harm a person or organization and is not appropriate for informal resolution under Standard 1.04, Informal Resolution of Ethical Violations, or is not resolved properly in that fashion, psychologists take further action appropriate to the situation. Such action might include referral to state or national committees on professional ethics, to state licensing boards, or to the appropriate institutional authorities. This standard does not apply when an intervention would violate confidentiality rights or when psychologists have been retained to review the work of another psychologist whose professional conduct is in question.

However, a review of the APA membership directory revealed that the play therapist was not an APA member. Therefore, APA could not impose sanctions, if indicated, on the alleged offender. Thus, the psychologist was left with the best option to be reporting to the state licensing board.

Assess the Outcome and Follow Up as Needed

Having filed a complaint with the state licensing board, the court-appointed psychologist found that there was little else that could be done to ensure that the alleged offender would adhere to the ethical standards and guidelines that require the withholding of an unsubstantiated opinion. The outcome of the complaint process was that the play therapist was again sanctioned by the state board, but shortly moved out of the area, so the court-appointed psychologist did not have further interaction with her. The process of researching options, especially the collegial consultations, proved time consuming but educative, and the forensic psychologist recognized that further action toward the play therapist might generate liability without an increasing probability of successful resolution. There was the further possibility that through the adversarial process of the family courts, the alleged offender's actions would continue to elicit the natural consequence of reduced credibility, and although vulnerable individuals might nevertheless be deprived of just services, the overarching value of justice would likely prevail.

Document the Process

It is wise to document the process of analyzing any ethical issue, and the matter of reporting a colleague for a possible ethics violation is no exception. The court-appointed psychologist maintained detailed documentation of all consultation-related matters involving this case, including the steps taken once the potential professional and ethical misconduct was detected. The thorough documentation served her particularly well when she filed the complaints.

GETTING IT RIGHT AFTER GETTING IT WRONG

Even competent, well-intentioned practitioners who strive to achieve and maintain high ethical standards make clerical mistakes and diagnostic errors. Despite appropriate training and best efforts, it is unrealistic to believe that a forensic practitioner can practice error-free over the course of their career. Such errors can range from minor mistakes involving test scoring to incorrect diagnoses, which can have considerable legal implications. Although many errors likely go undetected and, therefore, remain unknown by the practitioner, forensic contexts often allow for one's methods and conclusions to be carefully and critically reviewed by colleagues.

Differences of opinion frequently exist among qualified practitioners, with no ethical implications. However, forensic practitioners who are confronted with persuasive evidence that mistakes were made or their original conclusions were incorrect, either via reports from opposing colleagues or during testimony, have the opportunity and ethical responsibility to acknowledge and correct the mistakes and revise their original conclusions. Although no responsible professional likes to learn that they made a mistake, it is how the mistake is handled after being made aware of it that has more direct ethical implications than whether the mistake was made. The APA Ethics Code (APA General Principle C: Integrity) advises psychologists to "seek to promote accuracy, honesty, and truthfulness in the science, teaching, and practice of psychology." Acknowledging and correcting errors when they are brought to one's attention reflects professional integrity. In contrast, taking a more defensive stance may reflect failure to consider whether the available evidence supports the original conclusions or partisan bias. Striving to balance confidence and humility helps position forensic practitioners to acknowledge and correct mistakes that are brought to their attention.

CONCLUSION

Forensic practice provides a context for colleagues, who often hold differing perspectives on both practice issues and the evidence base that underlies professional options, to review each others' work. Whether retained specifically to perform a peer review or simply observing the practices of colleagues involved in a case, such exposure to other psychological work products affords psychologists the opportunity and responsibility to critically examine their own practices as well as those of colleagues. When substandard and potentially harmful practices are evident in one's own work or the work of a colleague, steps should be taken to address and improve the practices. A structured process for approaching the apparent ethical misconduct of colleagues can facilitate the process. All practitioners are vulnerable to making mistakes and diagnostic errors over the course of a career; it is how one handles the situation when made aware of the mistakes that reflects one's professional integrity and commitment to ethical practice.

Afterword

Psychologists who are ethically competent and committed to high standards of ethical practice provide a valuable service to the justice system. However, the practice of forensic psychology is susceptible to ethical misconduct on many fronts, from unintentional missteps to strong enticements to sacrifice moral principles. Maintaining professional competence and ethical behavior requires a lifelong commitment to high moral standards and continuing education. We believe that, in the abstract, nearly all psychologists would embrace a commitment to the highest standards of ethical practice. However, embracing a commitment to ethical practice in the abstract, such as while one is discussing cases with colleagues at a conference, is quite different from embracing it when faced with a sympathetic examinee, persuasive attorney, or considerable financial incentive.

Forensic psychologists must reaffirm their commitment to the highest standards of ethical practice not just when practice is going smoothly but particularly when faced with enticement to ethical misconduct. Such enticements may take many forms, such as receiving a referral for which professional competence may be lacking or the promise of remuneration for offering opinions that lack proper support. For example, forensic psychologists may, at some point, experience something similar to the following:

> An attorney calls and says, "I received your report. It was great. Thanks very much. I'm putting your check in the mail right now, and I want to talk to you about a couple of new cases, but first, I have a question about that last sentence

http://dx.doi.org/10.1037/0000164-009
Ethical Practice in Forensic Psychology, Second Edition: A Guide for Mental Health Professionals, by S. S. Bush, M. Connell, and R. L. Denney

of your report. Would you mind changing the statement ". . . and seems to be disabled due to the emotional distress that emerged or worsened following the accident" to ". . . is permanently disabled as a result of the accident"?

It is precisely when we consider engaging in professional conduct that we suspect or know to be ethically inappropriate, or our colleagues may consider ethically questionable, that we must reaffirm our commitment to high ethical standards of practice.

Although the financial temptations associated with forensic practice may at times represent the most obvious and most emphasized threats to ethical practice, psychologists in forensic practice confront wide-ranging ethical challenges. The challenges associated with becoming and remaining knowledgeable about ethical standards and guidelines, overcoming personal biases, and recognizing the potential for harm, are equally important.

A proactive approach to ethical practice may help to reduce the occurrence of, or problems that arise from, ethical dilemmas. That is, anticipating ethical issues and challenges can help to avoid dilemmas or to address dilemmas when they occur. In addition to continuing education, forensic psychologists are advised to pursue informal peer consultation that focuses specifically on professional ethics. For example, psychologists may find it beneficial to periodically send a copy of a report to a respected colleague, asking that the report be reviewed for the existence of ethically questionable statements or practices. Honest, objective feedback about one's practices can help to refine behaviors so that high ethical standards of practice are maintained. Although agreement among forensic psychologists, including those who present and write about ethics, regarding what constitutes ethical practice in all situations is not unanimous, differences of opinion can further an understanding of the complexity of an issue and heighten awareness of potential ethical pitfalls. Obtaining the perspectives of colleagues, whose opinions may differ from one another or from one's own, can be of considerable value in improving ethical compliance and avoiding ethical misconduct.

Forensic psychologists bear a considerable responsibility to individuals, institutions, and society when providing services. Once a commitment to maintaining the highest ethical standards has been affirmed, published and interpersonal resources can help psychologists negotiate the unique details of a given ethical challenge. The American Psychological Association's (APA's; 2017a) *Ethical Principles of Psychologists and Code of Conduct* and the APA's (2013) *Specialty Guidelines for Forensic Psychology* are among the many published resources of value to forensic practitioners. The practice of forensic psychology can be both challenging and rewarding; perhaps the greatest challenge is in keeping one's values in perspective. As forensic psychologists, we must remember that we are scientists and scholars as well as practitioners, and it is the understanding of science and ability to apply the science within the justice system that makes our services valuable.

REFERENCES

American Academy of Clinical Neuropsychology. (2001). Policy statement on the presence of third party observers in neuropsychological assessments. *The Clinical Neuropsychologist, 15,* 433–439. http://dx.doi.org/10.1076/clin.15.4.433.1888

American Academy of Clinical Neuropsychology. (2003). Official position of the American Academy of Clinical Neuropsychology on ethical complaints made against clinical neuropsychologists during adversarial proceedings. *The Clinical Neuropsychologist, 17,* 443–445. http://dx.doi.org/10.1076/clin.17.4.443.27943

American Academy of Psychiatry and the Law. (2005). *Ethics guidelines for the practice of forensic psychiatry.* Bloomfield, CT: Author.

American Bar Association. (2016). *Criminal justice standards on mental health.* Washington, DC: Author. Retrieved from http://www.americanbar.org/content/dam/aba/publications/criminal_justice_standards/mental_health_standards_2016.authcheckdam.pdf

American Bar Association/American Psychological Association, Assessment of Capacity in Older Adults Project Working Group. (2008). *Assessment of older adults with diminished capacity: A handbook for psychologists.* Washington, DC: Authors.

American Board of Forensic Psychology. (2015). *Core competencies in forensic psychology.* Retrieved from https://abpp.org/BlankSite/media/Forensic-Psychology-Documents/ABFP-Core-Competencies.pdf

American Educational Research Association, American Psychological Association, & National Council on Measurement in Education. (2014). *Standards for educational and psychological testing.* Washington, DC: American Educational Research Association.

American Psychological Association. (2007). Record keeping guidelines. *American Psychologist, 62,* 993–1004. http://dx.doi.org/10.1037/0003-066X.62.9.993

American Psychological Association. (2010). Guidelines for child custody evaluations in family law proceedings. *American Psychologist, 65,* 863–867. http://dx.doi.org/10.1037/a0021250

American Psychological Association. (2013). Specialty guidelines for forensic psychology. *American Psychologist, 68,* 7–19. http://dx.doi.org/10.1037/a0029889

American Psychological Association. (2017a). *Ethical principles of psychologists and code of conduct* (2002, Amended June 1, 2010, and January 1, 2017). Retrieved from http://www.apa.org/ethics/code/index.aspx

American Psychological Association. (2017b). *Professional practice guidelines for occupationally mandated psychological evaluations.* Retrieved from https://www.apa.org/practice/guidelines/occupationally-mandated-psychological-evaluations.pdf

American Psychological Association, Committee on Legal Issues. (2006). Strategies for private practitioners coping with subpoenas or compelled testimony for client records or test data. *Professional Psychology: Research and Practice, 37,* 215–222. http://dx.doi.org/10.1037/0735-7028.37.2.215

American Psychological Association, Committee on Psychological Tests and Assessment. (2007). *Statement on third party observers in psychological testing and assessment: A framework for decision making.* Retrieved from https://www.apa.org/science/programs/testing/third-party-observers.pdf

American Psychological Association, Joint Task Force for the Development of Telepsychology Guidelines for Psychologists. (2013). Guidelines for the practice of telepsychology. *American Psychologist, 68,* 791–800. http://dx.doi.org/10.1037/a0035001

Appelbaum, P. S., & Grisso, T. (1995). The MacArthur Treatment Competence Study. I: Mental illness and competence to consent to treatment. *Law and Human Behavior, 19,* 105–126. http://dx.doi.org/10.1007/BF01499321

Applied Innovations, Inc. v. Regents of University of Minnesota, 876 F.2d 626, 634–636 (8th Cir. 1989).

Archer, E. M., Hagan, L. D., Mason, J., Handel, R., & Archer, R. P. (2012). MMPI-2-RF characteristics of custody evaluation litigants. *Assessment, 19,* 14–20. http://dx.doi.org/10.1177/1073191110397469

Archer, R. P., Buffington-Vollum, J. K., Stredny, R. V., & Handel, R. W. (2006). A survey of psychological test use patterns among forensic psychologists. *Journal of Personality Assessment, 87,* 84–94. http://dx.doi.org/10.1207/s15327752jpa8701_07

Arkes, H. R. (1981). Impediments to accurate clinical judgment and possible ways to minimize their impact. *Journal of Consulting and Clinical Psychology, 49,* 323–330. http://dx.doi.org/10.1037/0022-006X.49.3.323

Arnoult, L. H., & Anderson, C. A. (1988). Identifying and reducing causal reasoning biases in clinical practice. In M. R. Leary & R. S. Miller (Eds.), *Social psychology and dysfunctional behavior: Origins, diagnosis, and treatment* (pp. 209–232). New York, NY: Springer-Verlag.

Association of State and Provincial Psychology Boards. (2018). *Code of conduct.* Retrieved from https://cdn.ymaws.com/www.asppb.net/resource/resmgr/guidelines/asppb_Code_of_Conduct_januar.pdf

Atkins v. Virginia, 536 U.S. 304 (2002).

Axelrod, B., Heilbronner, R., Barth, J., Larrabee, G., Faust, D., Pliskin, N., . . . Silver, C. (2000). Test security: Official position statement of the National

Academy of Neuropsychology. *Archives of Clinical Neuropsychology, 15,* 383–386. http://dx.doi.org/10.1093/arclin/15.5.383

Bagby, R. M., Nicholson, R. A., Buis, T., Radovanovic, H., & Fidler, B. J. (1999). Defensive responding on the MMPI-2 in family custody and access evaluations. *Psychological Assessment, 11,* 24–28. http://dx.doi.org/10.1037/1040-3590.11.1.24

Barsky, A. E. (2012). *Clinicians in court: A guide to subpoenas, depositions, testifying, and everything else you need to know* (2nd ed.). New York, NY: Guilford Press.

Barsky, A. E., & Gould, J. W. (2002). *Clinicians in court: A guide to subpoenas, depositions, testifying, and everything else you need to know.* New York, NY: Guilford Press.

Bartol, C. R., & Bartol, A. M. (2019). *Introduction to forensic psychology: Research and application* (5th ed.). Thousand Oaks, CA: Sage.

Bathurst, K., Gottfried, A. W., & Gottfried, A. E. (1997). Normative data for the MMPI-2 in child custody litigation. *Psychological Assessment, 9,* 205–211. http://dx.doi.org/10.1037/1040-3590.9.3.205

Bauer, R. M., Iverson, G. L., Cernich, A. N., Binder, L. M., Ruff, R. M., & Naugle, R. I. (2012). Computerized neuropsychological assessment devices: Joint position paper of the American Academy of Clinical Neuropsychology and the National Academy of Neuropsychology. *The Clinical Neuropsychologist, 26,* 177–196. http://dx.doi.org/10.1080/13854046.2012.663001

Beauchamp, T. L., & Childress, A. F. (2013). *Principles of biomedical ethics* (7th ed.). New York, NY: Oxford University Press.

Behnke, S. (2003). Release of test data and APA's new ethics code. *Monitor on Psychology, 34,* 70–72.

Behnke, S. H., Perlin, M. L., & Bernstein, M. (2003). *The essentials of New York mental health law: A straightforward guide for clinicians of all disciplines.* New York, NY: Norton.

Bennett, B. E., Bricklin, P. M., Harris, E., Knapp, S., VandeCreek, L., & Younggren, J. N. (2006). *Assessing and managing risk in psychological practice: An individualized approach.* Rockville, MD: The Trust. http://dx.doi.org/10.1037/14293-000

Bieliauskas, L. A. (1999). The measurement of personality and emotional functioning. In J. J. Sweet (Ed.), *Forensic neuropsychology: Fundamentals and practice* (pp. 121–143). Lisse, The Netherlands: Swets & Zeitlinger.

Blau, T. H. (1998). *The psychologist as expert witness* (2nd ed.). New York, NY: John Wiley.

Boccaccini, M. T., Turner, D. B., & Murrie, D. C. (2008). Do some evaluators report consistently higher or lower PCL-R scores than others? Findings from a statewide sample of sexually violent predator evaluations. *Psychology, Public Policy, and Law, 14,* 262–283. http://dx.doi.org/10.1037/a0014523

Borkosky, B. G., Pellett, J. M., & Thomas, M. S. (2014). Are forensic evaluations "health care" and are they regulated by HIPAA? *Psychological Injury and Law, 7,* 1–8. http://dx.doi.org/10.1007/s12207-013-9158-7

Brodsky, S. L. (2013). *Testifying in court: Guidelines and maxims for the expert witness* (2nd ed.). Washington, DC: American Psychological Association. http://dx.doi.org/10.1037/14037-000

Brodsky, S. L., & Gutheil, T. G. (2016). *The expert expert witness: More maxims and guidelines for testifying in court* (2nd ed.). Washington, DC: American Psychological Association. http://dx.doi.org/10.1037/14732-000

Bush, S. S. (2005a). Ethical challenges with ethnically and culturally diverse populations in neuropsychology. In S. S. Bush (Ed.), *A casebook of ethical challenges in neuropsychology* (pp. 159–161). New York, NY: Psychology Press.

Bush, S. S. (2005b). Ethical issues in forensic neuropsychology: Introduction. *Journal of Forensic Neuropsychology, 4*, 1–9. http://dx.doi.org/10.1300/J151v04n03_01

Bush, S. S. (2005c). Introduction to ethical challenges in forensic neuropsychology. In S. S. Bush (Ed.), *A casebook of ethical challenges in neuropsychology* (pp. 10–14). New York, NY: Psychology Press.

Bush, S. S. (2009). *Geriatric mental health ethics: A casebook.* New York, NY: Springer.

Bush, S. S. (2015). Ethical guidelines in forensic psychology. In R. L. Cautin & S. O. Lilienfeld (Eds.), *The encyclopedia of clinical psychology* (Vol. 2, pp. 1115–1124). West Sussex, England: Wiley Blackwell. http://dx.doi.org/10.1002/9781118625392.wbecp345

Bush, S. S. (2018a). *Ethical decision making in clinical neuropsychology* (2nd ed.). New York, NY: Oxford University Press.

Bush, S. S. (2018b). Ethical issues in forensic geropsychology. In S. S. Bush & A. L. Heck (Eds.), *Forensic geropsychology: Practice essentials* (pp. 11–23). Washington, DC: American Psychological Association. http://dx.doi.org/10.1037/0000082-002

Bush, S. S., Allen, R. S., & Molinari, V. A. (2017). *Ethical practice in geropsychology.* Washington, DC: American Psychological Association. http://dx.doi.org/10.1037/0000010-000

Bush, S. S., Barth, J. T., Pliskin, N. H., Arffa, S., Axelrod, B. N., Blackburn, L. A., . . . Silver, C. H. (2005). Independent and court-ordered forensic neuropsychological examinations: Official statement of the National Academy of Neuropsychology. *Archives of Clinical Neuropsychology, 20*, 997–1007. http://dx.doi.org/10.1016/j.acn.2005.06.003

Bush, S. S., Connell, M. A., & Denney, R. L. (2006). *Ethical practice in forensic psychology: A systematic model for decision making.* Washington, DC: American Psychological Association. http://dx.doi.org/10.1037/11469-000

Bush, S. S., Heilbronner, R. L., & Ruff, R. M. (2014). Psychological assessment of symptom and performance validity, response bias, and malingering: Official position of the Association for Scientific Advancement in Psychological Injury and Law. *Psychological Injury and Law, 7*, 197–205. http://dx.doi.org/10.1007/s12207-014-9198-7

Bush, S. S., & Morgan, J. E. (2017). Ethical practice in forensic neuropsychology. In S. S. Bush, G. J. Demakis, & M. L. Rohling (Eds.), *APA handbook of forensic neuropsychology* (pp. 23–37). Washington, DC: American Psychological Association. http://dx.doi.org/10.1037/0000032-002

Bush, S. S., Naugle, R., & Johnson-Greene, D. (2002). The interface of information technology and neuropsychology: Ethical issues and recommendations. *The Clinical Neuropsychologist, 16*, 536–547.

Bush, S. S., Rapp, D. L., & Ferber, P. S. (2010). Maximizing test security in forensic neuropsychology. In A. M. Horton, Jr., & L. C. Hartlage (Eds.), *Handbook of forensic neuropsychology* (2nd ed., pp. 177–195). New York, NY: Springer.

Bush, S. S., Ruff, R. M., Tröster, A. I., Barth, J. T., Koffler, S. P., Pliskin, N. H., . . . Silver, C. H. (2005). Symptom validity assessment: Practice issues and medical necessity. *Archives of Clinical Neuropsychology, 20*, 419–426. http://dx.doi.org/10.1016/j.acn.2005.02.002

Bush, S. S., & Schatz, P. (2017). Advanced technology and assessment: Ethical and methodological considerations. In T. D. Parsons & R. Kane (Eds.), *The role of technology in clinical neuropsychology* (pp. 457–469). New York, NY: Oxford University Press.

Bush, S. S., Sweet, J. J., Bianchini, K. J., Johnson-Greene, D., Dean, P. M., & Schoenberg, M. R. (2018). Deciding to adopt revised and new psychological and neuropsychological tests: An inter-organizational position paper. *The Clinical Neuropsychologist, 32*, 319–325. http://dx.doi.org/10.1080/13854046.2017.1422277

Campbell, L. F., Millán, F., Martin, J. N. (Eds.). (2018). *A telepsychology casebook: Using technology ethically and effectively in your professional practice.* Washington, DC: American Psychological Association.

Canadian Psychological Association. (2017). *Canadian code of ethics for psychologists* (4th ed.). Ottawa, Ontario, Canada: Author.

Cantor, N., & Mischel, W. (1979). Prototypes in person perception. *Advances in Experimental Social Psychology, 12*, 3–52.

Carpenter v. Superior Court, 141 Cal. App. 4th 249 (Cal. Ct. App. 2006).

Caudill, O. B., & Pope, K. S. (1995). *Law and mental health professionals: California.* Washington, DC: American Psychological Association.

Ceci, S. J., & Bruck, M. (1995). *Jeopardy in the courtroom: A scientific analysis of children's testimony.* Washington, DC: American Psychological Association. http://dx.doi.org/10.1037/10180-000

Ceci, S. J., & Hembrooke, H. (Eds.). (1998). *Expert witnesses in child abuse cases: What can and should be said in court.* Washington, DC: American Psychological Association. http://dx.doi.org/10.1037/10272-000

Chevalier, C. S., Boccaccini, M. T., Murrie, D. C., & Valora, J. G. (2015). Static-99R reporting practices in sexually violent predator cases: Does norm selection reflect adversarial allegiance? *Law and Human Behavior, 39*, 209–218.

Chicago Bd. of Educ. v. Substance, Inc., 354 F.3d 624, 627 (7th Cir. 2003), *cert. denied*, 543 U.S. 816 (2004).

Chiperas v. Rubin, 1998 WL 765126 (D.D.C. 1998).

Chrobak, Q. M., & Zaragoza, M. S. (2013). The misinformation effect: Past research and recent advances. In A. M. Ridley, F. Gabbert, & D. J. La Rooy (Eds.), *Suggestibility in legal contexts: Psychological research and forensic implications* (pp. 21–44). Chichester, England: Wiley-Blackwell. http://dx.doi.org/10.1002/9781118432907.ch2

Connell, M. (2019). The varied roles of the psychologist in military proceedings. In C. T. Stein & J. N. Younggren (Eds.), *Forensic psychology in military courts* (pp. 103–124). Washington, DC: American Psychological Association.

Connell, M., & Koocher, G. (2003). HIPAA & forensic practice. *American Psychology-Law Society News, 23*, 16–19.

Connell, M. A. (2003). A psychobiographical approach to the evaluation for sentence mitigation. *The Journal of Psychiatry & Law, 31*, 319–354. http://dx.doi.org/10.1177/009318530303100304

Constantinou, M., Ashendorf, L., & McCaffrey, R. J. (2002). When the third party observer of a neuropsychological evaluation is an audio-recorder. *The Clinical Neuropsychologist, 16*, 407–412. http://dx.doi.org/10.1076/clin.16.3.407.13853

Constantinou, M., Ashendorf, L., & McCaffrey, R. J. (2005). Effects of a third party observer during neuropsychological assessment: When the observer is a video camera. *Journal of Forensic Neuropsychology, 4,* 39–47. http://dx.doi.org/10.1300/J151v04n02_04

Constantinou, M., & McCaffrey, R. J. (2003). The effects of third party observation: When the observer is a video camera [Abstract]. *Archives of Clinical Neuropsychology, 18,* 788–789.

Crown, B. M., Fingerhut, H. S., & Lowenthal, S. J. (2003). Conflicts of interest and other pitfalls for the expert witness. In A. M. Horton, Jr., & L. C. Hartlage (Eds.), *Handbook of forensic neuropsychology* (pp. 383–421). New York, NY: Springer.

Cunningham, M. D. (in press). Competency for execution. In R. D. Morgan (Ed.), *The SAGE encyclopedia of criminal psychology.* Thousand Oaks, CA: Sage.

Cunningham, M. D., & Reidy, T. J. (2001). A matter of life or death: Special considerations and heightened practice standards in capital sentencing evaluations. *Behavioral Sciences & the Law, 19,* 473–490. http://dx.doi.org/10.1002/bsl.460

Cutler, B. L., & Zapf, P. A. (Eds.). (2015). *APA handbook of forensic psychology.* Washington, DC: American Psychological Association.

Daubert v. Merrell Dow Pharmaceuticals, Inc., 509 U.S. 579 (1993).

Deidan, C., & Bush, S. (2002). Addressing perceived ethical violations in clinical neuropsychology. In S. S. Bush & M. L. Drexler (Eds.), *Ethical issues in clinical neuropsychology* (pp. 281–305). Lisse, The Netherlands: Swets & Zeitlinger.

DeJesus-Zayas, S. R., Buigas, R., & Denney, R. L. (2012). Evaluation of culturally diverse populations. In D. Faust (Ed.), *Coping with psychiatric and psychological testimony* (6th ed., pp. 248–265). New York, NY: Oxford University Press.

DeMatteo, D., Murrie, D. C., Anumba, N. M., & Keesler, M. E. (2011). *Forensic mental health assessments in death penalty cases.* New York, NY: Oxford University Press.

Denney, R. L. (2005a). Ethical challenges in forensic neuropsychology, Part I. In S. S. Bush (Ed.), *A casebook of ethical challenges in neuropsychology* (pp. 15–22). New York, NY: Psychology Press.

Denney, R. L. (2005b). Gambling, money laundering, competency, sanity, neuropathology, and intrigue. In R. L. Heilbronner (Ed.), *Forensic neuropsychology casebook* (pp. 305–325). New York, NY: Guilford Press.

Denney, R. L. (2012a). Criminal forensic neuropsychology and assessment of competency. In G. J. Larrabee (Ed.), *Forensic neuropsychology: A scientific approach* (2nd ed., pp. 438–472). New York, NY: Oxford University Press.

Denney, R. L. (2012b). Criminal responsibility and other criminal forensic issues. In G. J. Larrabee (Ed.), *Forensic neuropsychology: A scientific approach* (2nd ed., pp. 473–500). New York, NY: Oxford University Press.

Denney, R. L., & Sullivan, J. P. (2008). Constitutional, judicial, and practice foundations of criminal forensic neuropsychology. In R. L. Denney & J. P. Sullivan (Eds.), *Clinical neuropsychology in the criminal forensic setting* (pp. 1–29). New York, NY: Guilford Press.

Denney, R. L., & Wynkoop, T. F. (2000). Clinical neuropsychology in the criminal forensic setting. *The Journal of Head Trauma Rehabilitation, 15,* 804–828. http://dx.doi.org/10.1097/00001199-200004000-00005

Detroit Edison Co. v. NLRB, 440 U.S. 301 (1979).

Duff, K., & Fisher, J. M. (2005). Ethical dilemmas with third party observers. *Journal of Forensic Neuropsychology, 4,* 65–82. http://dx.doi.org/10.1300/J151v04n02_06

Edens, J. F., & Boccaccini, M. T. (2017). Taking forensic mental health assessment "out of the lab" and into "the real world": Introduction to the special issue on the field utility of forensic assessment instruments and procedures. *Psychological Assessment, 29*, 599–610. http://dx.doi.org/10.1037/pas0000475

Erickson, S. K., Lilienfeld, S. O., & Vitacco, M. J. (2007). A critical examination of the suitability and limitations of psychological tests in family court. *Family Court Review, 45*, 157–174. http://dx.doi.org/10.1111/j.1744-1617.2007.00136.x

Estelle v. Smith, 451 U.S. 454 (1981).

Exclusive Rights in Copyrighted Works, 17 U.S. § 106 (2017).

Faust, D. (1986). Research on human judgment and its application to clinical practice. *Professional Psychology: Research and Practice, 17*, 420–430. http://dx.doi.org/10.1037/0735-7028.17.5.420

Fazio, R. L., Roebuck Spencer, T., Denney, R. L., Glen, E. T., Bianchini, K. J., Garmoe, W. S., . . . Scott, J. G. (2018). *The role of the neuropsychologist in selecting neuropsychological tests in a forensic evaluation: A position statement by the National Academy of Neuropsychology Policy & Planning Committee.* Retrieved from https://nanonline.org/docs/ResearchandPublications/PositionPapers/Test%20Selection%20Statement%20Approved%202-15-2018%20(002).pdf

Fischhoff, B. (1982). Debiasing. In D. Kahneman, P. Slovic, & A. Tversky (Eds.), *Judgment under uncertainty: Heuristics and biases* (pp. 424–444). Cambridge, England: Cambridge University Press. http://dx.doi.org/10.1017/CBO9780511809477.032

Fisher, C. B. (2003). Test data standard most notable change in new APA ethics code. *The National Psychologist, Jan/Feb*, 12–13.

Flynn, J. R. (2007). *What is intelligence? Beyond the Flynn effect.* Cambridge, England: Cambridge University Press

Forensic Specialty Council. (2007). *Education and training guidelines for forensic psychology.* Retrieved from http://www.apadivisions.org/division-41/education/guidelines.pdf

Fouad, N. A., Grus, C. L., Hatcher, R. L., Kaslow, N. J., Smith Hutchings, P., Madson, M. B., . . . Crossman, R. E. (2009). Competency benchmarks: A model for understanding and measuring competence in professional psychology across training levels. *Training and Education in Professional Psychology, 3*(4 Suppl.), S5–S26.

Frye v. United States, 293 F. 1013 (D.C. Cir. 1923).

Gavett, B. E., Lynch, J. K., & McCaffrey, R. J. (2005). Third party observers: The effect size is greater than you might think. *Journal of Forensic Neuropsychology, 4*, 49–64. http://dx.doi.org/10.1300/J151v04n02_05

Gavett, B. E., & McCaffrey, R. J. (2007). The influence of an adaptation period in reducing the third party observer effect during a neuropsychological evaluation. *Archives of Clinical Neuropsychology, 22*, 699–710. http://dx.doi.org/10.1016/j.acn.2007.05.002

General Provisions for Chapter, 18 U.S. § 4247 (2017).

Glancy, G. D., Ash, P., Bath, E. P. J., Buchanan, A., Fedoroff, P., Frierson, R. L., . . . Zonana, H. V. (2015). AAPL practice guideline for the forensic assessment. *Journal of the American Academy of Psychiatry and the Law, 43* (Suppl.), S3–S53.

Goodman, K. W. (1998). Bioethics and health informatics: An introduction. In K. W. Goodman (Ed.), *Ethics, computing, and medicine: Informatics and the transformation of health care* (pp. 1–31). Cambridge, England: Cambridge University Press.

Gottlieb, M. C., & Younggren, J. N. (2019). Addressing potential role conflicts in military courts-martial. In C. T. Stein and J. N. Younggren (Eds.), *Forensic psychology in military courts* (pp. 91–102). Washington, DC: American Psychological Association. http://dx.doi.org/10.1037/0000141-006

Green, R. G. (1983). Evaluation apprehension and the social facilitation/inhibition of learning. *Motivation and Emotion, 7,* 203–211. http://dx.doi.org/10.1007/BF00992903

Greenberg, L. R., & Gould, J. W. (2001). The treating expert: A hybrid role with firm boundaries. *Professional Psychology: Research and Practice, 32,* 469–478. http://dx.doi.org/10.1037/0735-7028.32.5.469

Greenberg, S. A., & Shuman, D. W. (1997). Irreconcilable conflict between therapeutic and forensic roles. *Professional Psychology: Research and Practice, 28,* 50–57. http://dx.doi.org/10.1037/0735-7028.28.1.50

Greenberg, S. A., & Shuman, D. W. (2007). When worlds collide: Therapeutic and forensic roles. *Professional Psychology: Research and Practice, 38,* 129–132.

Greve, K. W., Ord, J. S., Bianchini, K. J., & Curtis, K. L. (2009). Prevalence of malingering in patients with chronic pain referred for psychologic evaluation in a medico-legal context. *Archives of Physical Medicine and Rehabilitation, 90,* 1117–1126. http://dx.doi.org/10.1016/j.apmr.2009.01.018

Grisso, T. (2003). *Evaluating competencies: Forensic assessments and instruments* (2nd ed.). New York, NY: Kluwer Academic/Plenum.

Grisso, T., & Appelbaum, P. S. (1998a). *Assessing competence to consent to treatment: A guide for physicians and other health professionals.* New York, NY: Oxford University Press.

Grisso, T., & Appelbaum, P. S. (1998b). *MacArthur Competence Assessment Tool for Treatment (MacCAT-T).* Sarasota, FL: Professional Resource Press.

Grote, C. L. (2005). Ethical challenges in forensic neuropsychology, part II. In S. S. Bush (Ed.), *A casebook of ethical challenges in neuropsychology* (pp. 23–29). New York, NY: Psychology Press.

Grote, C. L., Lewin, J. L., Sweet, J. J., & van Gorp, W. G. (2000). Responses to perceived unethical practices in clinical neuropsychology: Ethical and legal considerations. *The Clinical Neuropsychologist, 14,* 119–134. http://dx.doi.org/10.1076/1385-4046(200002)14:1;1-8;FT119

Gudjonsson, G. H., Sveinsdottir, T., Sigurdsson, J. F., & Jonsdottir, J. K. (2010). The ability of suspected victims of childhood sexual abuse (CSA) to give credible evidence: Findings from the Children's House in Iceland. *Journal of Forensic Psychiatry & Psychology, 21,* 569–586. http://dx.doi.org/10.1080/14789940903540784

Guerin, B. (1986). Mere presence effects in humans: A review. *Journal of Experimental Social Psychology, 22,* 38–77. http://dx.doi.org/10.1016/0022-1031(86)90040-5

Hall v. Florida, 572 U.S. 701 (2014).

Halleck, S. L. (1980). *Law in the practice of psychiatry: A handbook for clinicians.* New York, NY: Plenum Press. http://dx.doi.org/10.1007/978-1-4684-7893-8

Hanson, S. L., Kerkhoff, T. R., & Bush, S. S. (2005). *Health care ethics for psychologists: A casebook.* Washington, DC: American Psychological Association. http://dx.doi.org/10.1037/10845-000

Health Insurance Portability and Accountability Act of 1996, §164.524(a)(1)(ii). Retrieved from http://www.hhs.gov/ocr/hipaa/

Heilbronner, R. L., Sweet, J. J., Morgan, J. E., Larrabee, G. J., Millis, S. R., & Conference Participants. (2009). American Academy of Clinical Neuropsychology Consensus Conference Statement on the neuropsychological assessment of effort, response bias, and malingering. *The Clinical Neuropsychologist, 23,* 1093–1129. http://dx.doi.org/10.1080/13854040903155063

Heilbrun, K. (1995). Child custody evaluation: Critically assessing mental health experts and psychological tests. *Family Law Quarterly, 29,* 63–78.

Heilbrun, K. (2001). *Principles of forensic mental health assessment.* New York, NY: Kluwer Academic/Plenum.

Heilbrun, K. (2003). Principles of forensic mental health assessment: Implications for the forensic assessment of sexual offenders. *Annals of the New York Academy of Sciences, 989,* 167–184. http://dx.doi.org/10.1111/j.1749-6632.2003.tb07304.x

Heilbrun, K., Grisso, T., & Goldstein, A. M. (2009). *Foundations of forensic mental health assessment.* New York, NY: Oxford University Press.

Heilbrun, K., Warren, J., & Picarello, K. (2003). Third party information in forensic assessment. In A. Goldstein (Ed.), *Handbook of forensic psychology* (pp. 69–86). Hoboken, NJ: John Wiley.

Hirschfeld v. Stone, 193 F.R.D. 175 (S.D.N.Y. 2000).

Horwitz, J. E., & McCaffrey, R. J. (2008). Effects of a third party observer and anxiety on tests of executive function. *Archives of Clinical Neuropsychology, 23,* 409–417. http://dx.doi.org/10.1016/j.acn.2008.02.002

House of Representatives, Committee on the Judiciary. (2018). *Federal Rules of Evidence for the United States Courts and Magistrates.* Washington, DC: U.S. Government Printing Office.

House of Representatives, Committee on the Judiciary. (2019). *Federal Rules of Civil Procedure.* Washington, DC: U.S. Government Printing Office.

Howe, L. L. S., & McCaffrey, R. J. (2010). Third party observation during neuropsychological evaluation: An update on the literature, practical advice for practitioners, and future directions. *The Clinical Neuropsychologist, 24,* 518–537. http://dx.doi.org/10.1080/13854041003775347

Hynan, D. J. (2013). Use of the Personality Assessment Inventory in child custody evaluation. *Open Access Journal of Forensic Psychology, 5,* 120–133.

Hynan, D. J. (2014). *Child custody evaluation: New theoretical applications and research.* Springfield, IL: Charles C Thomas.

International Test Commission. (2013). *ITC guidelines on test use.* Retrieved from www.intestcom.org/files/guideline_test_use.pdf

International Test Commission. (2015). *Guidelines for practitioner use of test revisions, obsolete tests, and test disposal.* Retrieved from http://www.intestcom.org/files/guideline_test_disposal.pdf

Iverson, G. L., & Slick, D. J. (2003). Ethical issues associated with psychological and neuropsychological assessment of persons from different cultural and linguistic backgrounds. In I. Z. Schultz & D. O. Brady (Eds.), *Psychological injuries at trial* (pp. 2066–2087). Chicago, IL: American Bar Association.

Kahneman, D., & Tversky, A. (1973). On the psychology of prediction. *Psychological Review, 80,* 237–251. http://dx.doi.org/10.1037/h0034747

Karson, M., & Nadkarni, L. (2013). *Principles of forensic report writing.* Washington, DC: American Psychological Association.

Kaslow, N. J., Rubin, N. J., Bebeau, M. J., Leigh, I. W., Lichtenberg, J. W., Nelson, P. D., . . . Smith, I. L. (2007). Guiding principles and recommendations for the assessment of competence. *Professional Psychology: Research and Practice, 38,* 441–451. http://dx.doi.org/10.1037/0735-7028.38.5.441

Kaufmann, P. M. (2005). Protecting the objectivity, fairness, and integrity of neuropsychological valuations in litigation. *Journal of Legal Medicine, 26,* 95–131. http://dx.doi.org/10.1080/01947640590918007

Kaufmann, P. M. (2009). Protecting raw data and psychological tests from wrongful disclosure: A primer on the law and other persuasive strategies. *The Clinical Neuropsychologist, 23,* 1130–1159. http://dx.doi.org/10.1080/13854040903107809

Kehrer, C. A., Sanchez, P. N., Habif, U. J., Rosenbaum, G. J., & Townes, B. D. (2000). Effects of a significant-other observer on neuropsychological test performance. *The Clinical Neuropsychologist, 14,* 67–71. http://dx.doi.org/10.1076/1385-4046(200002)14:1;1-8;FT067

Keilin, W. G., & Bloom, L. J. (1986). Child custody evaluation practices: A survey of experienced professionals. *Professional Psychology, Research and Practice, 17,* 338–346. http://dx.doi.org/10.1037/0735-7028.17.4.338

Knapp, S., & VandeCreek, L. (2003). *A guide to the 2002 revision of the American Psychological Association's Ethics Code.* Sarasota, FL: Professional Resource Press.

Knapp, S., Younggren, J. N., VandeCreek, L., Harris, E., & Martin, J. N. (2013). *Assessing and managing risk in psychological practice: An individualized approach* (2nd ed.). Rockville, MD: The Trust.

Knapp, S. J., VandeCreek, L. D., & Fingerhut, R. (2017). *Practical ethics for psychologists: A positive approach* (3rd ed.). Washington, DC: American Psychological Association. http://dx.doi.org/10.1037/0000036-000

Kois, L. (2017). Navigating conflicts with systems and other professionals. In G. Pirelli, R. A., Beatty, & P. A. Zapf (Eds.), *The ethical practice of forensic psychology: A casebook* (pp. 126–158). New York, NY: Oxford University Press. http://dx.doi.org/10.1093/acprof:oso/9780190258542.003.0005

Kumho Tire Co. v. Carmichael, 526 U.S. 137 (1999).

LaDuke, C., Barr, W., Brodale, D. L., & Rabin, L. A. (2018). Toward generally accepted forensic assessment practices among clinical neuropsychologists: A survey of professional practice and common test use. *The Clinical Neuropsychologist, 32,* 145–164. http://dx.doi.org/10.1080/13854046.2017.1346711

Lally, S. J. (2003). What tests are acceptable for use in forensic evaluations? A survey of experts. *Professional Psychology: Research and Practice, 34,* 491–498. http://dx.doi.org/10.1037/0735-7028.34.5.491

Lamade, R. V. (2017). Identifying the client and professional services. In G. Pirelli, R. A. Beattey, & P. A. Zapf (Eds.), *The ethical practice of forensic psychology: A casebook* (pp. 64–98). New York, NY: Oxford University Press. http://dx.doi.org/10.1093/acprof:oso/9780190258542.003.0003

La Rooy, D., Brubacher, S. P., Aromäki-Stratos, A., Cyr, M., Hershkowitz, I., Korkman, J., . . . Lamb, M. E. (2015). The NICHD protocol: A review of an internationally-used evidence-based tool for training child forensic interviewers. *Journal of Criminological Research. Policy & Practice, 1,* 76–89. http://dx.doi.org/10.1108/jcrpp-01-2015-0001

Larrabee, G. J. (2012). Performance validity and symptom validity in neuropsychological assessment. *Journal of the International Neuropsychological Society, 18,* 625–630. http://dx.doi.org/10.1017/S1355617712000240

Lewandowski, A., Baker, W. J., Sewick, B., Knippa, J., Axelrod, B., & McCaffrey, R. J. (2016). Policy Statement of the American Board of Professional Neuropsychology regarding third party observation and the recording of psychological test administration in neuropsychological evaluations. *Applied Neuropsychology: Adult, 23*, 391–398. http://dx.doi.org/10.1080/23279095.2016.1176366

Lezak, M. D., Howieson, D. B., Bigler, E. D., & Tranel, D. (2012). *Neuropsychological assessment* (5th ed.). New York, NY: Oxford University Press.

Loftus, E., & Ketcham, K. (1994). *The myth of repressed memory: False memories and allegations of sexual abuse.* New York, NY: St. Martin's Griffin.

Lynch, J. K. (1997). The effect of observer's presence on neuropsychological test performance: A test of the social facilitation phenomenon. *Dissertation Abstracts International: Section B. The Sciences and Engineering, 57*, 7230.

Manly, J. J., & Jacobs, D. M. (2002). Future directions in neuropsychological assessment with African Americans. In F. R. Ferraro (Ed.), *Minority and cross-cultural aspects of neuropsychological assessment* (pp. 79–96). Lisse, The Netherlands: Swets & Zeitlinger.

Martelli, M. F., Bush, S. S., & Zasler, N. D. (2003). Identifying, avoiding, and addressing ethical misconduct in neuropsychological medicolegal practice. *International Journal of Forensic Psychology, 1*, 26–44.

Martin, P. K., Schroeder, R. W., & Odland, A. P. (2015). Neuropsychologists' validity testing beliefs and practices: A survey of North American professionals. *The Clinical Neuropsychologist, 29*, 741–776. http://dx.doi.org/10.1080/13854046.2015.1087597

Martindale, D. A., & Gould, J. W. (2004). The forensic model: Ethics and scientific methodology applied to custody evaluations. *Journal of Child Custody, 1*, 1–22. http://dx.doi.org/10.1300/J190v01n02_01

Massey, C. (2017). Professional competence. In G. Pirelli, R. A. Beattey, & P. A. Zapf (Eds.), *The ethical practice of forensic psychology: A casebook* (pp. 32–63). New York, NY: Oxford University Press. http://dx.doi.org/10.1093/acprof:oso/9780190258542.003.0002

McCaffrey, R. J. (Ed.). (2005). Third party observers. *Journal of Forensic Neuropsychology, 4* (2).

McLearen, A. M., Pietz, C. A., & Denney, R. L. (2004). Evaluation of psychological damages. In W. T. O'Donohue & E. R. Levensky (Eds.), *Handbook of forensic psychology* (pp. 267–299). San Diego, CA: Elsevier Academic Press. http://dx.doi.org/10.1016/B978-012524196-0/50014-0

Melton, G. B., Petrila, J., Poythress, N. G., Slobogin, C., Otto, R. K., Mossman, D., & Condie, L. O. (2018). *Psychological evaluations for the courts: A handbook for mental health professionals and lawyers* (4th ed.). New York, NY: The Guilford Press.

Metzner, J. L., & Ash, P. (2010). Commentary: The mental status examination in the age of the internet—challenges and opportunities. *The Journal of the American Academy of Psychiatry and the Law, 38*, 27–31. http://www.jaapl.org/content/38/1/27.full

Miller, J. B., & Barr, W. B. (2017). The technology crisis in neuropsychology. *Archives of Clinical Neuropsychology, 32*, 541–554. http://dx.doi.org/10.1093/arclin/acx050

Miller, L., Sadoff, R. L., & Dattilio, F. M. (2011). Personal injury: The independent medical examination in psychology and psychiatry. In E. Y. Drogin, F. M. Dattilio,

R. L. Sadoff, & T. G. Gutheil (Eds.), *Handbook of forensic assessment: Psychological and psychiatric perspectives* (pp. 277–302). Hoboken, NJ: Wiley.

Moye, J., Karel, M. J., Edelstein, B., Hicken, B., Armesto, J. C., & Gurrera, R. J. (2007). Assessment of the Capacity to Consent to Treatment (ACCT). *Clinical Gerontologist, 31,* 37–66. http://dx.doi.org/10.1080/07317110802072140

Mrad, D. (1996, September). *Criminal responsibility evaluations.* Paper presented at Issues in Forensic Assessment Symposium, Federal Bureau of Prisons, Atlanta, GA.

Murrie, D. C., Boccaccini, M. T., Guarnera, L. A., & Rufino, K. A. (2013). Are forensic experts biased by the side that retained them? *Psychological Science, 24,* 1889–1897. http://dx.doi.org/10.1177/0956797613481812

Murrie, D. C., Boccaccini, M. T., Johnson, J. T., & Janke, C. (2008). Does inter-rater (dis)agreement on Psychopathy Checklist scores in sexually violent predator trials suggest partisan allegiance in forensic evaluations? *Law and Human Behavior, 32,* 352–362. http://dx.doi.org/10.1007/s10979-007-9097-5

Nagy, T. F. (2000). *Ethics in plain English: An illustrative casebook for psychologists.* Washington, DC: American Psychological Association.

National Academy of Neuropsychology Policy and Planning Committee. (2000). Presence of 3rd party observers during neuropsychological testing: Official statement of the National Academy of Neuropsychology. *Archives of Clinical Neuropsychology, 15,* 379–380. http://dx.doi.org/10.1016/S0887-6177(00)00053-6

National Academy of Neuropsychology Policy and Planning Committee. (2003). *Test security: An update. Official statement of the National Academy of Neuropsychology.* Retrieved from https://www.nanonline.org/docs/PAIC/PDFs/NANTestSecurity Update.pdf

NCS Pearson. (2009). *Administration and scoring manual for the WAIS-IV and WMS-IV.* San Antonio, TX: Author.

Neal, T. M. S. (2017). Identifying the forensic psychology role. In G. Pirelli, R. A. Beattey, & P. A. Zapf (Eds.), *The ethical practice of forensic psychology: A casebook* (pp. 1–31). New York, NY: Oxford University Press.

Neal, T. M. S., & Brodsky, S. L. (2016). Forensic psychologists' perceptions of bias and potential correction strategies in forensic mental health evaluations. *Psychology, Public Policy, and Law, 22,* 58–76. http://dx.doi.org/10.1037/law0000077

Neal, T. M. S., & Grisso, T. (2014). The cognitive underpinnings of bias in forensic mental health evaluations. *Psychology, Public Policy, and Law, 20,* 200–211. http://dx.doi.org/10.1037/a0035824

Neimark, G., Hurford, M. O., & DiGiacomo, J. (2006). The internet as collateral informant [Letter to the editor]. *The American Journal of Psychiatry, 163,* 1842. http://dx.doi.org/10.1176/ajp.2006.163.10.1842

New York State Workers' Compensation Board *Statement of Rights and Obligations, Independent Medical Examinations.* Retrieved from https://www.nysenate.gov/legislation/laws/WKC/137

Ochs v. Ochs, 193 Misc. 2d 502 (N.Y. Sup. Ct., 2002).

Otgaar, H., & Baker, A. (2018). When lying changes memory for the truth. *Memory, 26,* 2–14. http://dx.doi.org/10.1080/09658211.2017.1340286

Otto, R. K., Buffington-Vollum, J. K., & Edens, J. F. (2003). Child Custody Evaluation. In A. M. Goldstein (Ed.), *Comprehensive handbook of psychology: Forensic psychology* (Vol. 11, pp. 179–208). New York, NY: Wiley.

Otto, R. K., DeMier, R. L., & Boccaccini, M. T. (2014). *Forensic reports & testimony: A guide to effective communication for psychologists & psychiatrists.* Hoboken, NJ: Wiley.

Otto, R. K., Goldstein, A. M., & Heilbrun, K. (2017). *Ethics in forensic psychology practice*. Hoboken, NJ: Wiley.

Otto, R. K., & Ogloff, J. R. P. (2013). Defining forensic psychology. In I. B. Weiner & R. K. Otto (Eds.), *The handbook of forensic psychology* (4th ed., pp. 35–56). Hoboken, NJ: Wiley.

Packer, I. K., & Grisso, T. (2011). *Specialty competencies in forensic psychology*. New York, NY: Oxford University Press.

Pearson Assessments (2018). *HIPAA disclosure of test record forms*. Retrieved from https://www.pearsonassessments.com/footer/legal-policies.html.

Peery, S., Byrd, D. A., & Strutt, A. M. (2017). Diversity considerations in forensic neuropsychology. In S. S. Bush, G. J. Demakis, & M. L. Rohling (Eds.), *APA handbook of forensic neuropsychology* (pp. 379–393). Washington, DC: American Psychological Association. http://dx.doi.org/10.1037/0000032-016

Pirelli, G., Beattey, R. A., & Zapf, P. A. (Eds.). (2017). *The ethical practice of forensic psychology: A casebook*. New York, NY: Oxford University Press.

Pirelli, G., Hartigan, S., & Zapf, P. A. (2018). Using the Internet for collateral information in forensic mental health evaluations. *Behavioral Sciences & the Law, 36*, 157–169. http://dx.doi.org/10.1002/bsl.2334

Pirelli, G., Otto, R. K., & Estoup, A. (2016). Using internet and social media data as collateral sources of information in forensic evaluations. *Professional Psychology: Research and Practice, 47*, 12–17. http://dx.doi.org/10.1037/pro0000061

Pivovarova, E. (2017). Forensic assessment IV: Conveying evaluation findings and opinions. In G. Pirelli, R. A. Beattey, & P. A. Zapf (Eds.), *The ethical practice of forensic psychology: A casebook* (pp. 262–299). New York, NY: Oxford University Press. http://dx.doi.org/10.1093/acprof:oso/9780190258542.003.0009

Poole, D. A., & Lamb, M. E. (1998). *Investigative interviews of children: A guide for helping professionals*. Washington, DC: American Psychological Association. http://dx.doi.org/10.1037/10301-000

Posthuma, A. B., & Harper, J. F. (1998). Comparison of MMPI-2 responses of child custody and personal injury litigants. *Professional Psychology: Research and Practice, 29*, 437–443. http://dx.doi.org/10.1037/0735-7028.29.5.437

Poythress, N. G., & Feld, D. B. (2002). "Competence Restored"—What forensic hospital reports should (and should not) say when returning defendants to court. *Journal of Forensic Psychology Practice, 2*, 51–58. http://dx.doi.org/10.1300/J158v02n04_03

Quinnell, F. A., & Bow, J. N. (2001). Psychological tests used in child custody evaluations. *Behavioral Sciences & the Law, 19*, 491–501. http://dx.doi.org/10.1002/bsl.452

Rapp, D. L., Ferber, P. S., & Bush, S. S. (2008). Unresolved issues about release of raw test data and test materials. In A. M. Horton, Jr., & D. Wedding (Eds.), *The neuropsychology handbook* (3rd ed., pp. 469–498). New York, NY: Springer.

Recupero, P. R. (2008). Forensic evaluation of problematic internet use. *Journal of the American Academy of Psychiatry and the Law, 36*, 505–514. Retrieved from http://www.jaapl.org/content/36/4/505.full?cited-byýyes&related-urlsýyes&legidýjaapl;36/4/505

Recupero, P. R. (2010). The mental status examination in the age of the internet. *The Journal of the American Academy of Psychiatry and the Law, 38*, 15–26.

Reynolds, C. R., & Kamphaus, R. W. (2003). *Reynolds Intellectual Assessment Scales and the Reynolds Intellectual Screening Test professional manual*. Lutz, FL: Psychological Assessment Resources.

Richards, P. M., & Wortzel, H. S. (2015). Avoiding dual agency in clinical and medicolegal practice. *Journal of Psychiatric Practice, 21,* 370–373. http://dx.doi.org/10.1097/PRA.0000000000000093

Rodolfa, E., Bent, R., Eisman, E., Nelson, P., Rehm, L., & Ritchie, P. (2005). A cube model for competency development: Implications for psychology educators and regulators. *Professional Psychology: Research and Practice, 36,* 347–354. http://dx.doi.org/10.1037/0735-7028.36.4.347

Roesch, R., Zapf, P. A., & Hart, S. D. (2010). *Forensic psychology and law.* Hoboken, NJ: Wiley.

Ross, L. (1977). The intuitive psychologist and his shortcomings: Distortions in the attribution process. In L. Berkowitz (Ed.), *Advances in experimental social psychology* (Vol. 10, pp. 173–220). New York, NY: Academic Press.

Rubenzer, S. (2018). *Assessing negative response bias in competency to stand trial evaluations.* New York, NY: Oxford University Press. http://dx.doi.org/10.1093/med-psych/9780190653163.001.0001

Russell, A., Russell, G., & Midwinter, D. (1992). Observer influences on mothers and fathers: Self-reported influence during a home observation. *Merrill-Palmer Quarterly, 38,* 263–283.

Ryba, N. L., Cooper, V. G., & Zapf, P. A. (2003). Juvenile competence to stand trial evaluations: A survey of current practices and test usage among psychologists. *Professional Psychology: Research and Practice, 34,* 499–507. http://dx.doi.org/10.1037/0735-7028.34.5.499

Saks, M. J. (1990). Expert witnesses, nonexpert witnesses, and nonwitness experts. *Law and Human Behavior, 14,* 291–313. http://dx.doi.org/10.1007/BF01068158

Sales, B. D., & Miller, M. O. (1993). Editor's preface. In J. S. Wulach (Ed.), *Law & mental health professionals: New York* (pp. 1–5). Washington, DC: American Psychological Association.

Sattler, J. M. (1988). *Assessment of children* (3rd ed.). San Diego, CA: Author.

Saywitz, K. J., & Snyder, L. (1996). Narrative elaboration: Test of a new procedure for interviewing children. *Journal of Consulting and Clinical Psychology, 64,* 1347–1357. http://dx.doi.org/10.1037/0022-006X.64.6.1347

Saywitz, K. J., & Snyder, L. (1996). Narrative elaboration: Test of a new procedure for interviewing children. *Journal of Consulting and Clinical Psychology, 64,* 1347–1357. http://dx.doi.org/10.1037/0022-006X.64.6.1347

Sbordone, R. J., Rogers, M. L., Thomas, V. A., & de Armas, A. (2003). Forensic neuropsychological assessment in criminal law cases. In A. M. Horton, Jr., & L. C. Hartlage (Eds.), *Handbook of forensic neuropsychology* (pp. 471–503). New York, NY: Springer.

Schatman, M. E., & Thoman, J. L. (2014). Erratum to: Cherry-picking records in independent medical examinations: Strategies for intervention to mitigate a legal and ethical imbroglio. *Psychological Injury and Law, 7,* 290–295. http://dx.doi.org/10.1007/s12207-014-9203-1

Schroeder, R. W., Martin, P. K., & Odland, A. P. (2016). Expert beliefs and practices regarding neuropsychological validity testing. *The Clinical Neuropsychologist, 30,* 515–535. http://dx.doi.org/10.1080/13854046.2016.1177118

Shapiro, D. L. (1999). *Criminal responsibility evaluations.* Sarasota, FL: Professional Resource Press.

Shapiro, D. L. (2012). What is all the fuss about *Daubert*? A re-analysis. *Psychological Injury and Law, 5,* 202–207. http://dx.doi.org/10.1007/s12207-012-9136-5

Shuman, D. W., & Greenberg, S. A. (1998, winter). The role of ethical norms in the admissibility of expert testimony. *The Judge's Journal*, 5–9 & 42.

Siegel, J. C. (1996). Traditional MMPI-2 validity indicators and initial presentation in custody evaluations. *The American Journal of Forensic Psychology*, 14, 55–63.

Siegel, J. C., Bow, J. D., & Gottlieb, M. C. (2012). The MMPI-2 in high conflict child custody cases. *The American Journal of Forensic Psychology*, 30, 21–34.

Siegel, J. C., & Langford, J. S. (1998). MMPI-2 validity scales and suspected parental alienation syndrome. *The American Journal of Forensic Psychology*, 16, 5–14.

Slick, D. J., & Sherman, E. M. S. (2013). Differential diagnosis of malingering. In D. A. Carone & S. S. Bush (Eds.), *Mild traumatic brain injury: Symptom validity assessment and malingering* (pp. 57–72). New York, NY: Springer.

Snyder, M., & Campbell, B. (1980). Testing hypotheses about other people: The role of the hypothesis. *Personality and Social Psychology Bulletin*, 6, 421–426. http://dx.doi.org/10.1177/014616728063015

Stafford, K. P., & Sadoff, R. L. (2011). Competence to stand trial. In E. Y. Drogin, F. M. Dattilio, R. L. Sadoff, & T. G. Gutheil (Eds.), *Handbook of forensic assessment: Psychological and psychiatric perspectives* (pp. 3–23). Hoboken, NJ: Wiley. http://dx.doi.org/10.1002/9781118093399.ch1

Stein, C. T., & Younggren, J. N. (Eds.). (2019). *Forensic psychology in military courts*. Washington, DC: American Psychological Association.

Stone, A. A. (1984). *Law, psychiatry, and morality: Essays and analysis*. Washington, DC: American Psychiatric Press.

Strasburger, L. H., Gutheil, T. G., & Brodsky, A. (1997). On wearing two hats: Role conflict in serving as both psychotherapist and expert witness. *The American Journal of Psychiatry*, 154, 448–456. http://dx.doi.org/10.1176/ajp.154.4.448

Sullivan, J. P., & Denney, R. L. (2008). A final word on authentic professional competence in criminal forensic neuropsychology. In R. L. Denney & J. P. Sullivan (Eds.), *Clinical neuropsychology in the criminal forensic setting* (pp. 391–400). New York, NY: Guilford Press.

Sweet, J. J. (1999). Malingering: Differential diagnosis. In J. J. Sweet (Ed.), *Forensic neuropsychology: Fundamentals and practice* (pp. 255–285). Lisse, The Netherlands: Swets & Zeitlinger.

Sweet, J. J., & Moulthrop, M. A. (1999). Self-examination questions as a means of identifying bias in adversarial assessments. *Journal of Forensic Neuropsychology*, 1, 73–88. http://dx.doi.org/10.1300/J151v01n01_06

U.S. Sec. Ins. Co. v. Cimino, 754 So. 2d 697 (Fla. 2000).

Vagni, M., Maiorano, T., Pajardi, D., & Gudjonsson, G. (2015). Immediate and delayed suggestibility among suspected child victims of sexual abuse. *Personality and Individual Differences*, 79, 129–133. http://dx.doi.org/10.1016/j.paid.2015.02.007

Wells, G. L. (1982). Attribution and reconstructive memory. *Journal of Experimental Social Psychology*, 18, 447–463. http://dx.doi.org/10.1016/0022-1031(82)90065-8

Williams, C. W., Lees-Haley, P. R., & Djanogly, S. E. (1999). Clinical scrutiny of litigants' self-reports. *Professional Psychology: Research and Practice*, 30, 361–367. http://dx.doi.org/10.1037/0735-7028.30.4.361

Wynkoop, T. F., & Denney, R. L. (1999). Exaggeration of neuropsychological deficit in competency to stand trial. *Journal of Forensic Neuropsychology*, 1, 29–53. http://dx.doi.org/10.1300/J151v01n02_04

Yantz, C. L., & McCaffrey, R. J. (2005). Effects of a supervisor's observation on memory test performance of the examinee: Third party observer effect confirmed. *Journal of Forensic Neuropsychology, 4*, 27–38. http://dx.doi.org/10.1300/J151v04n02_03

Yantz, C. L., & McCaffrey, R. J. (2009). Effects of parental presence and child characteristics on children's neuropsychological test performance: Third party observer effect confirmed. *The Clinical Neuropsychologist, 23*, 118–132. http://dx.doi.org/10.1080/13854040801894722

Young, G. (2014). *Malingering, feigning, and response bias in psychiatric/psychological injury: Implications for practice and court.* Dordrecht, The Netherlands: Springer Science. http://dx.doi.org/10.1007/978-94-007-7899-3

Youtsey v. United States, 97 F. 937, 940 (6th Cir. 1899).

Zapf, P. A., Boccaccini, M. T., & Brodsky, S. L. (2003). Assessment of competency for execution: Professional guidelines and an evaluation checklist. *Behavioral Sciences & the Law, 21*, 103–120. http://dx.doi.org/10.1002/bsl.491

INDEX

ABOUT THE AUTHORS

Shane S. Bush, PhD, ABPP, is director of Long Island Neuropsychology, PC, a neuropsychologist with the VA New York Harbor Healthcare System, and an adjunct faculty member in the department of psychology at the University of Alabama. He is board certified in clinical neuropsychology, rehabilitation psychology, clinical psychology, and geropsychology. Dr. Bush has been awarded fellow status in Divisions 12, 18, 20, 22, 40, and 42 of the American Psychological Association. He is a past president and fellow of the National Academy of Neuropsychology. He has also held elected positions or served as a committee member for the American Academy of Clinical Neuropsychology, the American Board of Professional Psychology, the American Board of Professional Neuropsychology, the American Board of Geropsychology, and multiple divisions of the American Psychological Association. Dr. Bush is currently a member of the American Board of Professional Psychology Ethics Committee. He has served as an editorial board member of *Applied Neuropsychology*, *Archives of Clinical Neuropsychology*, *Clinical Gerontologist*, *Ethics and Behavior*, *Journal of Forensic Neuropsychology*, *Journal of Head Trauma Rehabilitation*, *Journal of Pediatric Neuropsychology*, *Psychological Injury and Law*, and *The Clinical Neuropsychologist*. Additionally, Dr. Bush has presented on issues relevant to forensic psychology at national and international conferences. He has more than 130 publications, including journal articles, book chapters, position papers for professional organizations, and more than 20 books, many of which are directly relevant to the practice of forensic psychology. In 2014, Dr. Bush was awarded the Outstanding Supervisor of the Year Award by the Department of Psychiatry at Stony Brook University Medical School. In 2019, he was the recipient of the American Psychological Association's Award for Distinguished Contributions to Independent Practice. He is a veteran of both the Marine Corps and Naval Reserve.

Mary Connell, EdD, ABPP, is board certified in forensic psychology and in clinical psychology by the American Board of Professional Psychology and is in independent practice in Fort Worth, Texas. Presently she works as a consultant and testifying expert in military courts-martial in matters primarily involving intimate partner violence, sexual assault, and child sexual abuse; in her local practice, Dr. Connell has focused on family court matters and currently engages in civil litigation regarding child sexual abuse. She has been active in professional organizations and has served on the Ethics Committee and the Committee on Professional Practice and Standards, as well as in office and on boards and committees for the American Psychology-Law Society, the American Academy of Forensic Psychology, and the Texas Psychological Association. Dr. Connell has published in the areas of child custody/access matters; parenting examinations; treatment considerations for children pending court litigation of sexual abuse allegations; ethics in forensic practice; interstate practice; death penalty mitigation; and on alcohol, blackouts, and sexual assault.

Robert L. Denney, PsyD, ABPP, is board certified in forensic psychology and clinical neuropsychology by the American Board of Professional Psychology. He is a fellow and a past president (2009) of the National Academy of Neuropsychology and fellow of APA Division 40 (Society for Clinical Neuropsychology). For over 20 years Dr. Denney was a forensic psychologist and neuropsychologist at the U.S. Medical Center for Federal Prisoners in Springfield, Missouri, and for 16 years he taught neuroanatomy, neuropathology, and neuropsychology courses at the Forest Institute. He currently maintains a consulting practice for prosecuting and defense attorneys, judges, and the insurance industry, in addition to holding a neuropsychology staff position at the Missouri Memory Center and Neurology Clinic at Citizens Memorial Hospital, Bolivar, Missouri. Dr. Denney has published over 50 book chapters and peer-reviewed papers in the scientific literature on such subjects as neuropsychological evaluation of criminal defendants, malingering, evaluating psychological damages, trauma and violence, ethical issues, and professional licensure. Additionally, he has served on the editorial boards of *The Clinical Neuropsychologist, Applied Neuropsychology, Journal of Forensic Neuropsychology*, and *Archives of Clinical Neuropsychology*. He is coeditor of *Clinical Neuropsychology in the Criminal Forensic Setting* (2008), coauthor of *Detection of Deception* (2007), and coeditor of *Detection of Response Bias in Forensic Neuropsychology* (2002). Dr. Denney has also presented throughout the United States and Canada on neurolitigation, the application of neuropsychology to criminal and civil forensic matters, neuroanatomy, brain injury, malingering, and admissibility of scientific evidence.